THE
WAR ON
PRICES

THE WAR ON PRICES

HOW POPULAR MISCONCEPTIONS ABOUT INFLATION, PRICES, AND VALUE CREATE BAD POLICY

EDITED BY RYAN A. BOURNE

Print ISBN: 978-1-952223-86-0
eBook ISBN: 978-1-952223-87-7

Cover: Molly von Borstel, Faceout Studio
Interior: Paul Nielsen, Faceout Studio

Library of Congress Cataloging Number: 2024932444

Printed in Canada.

CATO INSTITUTE
1000 Massachusetts Ave. NW
Washington, DC 20001
www.cato.org

CONTENTS

PART 2: PRICES AND PRICE CONTROLS

PART 3: VALUE

The War on Prices

Ryan Bourne, February 2024

In the span of just over two years, American households experienced a surge in the prices of everyday essentials. From January 2021 to May 2023, food prices increased by over 19 percent.[1] Used car prices, which had been flat from 1994 until just before the pandemic, skyrocketed by 31 percent.[2] Electricity prices shot up by 21 percent.[3] Even the price of coffee surged by 22 percent.[4]

With industries locked down and disrupted during the COVID-19 pandemic, significant price volatility after the reopening from shutdowns was expected. During the lockdowns, the economy shifted from a service-oriented focus toward an emphasis on manufactured goods, before gradually finding its way toward a new normal as restrictions were lifted and life adjusted. As I wrote in my last book, *Economics in One Virus*, that transition was bound to produce temporary dislocations, shortages, and big price swings as resources were redirected toward different uses in a world of very different supply-and-demand patterns.

But this rising cost of essentials was something different. It wasn't just reflective of certain prices fluctuating wildly as the economy restructured, nor was it a case of some prices rising sharply, offset by others falling. No, this broad rise in prices reflected a revival of high inflation—a sharp, sustained rise in the overall level of prices of a magnitude last seen in the 1970s.

The Federal Reserve, tasked with controlling inflation, traditionally targets an average of 2 percent inflation per year, as measured by the growth of the Personal Consumption Expenditures (PCE) price index. Yet by June 2022, the Fed's preferred annual inflation measure had peaked at a staggering 7 percent, its highest level since 1981. The Consumer Price Index, another widely cited inflation measure, had topped out higher still (at almost 9 percent).

Between January 2021 and May 2023, we would have expected a 4.7 percent increase in the price level of goods and services measured by the PCE index, if the Fed had been right on target. Instead, prices skyrocketed by 13.1 percent. We'd seen more than six years' worth of "normal" inflation in just two years and four months.

The impact on households was painful. Prices surged, but earnings initially failed to keep pace. Average real (inflation-adjusted) hourly compensation was lower in the opening months of 2023 than just before the pandemic.[5]

It soon became clear that something had gone badly wrong with macroeconomic policy to cause this. Given that monetary policy is tasked with ensuring price stability, the focus should have fallen on the Federal Reserve.

The Inflation Narrative

At first, monetary policymakers dismissed this inflation as "transitory" and something they could do little about. Inflation was concentrated in certain sectors (such as used cars and semiconductors), they said, over which they had no control. They saw inflation as a result of sector-specific bottlenecks and supply shocks that arose as the economy reopened from lockdowns, rather than anything to do with excess monetary stimulus.

Once those bottlenecks unwound themselves, the argument went, inflationary pressure would quickly dissipate, and some prices would perhaps even fall back down to their old levels, if the supply shocks reversed completely. We were talking months, not years, for this to play out. The policy implication was that the Fed tightening monetary policy to choke off this inflationary pressure would be both unnecessary and damaging to economic growth. Inflation would soon fall to target anyway.

As price pressures then spread across other industries, the war in Ukraine, with its attendant spike in global gas prices, provided another convenient nonmonetary culprit for inflation after February 2022. Central banks could not produce gas, after all. Tightening monetary conditions to offset the undoubted price-boosting effects of this supply shock, which undermined the production of goods and services, would risk shrinking output and employment further, maybe even generating a recession.

In reality, of course, central banks had let the inflation genie out of the bottle long before the war. The Fed's preferred PCE inflation measure, for example, had already risen to 6.5 percent before Putin's tanks had rolled into Ukraine. By the turn of the year in 2021, some members of the original "team transitory" were already acknowledging that this inflation was broad-based. As time went on, it became obvious that overall spending (or aggregate demand) was running way ahead of its pre-pandemic trend, which indicated that excess stimulus could explain a big component of the rise in the price level.

In response, the Fed tightened monetary conditions in spring 2022 in an attempt to combat inflation, an about-face from its previous complacency. Fed Chairman Jay Powell repeatedly articulated his commitment to curbing excess inflation after that, to keep the public's expectations for inflation anchored and prevent workers from pricing themselves out of jobs with their wage demands. However, even those delayed actions failed to convince many politicians, commentators, and segments of the public that this inflation had monetary causes.

As early as November 2021, prominent politicians, such as Sen. Elizabeth Warren (D-MA), had blamed other bogeymen for inflation, such as "plain-old corporate greed." By April 2022, when I testified before Congress, the Democratic select committee chair Jim Himes (D-CT) talked as if it were obvious that companies with "pricing power" were really responsible for driving up inflation.[6]

At no time during the hearing would he or other committee members acknowledge that, in a free economy, companies are disciplined in what they can charge by their competitors and by consumers' willingness and ability to pay. In monetary terms, that means that businesses, in any industry, could only raise prices so aggressively when an excess supply of money—or something else—helps drive consumer demand to higher levels. Otherwise, customers could not afford those higher prices, or some businesses could capitalize on their competitors' greed and undercut them by lowering prices.

Blaming "corporate greed" and one-off supply shocks nevertheless became a prevailing narrative that obscured the role of monetary mismanagement in fostering inflation. Rather than tighten monetary and fiscal conditions, many political commentators urged the federal government to invest in expanding capacity in sectors suffering from bottlenecks, to use antitrust policy to make markets more competitive, or even to control prices directly—basically, anything other than deliver the monetary medicine for inflation that has been accepted among economists as the (at times painful) cure since the late 1970s.

These off-the-mark views on inflation and its causes seeped into public opinion. A YouGov poll undertaken in June 2023 asked Americans what or who they blamed for inflation. The top answer was "large corporations seeking maximum profits."[7] Strikingly, despite the extensive coverage of the Fed's responsibility for managing inflation, YouGov hadn't even included the Federal Reserve or monetary policy as an option for the cause of inflation. When asked about effective policy ideas to curb inflation, public respondents' top answers were (a) increasing domestic oil production, (b) strengthening supply chains, and (c) the government imposing explicit limits or legal restrictions on price increases.[8] Raising interest rates was way down their list, with more people thinking this would increase inflation than reduce it.

Why does the American public hold such idiosyncratic economic views on inflation? The most charitable explanation is that they see inflation as synonymous with rising living expenses, rather than as a macroeconomic phenomenon of too much money chasing too few goods. So anything that they think might reduce their out-of-pocket costs or the prices of goods they buy—lower taxes, lower mortgage rates, companies keeping prices lower, unions making less aggressive wage demands—is deemed helpful for reducing inflation.

Part of the problem, no doubt, is plain old political partisanship. Republicans were much more likely to blame high federal spending for inflation and to see more oil production as a solution to it, for example, whereas Democrats blamed large corporations and saw price controls as an answer.

Yet it's surely also the case that a lack of basic economic literacy contributed to these views—which was not helped by much of the news reporting on inflation. As inflation persisted at high levels, all sorts of speculative "greedflation" theories gained popularity in explaining how businesses drove inflation. Dubbed "profit-led" inflation or "sellers' inflation," the most sophisticated story—entertained seriously by some media commentators but not most economists— went that companies across industries had capitalized on the public's awareness of rising business costs brought on by the COVID-19 pandemic and the war in Ukraine by jacking up prices way beyond their cost increases, raising both profit margins and inflation.

This sort of reasoning echoed the long-debunked 1970s' arguments that different economic interest groups (in that case, workers in heavily unionized industries) had the power to drive inflation, rather than just affect who was hurt by it. As then, it led politicians to demand "targeted" price controls, anti-price-gouging legislation, or voluntary price and wage restraint by companies. After all, if prices were going up because of firms' decisions rather than the economic fundamentals, shouldn't governments lean on businesses to correct things?

The War on Prices

The United States thankfully escaped a rerun of the World War II and Nixon-era price controls, despite the attempts of some politicians, intellectuals, and pundits to rehabilitate them as a viable solution to our recent inflation.[9] Some European countries ended up capping energy prices; Hungary imposed extensive controls on basic foods. But here, in our Congress, much of the energy was reduced to bizarre legislation to eradicate "junk fees" or else federalize anti-price-gouging legislation.

That said, the steady drumbeat of people blaming inflation on a range of one-off factors and malevolent actors, ignoring monetary and fiscal mismanagement, threatens to entrench a faulty history of the period in the public's memory. This could lead to bad policy outcomes the next time inflation surges.

In fact, recent media narratives reveal widespread misconceptions about what inflation is and how it differs from price movements in individual product markets. Even President Biden is not immune to these errors.[10] In November 2023, he tweeted that companies failing to reduce prices "as inflation has come down" were "price gouging." He seemingly forgot that a positive inflation rate means that, overall, prices are still rising, not falling. In any case, even deflation (in which prices in general were falling) need not mean every single business's price is falling, just as measured inflation (calculated as a weighted average of price changes) does not mean every single good's price is rising.

More worryingly, as inflation has dropped toward the Federal Reserve's target, some high-profile economists who admitted misjudging the persistence of inflation are again minimizing the role of monetary policy in reducing it.[11] Nobel Prize-winning economist Paul Krugman, for example, has argued that the disinflation to date, occurring alongside low unemployment, indicates that the recent high inflation was transitory and was mainly due to negative supply shocks, which have since been resolved.[12] This view does not accord with the evidence.

The Fed oversaw a sharp tightening in the growth of the money supply starting in 2021 and committed publicly to eradicating high inflation from spring 2022 onward. These actions were followed by a sustained slowdown in the growth of total spending, or demand, across the economy, which we would fully expect to dampen inflation.[13] Yet with major politicians and well-known economists arguing that corporate greed and supply shocks have caused inflation's ups and downs, we risk moving forward from this episode with the public largely unaware of money's crucial role.

Refuting such misconceptions was the original inspiration for this book. I wanted to explore not just how inflation stemming from monetary mismanagement damaged the fabric of the market price system, but how faulty thinking about inflation and its causes led to bad policy ideas, like price controls, that could do immense economic harm. As I pondered and mapped out the concept, however, I came to realize that many economic misperceptions about inflation stem not just from misunderstandings about macroeconomic policy, but, more broadly, from a lack of appreciation for the important functions of market prices in general.

The sorts of misconceptions about supply and demand that drove bad inflation theories have also been the intellectual bedrock for attempts to control prices in individual product markets. Across the country, state and local governments directly control rents, interest rates on short-term loans, goods' prices in emergencies, and low wages, all in the name of helping the poor. The federal government imposes less explicit but meaningful price controls throughout the health care system, through regulation of businesses' fees and charges, and bans certain items, such as donated kidneys, from being exchanged for money at all.

Moreover, many of the moral intuitions and faulty theories behind the inflation narrative apply to people's attitudes toward other market prices. When prices rise sharply, it is widely considered a result not of some market process of supply and demand, but of businesses being greedy or having market power. Much of the public seems to consider price increases acceptable only if they are caused by a firm facing rising costs, not an explosion of demand from customers. There is little appreciation for the crucial role that market prices play in efficiently coordinating economic activity by providing signals and incentives to consumers and businesses.

Many market prices or wages are seen as being simply wrong or even immoral, if they don't comport to the value ascribed to the good or service by the individuals complaining. For example, CEOs and sports stars are widely derided for being paid "too much," rents are considered "too high," and pricing differently to customers at different times is viewed as unjust. All these sentiments—based on claims of fairness—drive many of the demands for government price controls and other regulatory interventions on business.

This book will explore all these themes—hence its title, *The War on Prices*. Like the "war on poverty" or the "war on drugs," this nomenclature hopefully encapsulates the growing fervor and rhetoric surrounding something viewed as a great ill—prices of certain goods or inflation being too high—and the ensuing clamor for government controls to solve the problem. The term "war" is appropriate, as it characterizes the desire for a state-led effort to usurp the free functioning of a market economy, the invocation of a moral imperative to do so, and the ultimate futility and destructiveness of the efforts.

To better explore all the underlying forces and misconceived arguments that animate *this* war, I have harnessed the talents of many economic thinkers to produce this volume. The chapters on specific topics are organized into three parts, titled "Inflation," "Prices and Price Controls," and "Value." Each part begins with a basic overview of the broad topic covered—inflation, market prices and price controls, and the concept of value—and how economists think about that topic. The rest of the book includes more detailed chapters that explore the many misconceptions and impulses that animate attempts to get governments to control prices, and the consequences when these controls are implemented.

Through rigorous analysis, historical context, and evidence-based arguments, this book aims to empower readers with a deeper understanding of inflation, the value of market prices, and the harmful consequences that result when governments usurp those prices with top-down controls.

PART 1

Inflation

Inflation: An Introduction

Ryan Bourne

According to Gallup, "mentions of inflation as the most important problem facing the nation averaged only 1 percent [of Americans] between 1990 and 2021."[1] By October 2022, on the eve of that year's midterm elections and after inflation had peaked at its highest level since 1981, 20 percent of the public said it was the key issue.[2]

By June 2023, Pew Research found that inflation was still identified as a "very big problem" by 65 percent of Americans—the highest share for any single issue.[3] Quite simply, the spike in inflation dominated political debates about economics for more than two years, with big downstream effects on policy.

What Is Inflation?

"Inflation" refers to a sustained rise in the general level of prices across goods and services in an economy, which results in each unit of currency buying fewer items. Essentially, it is a decrease in the purchasing power of money. The opposite of inflation—a sustained fall in the general level of money prices—is called deflation.

Inflation is not the same as a rising price for an individual good or service, which can also be driven by changing consumer tastes or disruptions to supply chains. Nor is inflation caused by a product price rising because of a new tax or regulation. Those affect the *relative* prices of goods and services to each other. Inflation is a sustained increase in the price of *all goods and services*, meaning a unit of money buys less. It is a macroeconomic phenomenon.

How Do We Measure Inflation?

Inflation cannot be observed directly. Government statistical agencies therefore estimate it by calculating the change in some weighted average of individual prices for a representative basket of goods over time (weights are determined by the amount of expenditure consumers allocate to each item relative to their total expenditure).

In the United States, the two main indexes used are the Consumer Price Index for urban consumers and the Personal Consumption Expenditures (PCE) price index.[4] The Federal Reserve uses the PCE for its average 2 percent yearly inflation target because of the PCE's broader scope and greater responsiveness to changing demand patterns. Even if the Fed hits its 2 percent target for the year, that weighted average is made up of millions of prices, some of which will have risen by 5, 10, or 20 percent, or more, whereas others fell significantly, due to relative price changes.

All inflation indexes face challenges in accurately capturing the general price level because of the regular introduction of new goods, changes in the quality of products, and rapid consumer substitution between items. These indexes are best viewed as approximate guides to underlying inflation.

What Has Happened to Inflation?

Measured inflation rates fluctuate. Since 1960, the monthly PCE inflation rate, calculated as a year-on-year percentage change, hit a high of 11.6 percent in March 1980 and a low of −1.5 percent (deflation) in July 2009.[5]

From 1992 to 2020, inflation averaged 1.9 percent, and it only fluctuated within a narrower range of −1.5 percent to 4 percent. Yet in 2021,

PCE inflation began to climb rapidly, swiftly increasing from 1.5 percent in January to a peak of 7 percent in June 2022. The inflationary surge that led to this proved more persistent than many—including Federal Reserve chair Jerome Powell—had initially expected.

What Are Inflation's Origins?

The "equation of exchange" provides a basis for understanding inflation's origins. It says

$$MV = PY,$$

where M signifies the money supply, V represents the velocity of money (how often a unit of money is used to buy goods and services in a year), P represents the price level, and Y depicts real income or output. In essence, this accounting identity just states that total dollar spending is, by definition, equivalent to total dollar income.

A delta in front of these variables represents the change in each of them, say over a year. When expressed dynamically, the equation therefore becomes

$$\%\Delta M + \%\Delta V = \%\Delta P + \%\Delta Y.$$

Given that inflation is the change in the price level ($\%\Delta P$), we can rearrange that identity to give

$$\%\Delta P = \%\Delta M + \%\Delta V - \%\Delta Y.$$

This shows that inflation is determined by the growth rates of the money supply, money's velocity, and real income. All else being equal, higher inflation can come from stronger growth in the money supply or money velocity, weaker growth in real income, or some combination of these effects.

Positive real income growth is the norm, driven by productivity growth stemming from innovation and better know-how. But real income can fall too, perhaps because of an oil price spike or supply disruption. These are called "negative supply shocks" and can lead to a higher price level.

Negative supply shocks can include everything from a bad tomato harvest to a destructive hurricane. However, such supply shocks rarely reduce the economy's productive capacity sufficiently to curb real income growth significantly. Consider the math above: other things equal, for a supply shock to explain a one percentage point increase in inflation, it must reduce the growth rate of real income by one percentage point. Over the decade before the COVID-19 pandemic, however, U.S. real growth in gross domestic product (GDP) averaged just 2.4 percent per year. Thus, to explain even one percentage point of inflation within a year, a supply shock would need to reduce the rate of growth for that one year by over 40 percent—an impossible feat for all but the most valuable commodities.

Even when supply shocks are large—such as during a pandemic or war or oil price shock—they tend to be one-offs, leading to a higher price level and increasing inflation only temporarily. For supply shocks to explain inflation rising persistently, one would need new negative supply shocks of increasing magnitude over time.

This rarely happens. Given that the growth rate of money's velocity tends to be relatively stable in the longer term too, the equation thus suggests a central role for money supply growth in driving sustained inflation.

What Is the Role of Money in Causing Inflation?

Nobel Prize–winning economist Milton Friedman, an advocate of the quantity theory of money, concluded:

> Inflation is always and everywhere a monetary phenomenon, in the sense that it is and can be produced only by a more rapid increase in the quantity of money than in output.[6]

Friedman was talking about the long run. Cross-country and long-term within-country differences in inflation rates have indeed historically correlated strongly with money supply growth (see Figure P1.1), with the link especially obvious during periods of high inflation or hyperinflation, when inflation accelerates rapidly to extremely high levels.[7] In the Weimar Republic, for example, the *monthly* inflation rate exceeded 29,500 percent by late 1923.

The quantity theory of money implies that to keep inflation low and stable, a central bank must keep the growth of the money supply at a low level. For instance, a 2 percent average inflation target is in line with the money supply growing two percentage points faster than annual real income growth when the growth rate of velocity is zero. If the money

FIGURE P1.1

Inflation is highly correlated with growth in the money supply

Annual inflation rate for all countries, 1960–2021, percent

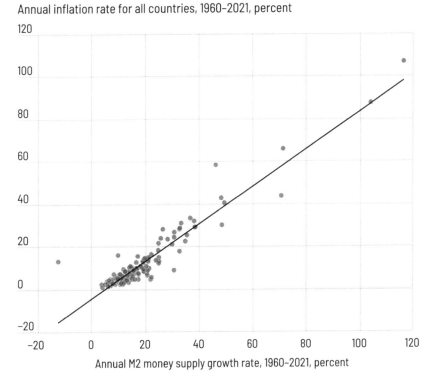

Annual M2 money supply growth rate, 1960–2021, percent

Source: World Bank (accessed September 23, 2023).[8]

supply grows rapidly, it can instead lead to a surge in inflation, as too much money in the economy chases the same amount of goods and services, with the excess spending driving up prices.

Although persistently high inflation requires a continued high money supply growth, even a one-off surge in the money supply can play out over several years, with certain prices adjusting faster than others because of fixed contracts, wage negotiations, and business costs associated with changing prices. These frictions exacerbate the costs of inflation (as will be outlined later). Changes in monetary conditions thus tend to affect measured inflation with a lag, with the full effects playing out over several years.

The effects of a sharp increase in the money supply on inflation can also look, at least initially, much like supply shocks. As more money circulating throughout the economy drives higher spending, industries with limited spare capacity can see their prices rising sharply at first. This observation creates the mistaken impression that these price increases are themselves being driven by industry-specific shortages or bottlenecks, rather than too much money creation.

What Is the Role of Central Banks in Inflation?

In the 1980s, central banks' attempts at targeting the money supply directly proved challenging. These days, monetary authorities instead target the desired outcome—future inflation rates—using various tools. In 2020, the Federal Reserve shifted away from a standard annual inflation target of 2 percent to a flexible average target of 2 percent, as part of its dual mandate to promote "stable prices" and "maximum employment."

In effect, the Fed tries to predict the path of real income or output in the near future, then uses various monetary tools to influence the money supply or money's velocity, and thus total spending in the economy, to achieve its inflation target in the future.

These tools include open-market operations—the buying and selling of government securities, such as Treasury bonds. When the Fed buys securities, it pays for them by adding money to the reserve accounts of the banks that sell them, increasing the total reserves in the banking system. As banks compete to lend out these excess reserves, the interest rate at which banks willingly lend to each other—the federal funds rate—falls. A lower rate is ultimately passed through to customers, making borrowing cheaper and encouraging businesses and consumers to take out loans and spend more. The opposite process plays out when the Fed sells government securities.

The interest rate the Fed pays on excess reserves—reserve bank holdings that exceed the level mandated by the Fed—can also influence banks' incentives to lend. If this rate is high relative to comparative market rates, banks might prefer to hold reserves rather than lend them out, which can reduce the money supply and limit inflation.

The Fed also uses quantitative easing, whereby it purchases large amounts of securities with longer maturities to push down long-term interest rates. Forward guidance—public communication about the likely path of interest rates—has also been used to anchor people's inflation expectations and, by extension, their spending behavior.

Fiscal policy—changes to government spending, taxation, and borrowing—can also create inflationary pressure. New government spending can increase the money supply if financed directly by central bank money creation. Deficit-financed spending can also push up inflation in the short run by transferring money to those more likely to spend. More government borrowing raises interest rates as the government competes for funds. If not offset by the central bank, these higher rates increase the opportunity cost of holding cash, meaning individuals and businesses have an incentive to reduce their cash holdings and invest instead in interest-bearing assets, such as bonds or savings accounts. As a result, money can be used more actively, leading to a temporarily higher money velocity (which then reverses). An inflation-targeting central bank should, in theory, offset these forces by tightening monetary policy to hit its inflation target, a principle often dubbed "monetary dominance."

Modern inflation-targeting by central banks makes the year-to-year link between the money supply and inflation less obvious in normal times, because of an issue that Milton Friedman analogized to a thermostat.[9] A thermostat targets a specific temperature. If it gets colder outside, the thermostat calls on more heat generation to keep the inside temperature steady. A good thermostat should thus show no correlation between heat generation—the policy tool—and the inside temperature—the outcome—because the latter shouldn't change if heat is generated at just the right time and level. This, of course, does not mean that heat generation has no effect on the inside temperature—quite the opposite, in fact.

In the same way, central banks target inflation by affecting monetary forces in light of their forecasts of changes to the economy's real income and money's velocity. If money velocity is expected to grow more slowly, an inflation-targeting central bank may increase the growth of the money supply to keep the inflation rate steady. Yet if it hits that target, a crude correlation will suggest that the money supply, which increased, and inflation rates, which stayed steady, are uncorrelated. We might only observe the true causal relationship between the money supply and inflation when very large, unexpected changes to the money supply occur—as happened between March 2020 and March 2022, when the M2 money supply grew by 39 percent, preceding inflation's takeoff.[10]

Who Is to Blame for Inflation?

Central bankers tend to talk as if they are inflation fighters, but it's more accurate to think of them as inflation creators. The overwhelming majority of modern episodes of high inflation have been caused by central banks, either directly, through money creation, or by errors in correctly forecasting the "real" conditions of the economy.

Consider a simple model of aggregate total spending growth ($\%\Delta M + \%\Delta V$) and real income growth ($\%\Delta Y$) affecting inflation ($\%\Delta P$). Inflation can result from a central bank injecting an excessive money supply or failing to counteract the stimulative effect of government borrowing or heightened consumer spending. This "demand-side" inflation is associated with excess spending. The central bank is clearly culpable for this.

The effect of excess spending on the price level in the short term tends to be more pronounced when the economy operates at or near its productive capacity (maximum Y), indicated by low unemployment and high levels of production. In assessing the likely impact of policy, the Fed and other economists often calculate "output gaps"—estimates of how far the economy is operating below its potential—to evaluate the likelihood that the Fed's monetary stance will lead to changes in inflation rather than in real income in the short-term. Misestimating this output gap is a major error that central banks often make in causing inflation.

Until the 1970s, policymakers thought a monetary and fiscal stimulus could be used to achieve lower unemployment—and higher real income—at the cost of higher inflation. They thought a direct tradeoff existed: less joblessness meant more inflation, or reducing inflation required more unemployment. Echoes of that thinking has permeated recent debates. But this perspective among economists was largely abandoned because of insights from Nobel Prize–winning economist Robert Lucas. He observed that if people expect a central bank to pump in more money to reduce unemployment, they'll expect more inflation and will raise prices and wages immediately. Little to no real increase in jobs or output would occur, even in the short term.

The broad consensus, then, is that monetary policy can, at best, only lower unemployment or raise real income in the short run, and even then, the policy change will have a big impact on real outcomes only when the expansionary policy is unexpected. In the longer term, once people become wise to the policy and prices adjust, money is "neutral." That is, an increase in the money supply only affects the price level, not real income.

By the same logic, tightening monetary policy to reduce inflation need not lead to a big spike in unemployment, at least in theory. Bringing down inflation without causing too much real harm requires the central bank to commit to a monetary policy path consistent with what it wants the public's inflation expectations to be. In reality, bringing down inflation from high levels has been historically difficult, and accompanied by painful recessions. This risk is one reason to avoid large inflationary spikes.

Supply shocks can temporarily cause inflation too, of course, and these are outside the control of the central bank, which can only affect spending—the demand side—through its policies. But if a central bank has a pure inflation target, it could, in theory, still try to counteract the impact of such shocks on the price level by squeezing demand.

In other words, supply-side inflation occurs if an inflation-targeting central bank overestimates the capacity of the real economy relative to monetary conditions or decides to temporarily abandon its inflation target. To give an example: Perhaps central banks underestimated how the COVID-19 pandemic and lockdowns would generate supply-side problems that undermined the economy's capacity to grow, meaning they underestimated the inflationary effects of their monetary policies. Or perhaps they understood these consequences but ignored them.

The reason the latter is feasible is that so far, for simplicity, we have talked as if the central bank does strictly target inflation. The real story is more complex. The Fed commits to hit an average of 2 percent inflation over time, but it is also mandated to pursue maximum employment. In achieving those goals, it only has tools to affect demand (MV).

Given these realities, many economists argue that monetary authorities' target should focus only on what they can influence: total spending. This perspective supports nominal GDP-level targeting, suggesting the central bank should aim to achieve a steady growth in total money spending $(PY$—which is equivalent to $MV)$, rather than a rate of inflation (growth in P).

With this approach, the central bank would respond in the same way to an inflation-targeting regime when inflationary pressure is driven by too much spending. However, when a negative supply shock like an oil-price spike hits, the policy response would be different. A central bank with a strict inflation target should tighten policy to offset the inflationary impact of the same money chasing fewer goods. In the immediate term, this decline in spending risks reducing real income (Y), making output more volatile and risking a recession and unemployment. A central bank pursuing a steady growth in PY would instead permit temporary higher inflation alongside the weaker real income growth to maintain steady total spending growth. It prioritizes reducing short-term output volatility at the expense of higher prices.

The opposite considerations would play out for positive supply shocks. If an innovation reduces costs across the economy and so reduces the price level, a pure inflation-targeting central bank would try to offset this by stimulating the money supply to keep inflation on track. A nominal GDP–targeting central bank would instead allow consumers to benefit from the lower prices, keeping total spending on trend, but at a lower inflation rate and with higher real income growth.

Viewing a stable growth in total spending as a reasonable proxy for what a modern central bank seeks to achieve can be clarifying in identifying whether an inflationary burst is driven by too much demand or uncontrollable supply shocks. For a demand-side inflation, we would expect to see nominal GDP—total spending—running above its desired trend. For inflation that is driven only by supply shocks, we would expect to see higher inflation coincide with lower real income growth, with nominal GDP growth still broadly at trend.

In either scenario, blame for a *persistent* above-target inflation lays firmly at the door of central banks, whether through policy error or a deliberate decision to facilitate rising prices.

What Are the Costs of Inflation?

High inflation, whether or not anticipated, carries numerous costs. It depreciates the value of money (often referred to as the "inflation tax"), which hurts those holding currency and prompts people to take expensive and inefficient measures to mitigate their losses. High inflation encourages consumers to rapidly spend or invest their cash, for example, leading to "shoe-leather costs"—the time and effort involved in managing a cash balance. Sellers also face higher "menu costs" and decisionmaking costs as they must update their prices more frequently, which can entail meetings, reprogramming systems, updating signage, and much more.

Tax laws often fail to effectively index thresholds and allowances to account for inflation. Higher inflation then causes sudden changes in people's real tax burdens. If personal income taxes are under-indexed, inflation driving higher wages can cause "fiscal drag," raising tax burdens as earners are dragged into higher marginal rate tax bands. Similarly, a lack of indexation for capital gains tax can increase the real tax burden on capital income and thus discourage saving and investment.

People most commonly associate inflation with rising living costs relative to wages. But all prices—including wages—should eventually adjust to an inflationary impulse from the money supply. The problem is that wages tend to adjust more slowly (economists say they are "stickier"), meaning monetary excess often leads to short-term falls in real (inflation-adjusted) wages.

When inflation is expected, it can be factored into contracts, and lenders can adjust interest rates for borrowers to account for it. That is, in a world where inflation is stable and predictable, and prices are flexible, the real costs of inflation tend to be smaller.

Unexpected inflation has more severe effects. The existence of those decisionmaking costs and fixed nominal price wage and debt contracts means that unforeseen inflation can cause significant changes in real wealth for households and businesses, distorting economic activity and redistributing wealth arbitrarily.

Far from leading to the seamless elevation of all prices in one fell swoop, an unexpected expansion of the money supply means that more money is first created and then transferred to certain sectors, especially the banking sector and industries to which banks lend heavily. That money infusion thus affects relative prices first, before rounds of pass-throughs as money is transferred throughout the economy, given the higher overall spending, leading to higher overall inflation.

Unexpected inflation can also make sellers and buyers unsure of whether a price increase reflects actual inflation or simply a relative price increase for that product. It therefore makes economic planning more difficult for businesses, consumers, and entrepreneurs. Resources get committed to unviable endeavors. All these groups then take steps to try to mitigate the effects of inflation (such as hiring financial experts for advice), rather than engaging in activities that yield real productive value. People start negotiating wages and debt contracts at more regular intervals, wasting additional time and money as well.

Unanticipated inflation can be highly damaging to real output and unemployment if it undermines confidence in the central bank's willingness and ability to get inflation back on target. If workers think that inflation will be higher than the central bank's policy would produce, and so demand higher pay, the result will be more layoffs, as workers price themselves out of jobs. This is one reason why economists obsess about keeping "inflation expectations" well anchored.

Unexpected inflation also leads to unpredictable wealth redistribution. Losers tend to be those holding large amounts of currency, people on fixed nominal wage contracts, retirees earning cash incomes, lenders, workers in competitive sectors, and businesses facing rising costs. Winners often include real asset investors, fixed-interest debt borrowers, highly indebted governments, workers with market power, and businesses seeing demand-driven price increases before their costs rise. These windfalls and losses are arbitrary. People might try to insulate themselves from those shocks. Workers might seek to unionize. Businesses might impose new (sometimes hidden) fees or reduce the quality or sizes of their products to increase prices in less obvious ways.

Misguided Policy Responses to Inflation

Rather than blaming monetary authorities for inflationary policies, public resentment over this redistribution is often targeted at those perceived to have benefited from inflation. In the 1970s, people blamed unionized workforces and their wage demands for inflationary pressures; during the recent inflation, it's been supposedly "greedy" companies, especially businesses enjoying windfall profits in sectors with near-term bottlenecks. The public seeks redress from policymakers to protect their income against supposedly rapacious businesses.

It can be in the interest of independent central bankers and politicians to encourage this deflection of blame. Policymakers often call for voluntary restraint on behalf of workers and businesses to curb wage or price increases, but these efforts prove futile when running against individuals' self-interest and too much money in circulation. Governments with high debt burdens can benefit from unexpected inflation because it reduces the real value of their debt. This, again, creates perverse incentives for central banks to tolerate higher inflation by setting monetary policy to keep government debt servicing costs low (so-called fiscal dominance).

Inflation also tends to persist for longer than necessary because stopping it requires contractionary monetary policy, which risks reducing output as well as prices in the short term. Central banks therefore often take a wait-and-see approach before committing to tightening policy. Given the time lag between changes in monetary policy and their effect showing up in prices, the public can become frustrated by governments' apparent lack of grip on the situation.

Thus, it is tempting for the public to demand, and for politicians to acquiesce to, damaging alternative policies that seek to mitigate the inflation's effects. As economist Axel Leijonhufvud wrote in 1975, complaints about inflation in general tend to get "quite drowned in the rising babble of specific demands and concrete proposals from identifiable interest groups—to compensate me, to regulate him, to control x's prices, and to tax y's 'excess profits,' etc."[11] These measures often endure for a long time (oil and gas price controls in the 1970s lasted a decade).

During World War II and in 1971 under President Richard Nixon, the U.S. government instituted broad-ranging wage and price controls to try to curb inflation. Banning prices from changing can obviously reduce *measured* inflation, but it doesn't mitigate its underlying monetary or supply-side causes. As such, price controls, at best, restrain measured inflation until those controls are removed. In the interim, they lead to concealed price increases in the form of reductions in goods' quality or volume, the discontinuation of products, queues, rationing, and black markets.

Most importantly, banning prices from changing fundamentally distorts the pattern of relative prices in the economy, and so creates huge inefficiencies. Remember that inflation, as measured, is a weighted average of prices throughout the economy, but in any given year some prices would ordinarily rise by 5, 10, or 20 percent, whereas others fall similarly sharply. Freezing prices or capping price increases thus distorts relative prices from accurately reflecting the supply-and-demand realities that help allocate resources appropriately (see Part 2 for more on specific price controls).

Thankfully, the United States has not instituted broad price controls this time around. But the unexpected inflation has led to misguided theories about inflation's causes—including attributing it solely to corporate greed and supply shocks. This, in turn, has led to advocacy for flawed policies that would not fix inflation, such as sector-level price controls, profit taxes, or even industrial policy.

These misconceptions about inflation are the first front in the war on prices, and they are explored in the chapters of Part 1.

CHAPTER 1

A Rising Product Price Doesn't Cause Inflation

Pierre Lemieux

Misconceptions about what causes inflation are widespread. Perhaps the worst is to view inflation as the result of increases in specific prices. Instead, the causality works the other way around: inflation adds to an otherwise rising price, or it attenuates or cancels the movement of an otherwise falling price.

Examples of this confusion between inflation and the movement of specific prices are all over the media. In the summer of 2022, for example, a *Washington Post* graphics editor mechanistically used the main categories of prices that make up the Consumer Price Index (CPI) to determine "what is causing inflation."[1] The financial press is not immune to the same error. In early 2023, the *Financial Times* informed its readers that "French inflation was mainly driven up by faster growth in food and services prices."[2]

The Difference between Relative Prices and Inflation

We must clearly distinguish the two different phenomena: relative price changes and changes in the general level of prices.

A relative price is the price of one good in relation to the price of another.[3] In the absence of inflation, it is clear that all prices are relative prices. If a bottle of water costs $3 and a bottle of Burgundy costs $30, the relative price of water in terms of Burgundy is one-tenth, and the relative price of Burgundy in terms of water is 10.

Relative prices are important because they guide economic behavior. If all prices double, including your wages or salary (the price of your labor), other things being equal, you will not change the basket of goods you buy. In any economy—a fortiori in a dynamic economy—relative prices change all the time because of changes in demand for, or supply of, myriad goods. For example, if the supply of gasoline decreases, its price will rise. If the demand for housing increases because of, say, a population increase, rents will go up.

Inflation, by definition, is an increase in the general or overall price level—that is, in all prices together. We are usually concerned with the prices of consumer goods, although inflation will also hit salaries and the prices of other intermediary inputs. To be called inflation, an increase in the price level must typically be sustained over some period of time, as opposed to a one-shot increase. In a period of inflation, some prices might be slower to increase, but with time, all prices will ultimately rise in the same proportion if nothing else changes in the economy.

In other words, inflation is an increase in the price of all goods in terms of money. It makes all goods more expensive in terms of money, which is equivalent to saying that money depreciates in terms of goods. If the general price level *decreases*, the phenomenon is called "deflation," but we will focus here on inflation, a more frequent concern.

The general price level (and thus inflation) is not technically observable as such and must be estimated, typically through some weighted average of observed individual prices, like in the CPI. But we must keep in mind the difference between what we are attempting to measure and its calculated estimate.

In the presence of inflation, the change of a given price will include both its relative change (without inflation) and the effect of inflation.

We may say that the "total" price change of a good, or a category of goods, is the sum of its relative change and the inflation rate:

total price change = relative price change + inflation.

As the formula encapsulates, the basic confusion comes from taking the total price change as an estimate of inflation as if there were no relative price changes, and then tracing back the cause of inflation to relative prices. If you obtain 3 by adding 2 to 1 (3 = 2 + 1), it does not make much sense, nor is it useful, to affirm that 3 "contributes to" or "drives" 1. If an observed price—say, the price of roast beef or of gasoline—comes from both a relative price change and inflation, the observed price cannot cause inflation.

Indexes Catch Both Inflation and Relative Price Changes

The following illustration provides another way to see this. Assume for the sake of argument that the CPI provides an accurate measure of inflation. Consider the period between mid-2014 and the end of 2019 (just before the COVID-19 pandemic), a short time frame that allows for an easy-to-read graph. In Figure 1.1, the CPI (rebased at 100 in June 2014) shows a modest inflationary trend as it increased fairly smoothly, by 7.8 percent over the period. Individual prices behaved differently. For example, gasoline prices, although on a general downward trend, went up and down repeatedly. The price of uncooked beef roasts also fluctuated. The rental price of primary residences increased continuously. College tuition and fees increased so much that their line would escape the chart.[4] While inflation, *as estimated by the change of the CPI*, goes on smoothly, some relative prices increase and decrease in patterns not attributable to inflation.

Let's continue to assume that the CPI curve depicts true inflation—that is, a general increase in the price level (all prices)—and

FIGURE 1.1

Individual goods' prices can be more volatile than the overall Consumer Price Index

Consumer Price Index (CPI) and selected components, June 2014 = 100

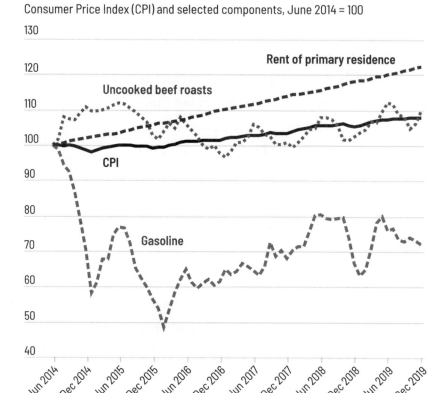

Source: Bureau of Labor Statistics (accessed April 26, 2023).[5]

focus on 2018. That year (from December 2017 to December 2018) was a year of mild inflation, at 1.9 percent. However, gasoline prices decreased by 2.1 percent, uncooked beef roasts increased by 1.7 percent, and rents of primary residences went up by 3.5 percent. Remembering that the "total" price change of a good is equal to its relative price change plus the rate of inflation, we can deduce that, without inflation, considering only relative prices, the price of gasoline would have decreased by 4 percent (−2.1 percent − 1.9 percent), the price of uncooked beef roasts would have decreased by 0.2 percent (1.7 percent − 1.9 percent), and residential rents would have increased by only 1.6 percent (3.5 percent − 1.9 percent). But these calculations are only accurate if we know that the true rate of inflation in 2018 was 1.9 percent.

In reality, the CPI does not provide the true rate of inflation. Indeed, the main point is that *index measures such as the CPI do not reliably estimate inflation because they cannot distinguish between relative price changes and inflation.* Statisticians estimate inflation with the only data they have available: a sample of total prices for a basket of goods and services representative of what the average urban consumer purchases every month. In the index, observed prices are weighted by the quantities consumed. If we assume that the relative price changes cancel each other out—the average change is 0 percent—then the estimate of the total price change would give a correct measure of inflation. But there is no reason why the net relative price increases would be 0 percent, because the quantities purchased generate different weights for the price changes. To repeat, the CPI catches both inflation (the rise in the general price level) and relative price changes.

The CPI is only one of several possible price indexes, which all share this problem. The Personal Consumption Expenditures price index, calculated by the Bureau of Economic Analysis and preferred by the Federal Reserve, shows lower inflation rates and a higher contribution of relative price changes in the measured index.[6]

It is worth noting that the Bureau of Labor Statistics (BLS), author of the CPI and guardian of its methodology, describes it not as a measure of inflation, but as "a measure of the average change over time in the prices of consumer items—goods and services that people buy for day-to-day living." It is technically a cost-of-living index. The BLS handbook doesn't often use the term "inflation."[7]

The BLS publishes a special aggregation that strips out the CPI's food and energy subcategories, "two of the most volatile components of the CPI." It notes that "some users" prefer this series "to measure the 'core' rate of inflation." One can view this as an effort to remove relative prices from the CPI, but it is an imperfect solution. The CPI and similar indexes can be useful *indicators* of, or alerts to, inflation, but only if we realize their inherent limitations.

Where Does Inflation Come From?

Some might object that relative price changes can, by themselves, produce inflation in the sense of an increase in some price index. This is mathematically possible, but it is also possible that the net result of relative price changes could be a decrease in the price index; it depends on the quantities demanded and on factors related to production. We should remember that the objective of an inquiry into prices is not to develop a price index, but to see how price movements affect economic prosperity and, ultimately, human welfare.[8] A clear view of these issues requires us to distinguish between, on the one hand, adjustments of relative prices brought about by supply and demand in different markets and, on the other hand, a general depreciation in the value of money—that is, inflation. If we mix the two phenomena into an intellectual blob, the concept of inflation becomes muddled. We cannot transform a cost-of-living index into a general macroeconomic theory.

It is also true that a supply shock—a sudden reduction of an economy's productive capacity—like we experienced during the COVID-19 pandemic or after the Russian invasion of Ukraine— could, while it lasts, cause a one-shot increase in the general price level because the same amount of money is chasing fewer goods. A supply shock can also cause changes in relative prices, but relative price movements themselves don't cause inflation, which is a macroeconomic phenomenon. (Those familiar with economic theory will understand that a supply shock shifts down an economy's "production possibility frontier," whereas a relative price change occurs along the frontier.)

The distinction between the microeconomics of relative prices and the macroeconomics of inflation becomes most obvious in episodes of hyperinflation—defined as inflation over 50 percent per month—as observed in countries such as Argentina, Turkey, Venezuela, Zimbabwe, and others. In 2008, the Reserve Bank of Zimbabwe's issuance of notes bearing the denomination "one hundred trillion [Zimbabwean] dollars" (Figure 1.2) was a sign of much human misery.

Inflation is quite clearly a distinct phenomenon, caused by an increased supply of money chasing the same quantity of goods or the same supply of money chasing fewer goods. Milton Friedman, a famous monetary theorist and laureate of the 1976 Nobel Prize in Economics, argued that "inflation is always and everywhere a monetary phenomenon in the sense that it is and can be produced only by a more rapid increase in the quantity of money than in output."[9] The fact that the velocity of money (how often a dollar is used in different

FIGURE 1.2

Zimbabwean 100 trillion dollar note, a result of hyperinflation

transactions) desired by the public can change depending on other factors does not change that basic insight.

Empirically, we do observe a correlation between the growth rate of the money supply and the level of inflation or hyperinflation across countries.[10] In the United States, the inflation outbreak that started in 2021 confirmed the same insight. During the three preceding years, the Federal Reserve had pushed up the U.S. money stock (measured as M2) by close to 50 percent. After a typical lag, inflation accelerated. By June 2021, the CPI increase reached 8.9 percent, the highest annual inflation rate in four decades. Federal Reserve chair Jerome Powell was among those who rejected the monetary theory of inflation. In February 2021, two months before the rapid takeoff of inflation, he declared, "The growth of M2, which is quite substantial, does not really have important implications for the economic outlook."[11]

Policy Implications

The confusion between inflation and relative price changes fuels the war on prices. General wage and price controls of the kind that President Richard Nixon decreed in the early 1970s is one front in the war. Fortunately, it now seems that governments and even interventionist economists have become disillusioned with economy-wide price controls as a macroeconomic strategy (but we should still beware of the tendency of failed policies to come back).[12]

Another common illusion is that governments can tame inflation by controlling specific prices. In late 2022, for example, the government of the United Kingdom, under new prime minister Liz Truss, seemed to believe that capping energy prices—which had jumped relative to other prices after the invasion of Ukraine—would dampen inflation.[13] This belief is understandable only if one thinks that the increase of specific prices causes inflation.

More generally, focusing on the increase of specific prices—which may be partly or mainly caused by changes in relative prices (one can always find some prices that increase)—serves as an easy excuse for denying the danger of inflation, as many did through 2021. In August of that year, as CPI increases had already surpassed 5 percent (monthly year-to-year rates), Federal Reserve Chair Jerome Powell declared:

> Inflation at these levels is, of course, a cause for concern. But that concern is tempered by a number of factors that suggest that these elevated readings are likely to prove temporary. . . . Durable goods alone contributed about 1 percentage point to the latest 12-month measures of headline and core inflation. Energy prices, which rebounded with the strong recovery, added another 0.8 percentage point to headline inflation, and from long experience we expect the inflation effects of these increases to be transitory. . . . Used car prices will soon be pulling measured inflation down.[14]

Confusing inflation and relative prices can have dire consequences, not only for understanding the economy, but for public policy as well. Diverting resources from one industry to another (as was done by the misleadingly named Inflation Reduction Act and other industrial policy interventions) will artificially modify relative prices, but cannot reduce inflation. Inflation can only be controlled by drying up its source, which lies in the Federal Reserve's monetary policy. Relative prices, on the other hand, must be free to adjust to movements of supply and demand. Therefore, there is much at stake in clearing up this mistaken conflation.

CHAPTER 2

There Is No Such Thing as a Wage-Price Spiral

Bryan P. Cutsinger

Following the COVID-19 pandemic, inflation surged in the United States and western Europe, triggering a resurgence of theories of inflation that economists had thoroughly debunked 50 years earlier. One such theory posits that demands by workers for higher wages can drive higher prices, which, in turn, cause additional demands for higher wages—leading to what some call a "wage-price spiral" that keeps inflation elevated, or even accelerates it. This theory was popular the last time the world experienced high inflation, in the 1970s, but it is just as wrong today as it was then.

The revival of the wage-price spiral theory can be seen among policy-makers. In early 2023, for example, Bank of England governor Andrew Bailey claimed that the United Kingdom was in the grip of a wage-price spiral.[1] Echoing Governor Bailey's remarks, Huw Pill, the Bank of England's chief economist, stated that workers needed "to accept that they're worse off and stop trying to maintain their real spending power by bidding up prices . . . through higher wages."[2] Federal Reserve officials did not fully embrace such thinking, but did point to rising wages as a driver of inflation. For example, Federal Reserve chair Jerome Powell, while initially admitting that rising wages were not "the principal story for why prices are going up," later testified to

Congress that "some part of the high inflation that we're experiencing is very likely related to an extremely tight labor market."[3]

The views expressed by Bailey, Pill, and Powell are intuitive to the public, to political commentators, and to business executives. Individual company managers see their nominal wage costs rising during an inflationary period, and they understandably feel as if these are driving them to raise prices. But this view confuses an effect of inflation caused by excessive monetary stimulus with its underlying cause. To see why the wage-price spiral is a faulty concept—both in theory and empirically—it is necessary to think through the economics of inflation from first principles.

Inflation, Total Money Expenditure, and Nominal Income

Inflation is a sustained increase in the overall level of prices, denominated in units of money.[4] The inflation rate refers to the percentage growth of one of the broad indexes of money prices that economists use to try to measure that price level, such as the Personal Consumption Expenditures price index.

The inflation rate depends on three factors. The first is the money supply, which in the United States is largely under the control of the Federal Reserve. The second factor is what economists call "money's velocity"—the rate at which a unit of currency circulates to purchase domestically produced goods or services. And third is the quantity of goods and services the economy produces, which economists call real income.

When the growth rates of the money supply or velocity increase relative to the growth rate of real income, the inflation rate will tend to rise. When the growth rate of real income increases relative to the growth rates of the money supply and velocity, the inflation rate will tend to fall. The interaction of these three factors determines the inflation rate. For example, if the money supply grows at 4 percent per year, velocity at 1 percent, and real income at 3 percent, the rate of inflation will be 2 percent per year.[5]

The growth rates of the money supply and velocity determine the growth rate of total money expenditure in the economy. If the money supply grows at 4 percent per year and velocity at 1 percent, then total money expenditure will grow at 5 percent per year. Since every dollar must ultimately be spent on domestically produced goods or services, the growth rate of total money expenditure is, by definition, equivalent to the growth rate of the money value of those goods and services.

Economists refer to this latter concept as nominal, or cash, income. Its growth rate depends on both the inflation rate and the growth rate of real income. For example, if total money expenditure grows at 5 percent per year, the sum of the inflation rate and the growth rate of real income must also be 5 percent. The economy's productive capacity is independent of total money expenditure in the long run, so changes in the growth rate of expenditure will tend to affect the inflation rate rather than real income growth.

The Wage-Price Spiral View of Inflation: Theory and Evidence

This basic framework provides a way to assess the validity of the wage-price spiral hypothesis. Let's suppose, for the sake of illustration, that the central bank can perfectly adjust the money supply to changes in money's velocity so that total money expenditure grows at a constant rate. This assumption rules out changes in the money supply or velocity as drivers of inflation and emphasizes changes in the growth rate of real income as inflation's source.

Under these assumptions, a wage-price spiral could be feasible if workers are able to push the prevailing wage rate above the market-clearing wage level, prompting employers to hire fewer workers and thus produce less output. With the growth rate of total money expenditure constant and the amount of goods and services produced by the economy growing slower than before, the inflation rate must increase to ensure that the growth of nominal income remains equal to that of total money expenditure.

Whatever purchasing power workers gained by pushing their wages above the prevailing wage rate is then offset by the higher prices of goods and services. To recapture this purchasing power, workers negotiate for higher wages again, forcing firms to use less labor and, by implication, to produce fewer goods still, pushing prices even higher. This process continues as workers and firms try to capture more of the economy's ever-shrinking output. Hence, the moniker "wage-price spiral."

Is this a plausible story for the 2021–2023 period? Well, it would require, first, an explanation for why workers across the economy suddenly had greater market power to command wages beyond competitive levels. That might occur, say, if we saw a sudden rise in trade union membership, reducing the amount of goods and services our economy produces and so pushing prices higher. Yet the proportion of employed workers represented by unions fell between 2020 and 2022.[6]

If workers had always had the power to force higher wages despite this, what explains the period of low inflation before 2021? A proponent of the wage-price spiral explanation might respond that the COVID-19 pandemic temporarily increased workers' leverage over employers, perhaps because of all the relief spending from the federal government and shifting demand patterns. Although that may be true of some labor markets, it stretches credulity to think this effect would have been large enough to reduce the growth rate of real income by the magnitude necessary to explain the inflation rates we have observed since 2021. For example, to explain a one percentage point increase in the inflation rate, higher wages from increased market power would need to reduce real income growth by a full percentage point (assuming a given rate of total money expenditure growth). This magnitude is implausibly large, as even a one percentage point decrease in real income growth would reduce the economy's usual real income growth rate by nearly half.

More importantly, if this story explained our current inflation, some obvious empirical evidence would exist to suggest so. First, assuming that total money expenditure is growing at a constant rate, a wage-price spiral would lead to higher inflation but not an increase in the growth rate of nominal income. Figure 2.1 illustrates the growth rate of nominal income since 2020 relative to the Federal Reserve's forecast at the

FIGURE 2.1

Total expenditure growth in 2021 and 2022 vastly exceeded the Federal Reserve's pre-pandemic forecast

Annual growth rate, percent

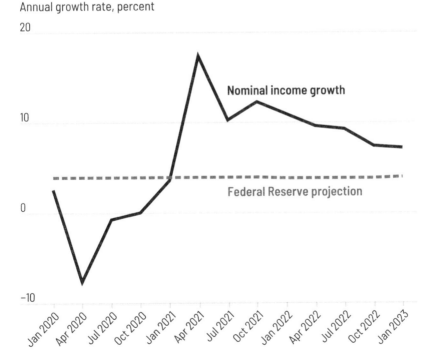

Sources: Bureau of Economic Analysis and Board of Governors of the Federal Reserve System (2019).[7]

end of 2019. As the figure shows, nominal income growth has been above the trend the Fed forecasted before the COVID-19 pandemic began. This result shows that the recent inflation has been driven, at least in part, by money supply growth and higher velocity rather than a wage-price spiral.

Second, the wage-price spiral view implies that the level of employment should fall as inflation rises. Figure 2.2 illustrates the inflation rate and level of employment.[8] The figure shows that inflation and employment both increased from May 2020 to June 2022, after which inflation started to decline while employment continued to grow. Although these observations are inconsistent with the wage-price spiral view, they are exactly what we would expect if nominal income growth exceeded the economy's productive capacity.

FIGURE 2.2

Inflation and employment both rose as total expenditure surged

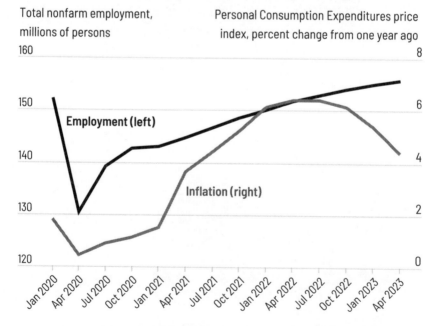

Total nonfarm employment, millions of persons

Personal Consumption Expenditures price index, percent change from one year ago

Sources: Bureau of Economic Analysis and Bureau of Labor Statistics.[9]

Third, if workers' efforts to maintain or increase the purchasing power of their wages is the main driver of inflation, as the wage-spiral view holds, we would expect nominal wages to at least keep pace with inflation. Figure 2.3 illustrates the evolution of inflation-adjusted average wages after January 2020 relative to their pre-pandemic trend.[10] As the figure shows, wages did not keep up with inflation, suggesting that a key source of rising prices over this period was excessive nominal income growth, which helped erode real wages.

FIGURE 2.3

Wages failed to keep pace with prices as inflation took off

Real average hourly earnings, January 2020 dollars

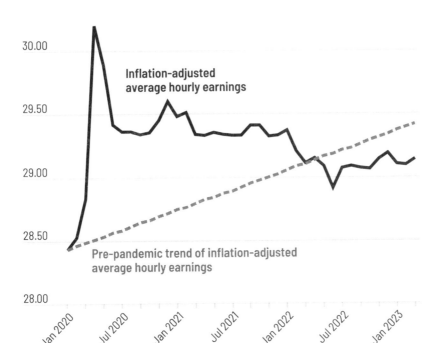

Source: Bureau of Labor Statistics.[11]

Confusing Cause with Effect

The wage-price spiral theory of inflation sounds plausible on first sight, because what looks like a wage-price spiral is often demand-driven inflation (a sharp rise in total expenditure) in disguise. Tracing the effects of an unexpected increase in the money supply can illustrate why.

Suppose the Federal Reserve unexpectedly increases the money supply, and people decide to spend the excess money on new appliances for their homes. Stores like Best Buy, Home Depot, and Lowe's sell more appliances than before, but since they do not know whether the increase in demand for appliances is permanent or transitory, they don't raise their prices immediately. Instead, they draw down their existing inventories to satisfy the increased demand.

These stores place orders with appliance manufacturers like General Electric, Maytag, and Whirlpool to replenish their inventories. The manufacturers must hire additional workers or convince their existing workers to work longer to fulfill the unusual increase in orders from appliance retailers. They do so by offering higher wages. Higher wages raise production costs, which the manufacturers pass along to the appliance retailers by charging them higher prices. Since their costs have also increased, the retailers behave similarly, passing along part of their higher costs to consumers by raising the retail prices of home appliances.

From the manufacturers' and retailers' perspectives, it certainly appears that higher wages are the source of the higher wholesale and retail prices. However, the unexpected increase in the money supply is what really drove demand higher and is thus ultimately responsible for both the higher retail prices and wages.

A similar process occurs throughout the economy as people rebalance their portfolios in response to the unexpected increase in their money balances. As before, firms respond by offering higher wages to attract additional workers and pass on part of their higher labor costs to consumers by charging higher prices.[12]

Unlike the wage-price spiral explanation, which predicts higher wages but lower employment, this view of inflation can account for both the rising prices and the increased employment we've seen. Greater demand for workers leads to higher wages, which in turn lead to both the creation of new jobs and the currently employed workers staying at their jobs longer, thereby reducing the unemployment rate temporarily. In other words, if nominal income growth exceeds growth in the economy's productive capacity, the unemployment rate will temporarily fall below the rate the economy can sustain without generating inflation, which economists refer to as the "natural unemployment rate."

However, once workers realize that the purchasing power of the higher wages employers offer is no greater than before the increase in total spending, the unemployment rate will tend to return to its natural rate (as workers realize the employment is less attractive than they thought), albeit at higher prices and nominal wages.

The COVID-19 pandemic also induced unexpected changes in demand patterns, which led to resources shifting from some industries to others. Some economists have pointed to this phenomenon, and the localized near-term shortages of workers it generates, as a source of inflation.[13] So suppose that instead of a rise in total expenditure driven by money supply growth, consumer behavior just suddenly shifts toward home production, increasing the demand for home appliances and the workers producing them.

The process plays out the same as before, except for one important difference: for a given level of total expenditure, the rising demand for workers who produce home appliances is offset this time by a falling demand for workers who produce commercial appliances. In consequence, employment, wages, and prices in the home appliance industry will rise, whereas employment, wages, and prices in the commercial appliance industry will fall.

This example illustrates an important difference between an increase in the growth rate of nominal income caused by unexpected increases in the money supply and a shift in consumption from one industry to another. In the first case, employment, wages, and prices will tend to increase across all industries temporarily as people spend their excess money. By contrast, in the second case, the net effect of the demand changes will generally offset one another. As a result, it is unlikely that such a shift would really affect the overall employment level, wages, or prices. In other words, a shift in the composition of demand shouldn't be expected to generate inflation.[14]

In short, basic economics and the empirical evidence from the past three years point to demand-driven inflation, not wage-price spirals, as a major underlying cause of the recent rise in wages and prices.

What Is at Stake?

This distinction is important, because the wage-price spiral view often lends intellectual support to wage and price controls. If higher wages drive higher prices—which, in turn, drive higher wages, in a continuous feedback loop—trying to break the cycle by making it illegal for wages and prices to increase becomes more attractive for policymakers. Using wage and price controls to fight inflation not only confuses cause and effect but also creates market distortions that misallocate resources, reduce productivity, and make society poorer.

Preventing wages and prices from increasing in response to higher nominal income will cause product and labor shortages. These controls prevent wages and prices from rising to clear the market, so people must adjust on other margins. For example, consumers may find that they must wait in long lines to purchase goods that seemed abundant before the price controls went into effect. Likewise, since wage controls prevent employers from offering higher wages to attract workers, they will be forced to offer other benefits that workers prefer less than higher wage rates.

Central bankers did not advocate for wage or price controls directly. But leaders at the Bank of England, at least, called for self-sacrifice on the part of workers—for workers to ignore their self-interest and simply accept lower wages by bargaining less aggressively. If acted on, such "soft" wage controls (or "voluntary restraint," as it was called in the 1970s) would have similar effects to actual wage controls. Importantly, they wouldn't reduce inflation.

Perhaps the biggest problem with misdiagnosing inflation by blaming it on wage-price spirals is that doing so diverts attention from the underlying cause of inflation—excessive money growth driven by the central banks responsible for managing the money supply. Focusing on wage-price spirals and other nonmonetary explanations of rising prices, like "greedflation," makes it difficult, if not impossible, to hold central banks accountable for creating the worst inflationary episode in 40 years. For that to happen, there must be clarity regarding inflation's underlying cause.

CHAPTER 3

Greed and Corporate Concentration Have Not Caused Inflation

Brian C. Albrecht

Inflation in the United States hit a 40-year high in early 2022. In response, the blame game started. Instead of the usual culprits, such as congressional spending or the Federal Reserve, prominent politicians like Sen. Elizabeth Warren (D-MA) pointed the finger at corporations, blaming rising prices on "plain-old corporate greed."[1]

By May 2022, *Washington Post* columnist Catherine Rampell used the phrase "greedflation" to describe a collection of theories and ideas about how greed, corporate power, and profits were driving inflation. She called it "a conspiracy theory [that] has been infecting the Democratic Party, its progressive base, even the White House."[2]

Fast-forward one year, and every news outlet from the *Wall Street Journal*, Bloomberg, and Axios to the *New York Times* was pointing to greedflation or greedflation-esque explanations for inflation.[3] Companies with market power, many argued, had found the inflationary moment caused by supply shocks to be a great opportunity to collectively take advantage of consumers, by raising prices far above marginal costs.[4] In other words, the sudden onset of inflation after a long period of price stability had made coordinated profit puffing easier. This, they thought, contributed to sustained inflation.

Politicians' statements and these news stories stand in contrast to how economists tend to think about why prices rise.[5] Inflation, represented through some *aggregate* price index, economists maintain, is caused by the interaction of aggregate supply and aggregate demand. Although different macroeconomists stress different explanations for how much the recent inflation was driven by supply shocks or rising demand, the overall framework helped ground analysis in a unified framework.

By contrast, politicians' pronouncements and media perspectives mysteriously left out the aggregate demand story. They sometimes mentioned aggregate supply, such as in the context of the COVID-19 pandemic or the war in Ukraine. But neither supply nor demand were the primary focus. Greedflation was supposed to occupy a novel space where corporations' desire for greater profits drove up inflation.[6]

Theories of Inflation

A theory of inflation should be causal. Causation relies on thinking through counterfactuals— that is, if X were different, then Y (in this case, inflation) would be different. For a noneconomic example, I may say that if I eat more calories, my weight will go up. That is a causal theory of my weight. That theory may be wrong in explaining my past weight gain or predicting my future weight gain. The cause may really have been aging. But it is at least plausibly a theory we could imagine manipulating to study the causes of my weight. I could systematically change my calorie intake. I can make predictions: if I lower my calories by X, my weight will drop Y.

To understand the causes of inflation, we must therefore identify likely changes to variables that we observed or will observe in the future, which we might have reason to believe would influence the price level. In this case, what changed just before or around 2021, when inflation rose rapidly? Was it greed, increased market power, collusion, or drivers of aggregate supply and aggregate demand? We will consider each in turn.

Is Greed to Blame for Inflation?

To establish causation, we need something we can imagine manipulating, like the dieter changing her calorie intake. Since greed is, to a first approximation, constant from year to year, we cannot attribute big changes in inflation to differences in levels of greed.

As I wrote with Texas Tech economist Alexander Salter after inflation peaked in early 2022, blaming inflation on greed is like blaming plane crashes on gravity.[7] Yes, if we had a machine that suddenly increased the amount of gravity, that would cause more plane crashes. But that variation does not and will not exist in the real world. Despite the popularity of the term "greedflation," then, people are not actually arguing that the level of greed suddenly increased. Instead, greedflation is a stand-in for a hodgepodge of different theories, all of which blame inflation on something besides supply and demand.

Is Corporate Concentration to Blame for Inflation?

Beyond comments by politicians scolding companies for price increases, the first economic work related to greedflation was about the relationship between market concentration (as a poor proxy for market power) and inflation.

Blaming high market concentration for the recent inflation can be interpreted in two ways. The first is that concentration rose and that created higher inflation. The problem with that story was that we did not have good data on concentration during the COVID-19 pandemic. (Even the "first look" results of the 2022 Economic Census were only released in March 2024.) The contemporary data, such as on new business formation, suggested that concentration may have fallen during the pandemic.[8]

Even if concentration did increase during the pandemic, the magnitudes matter here. Inflation rose to over three times the Federal Reserve's target of 2 percent. It is nearly impossible for concentration to increase enough in one year to cause a multiple-percentage-point increase in inflation.

The second possibility is that concentration was high going into the pandemic, worsening inflation. The best example of this argument is from a May 2022 Boston Fed policy brief (and subsequent working paper) from Falk Bräuning, José L. Fillat, and Gustavo Joaquim that received lots of media attention.[9] The basic idea was that high concentration levels going into the pandemic meant that any supply shocks pushed up prices more than they would have with lower levels of concentration. The theoretical justification is that greater concentration may enable firms to have more market power. This premise is debatable but could be true. Firms with more market power can pass on any cost shocks—such as when oil prices rise—to consumers to a greater extent than they could in a more competitive market. Although hard to tease out in the data, this is a possible causal theory in that you can imagine varying concentration levels and measuring what happens to prices.

There are two major empirical problems with using the Boston Fed paper to explain inflation, even for the period on which it focuses, which is before the pandemic. First, the paper uses concentration measures calculated from data only for publicly traded firms. That is only a subset of companies. An extremely low correlation exists between these concentration measures and the more accurate concentration measures found using the best available data, which come from the Economic Census.[10]

Second, the paper (and others like it) relies on regressing producer price increases on concentration to estimate the relationship between the two. As a collection of esteemed industrial organization econ-omists—including Nathan Miller, Steven Berry, Ariel Pakes, and others—wrote in a paper arguing against these regressions:

> The underlying problem with regressions of price on concentration is that the relationship between price and the concentration is not causal. Instead, both are equilibrium outcomes that are determined by demand, supply, and the factors that drive them.[11]

Although concentration could plausibly increase the inflationary impact of a supply shock—in the sense that it would lead to a bigger jump in prices—the evidence it did so is weak. Regressing inflation on concentration will not answer the relevant question.

Are Profits to Blame for Inflation?

A newer greedflation idea is that profits caused the recent inflation through a so-called profits-price spiral. This is far from a fringe the-ory; even some staff members at the European Central Bank were pushing this narrative.[12] Yet the profit-price spiral idea suffers from the same problems Bryan Cutsinger points out in Chapter 2 about the more traditional wage-price spirals; there is no reason to believe the causal arrow runs from profits or wages to prices.

Proponents of greedflation used basic accounting identities to tell this story. If profit on a unit of a good sold is the price minus marginal cost, then we can rearrange the equation to get price equal to the mar-ginal cost plus profit. If profit margins are up, were these not "driving" higher prices?

Such accounting identities complicate matters when thinking through causal arguments, though. Returning to the example of weight loss, my total weight drops if my lower body loses weight. Is that causal? Yes, if I cut off my leg, my total weight falls. But that is not the sort of causal manipulation we have in mind when we wonder, "How can I lose weight?" Again, like the regression of concentration on

prices, we have the issue that other factors cause both profits and inflation together. They are both endogenous. Simply pointing to profits
and inflation moving together—which is not always the case—tells us
nothing about the cause.

One way that profits might have risen is through collusion. Companies deciding to collude could be the causal change. When firms
collude, they agree to raise prices, and the quantity of goods sold in
their industry falls as a result.

For collusion to cause the broad inflation we've seen, it would
require collusion in nearly every sector of the economy. Yet many
greedflation-esque theories rely on some form of implicit collusion
between firms due to recent circumstances. For example, University of
Massachusetts Amherst economists Isabella Weber and Evan Wasner
called it "sellers' inflation," whereby "firms are price makers, but they
only engage in price hikes if they expect their competitors to do the
same. This requires an implicit agreement which can be coordinated
by sector-wide cost shocks and supply bottlenecks."[13] Some writers in
the popular press have used the term "excuseflation" to capture the
same idea.[14] Firms were able to raise prices above any increase in their
costs, since they had an excuse that customers were willing to accept,
such as supply chain bottlenecks or rising energy costs.

One major problem with the sellers' inflation theory (to the extent
that it differs from supply and demand) is that it does not take consumers seriously. Why are consumers willing and able to pay elevated
prices? What changed about their position? Instead, greedy corporations are talked about as if they can just set prices at whatever levels they
like, undisciplined by competition or customers' willingness to pay.

Beyond ignoring buyers, standard collusion stories make less sense
when applied to the broad inflation of the entire economy. One complication is that to produce inflation, this behavior needs to happen
across many markets and those effects fight against each other; if

profits and prices are high because of market power in one market, that will drive down prices in another market. For example, suppose prices start at $1 for an apple and $1 for a banana, and each consumer spends $10 to buy apples and bananas. Suddenly, apple producers conspire to raise the price of an apple to $2. It is tempting to believe this collusion will generate inflation; after all, the apple price rose. But since the consumer has only $10 to spend, any price increase in the apple market will reduce spending on bananas, driving down banana prices.

Furthermore, the collusion and market power theories would require implausibly large effects on the real economy to generate the inflation we have seen. For a quick calculation of the magnitudes we are talking about, suppose the central bank were targeting nominal income growth (ΔPY) at 4 percent, as David Beckworth assumes in Chapter 4 (where P is the price level and Y is real output). To a first approximation, this can be decomposed into $\Delta PY \approx \Delta P + \Delta Y$. Suppose that, in normal times, prices are increasing at 2 percent ($\Delta P = 2$) and output is growing at 2 percent ($\Delta Y = 2$). For inflation to hit 9 percent ($\Delta P = 9$)—as the Consumer Price Index did from mid-2021 to 2022— real income would need to *drop by* 5 percent ($\Delta Y = -5$) to maintain that constant 4 percent nominal income growth. For inflation to remain high for multiple years, real output would need to continue to fall relative to the trend year over year.

But as Bryan Cutsinger showed in Chapter 2, inflation and real output increased in tandem during 2021. In fact, real output increased so much that it had returned to its pre-COVID-19-crisis level by the end of that year. That tells us that inflation saw a major demand-side component; that is, it was in part caused by a large increase in overall nominal spending.

If we extend the story to include profits, we have even more support for the view that demand increases caused a significant portion of the inflation. As University of Mississippi economist Josh Hendrickson has pointed out, in a standard model of a seller with market power, if we see prices and profits rising together, then demand must have increased because, say, the Fed increased the growth of the money supply.[15]

Not only did real output and prices rise together in 2021, but that year is precisely the period when profits were supposed to start driving inflation, according to a May 2023 Kansas City Fed report from Andrew Glover, José Mustre-del-Río, and Jalen Nichols.[16] The most cited paper in the press, by Weber and Wasner, shows profits rising in the same period.[17] Rather than rising profits being evidence of a profit-driven inflation, the profit data further support the argument that a major cause of inflation (and rising profits) was overly stimulatory demand-side policy.

What Causes Inflation? Supply and Demand

Inflation, always and everywhere, results from too much purchasing power chasing too few goods. Over the past few years, the United States has experienced both. Surging demand amid flagging supply is the best explanation for inflation in any short period in which market power is relatively stable. Corporate greed or increased concentration doesn't get us the sudden, economy-wide price hikes we saw in 2021.

Supply and demand provide a simple framework for breaking down the causes of inflation.[18] If inflation arises from a positive demand shock (such as the Federal Reserve printing lots of money), prices and real output will rise together. If it is from a negative supply shock (such as the war in Ukraine), prices will rise, but real output will fall. As of May 2022, real output was roughly on trend, whereas prices were well above trend. Since output was on trend, this suggests equally offsetting demand and supply shocks (as illustrated by a simple supply-and-demand model in Figure 3.1). A more rigorous analysis from Adam Shapiro of the San Francisco Fed found roughly the same demand and supply split up to that point in time.[19]

FIGURE 3.1

How aggregate demand and supply shocks affect output and prices

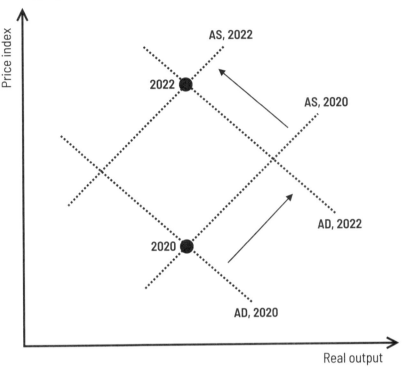

Note: AS = aggregate supply; AD = aggregate demand.

After May 2022, real output fell slightly below trend, suggesting that the supply shock dominated (although not completely). Shapiro's framework agrees for 2022.[20] For a price index, Shapiro uses the Personal Consumption Expenditures (PCE) price index. For 2022, the overall headline PCE inflation was around 5.2 percent. He breaks down that overall figure into 2.58 percent attributable to supply factors, 1.85 percent to demand factors, and the remaining 0.8 percent being ambiguous. For the year leading up to April 2023, he finds 1.6 percent from supply, 1.89 percent from demand, and 0.86 percent ambiguous. For reference, in 2019, he finds that the headline PCE inflation of 1.6 percent was 0.57 percent supply, 0.85 percent demand, and 0.21 percent ambiguous. We can debate the exact methodology and tell stories for each period, but this basic framework shows that both supply and demand factors have driven high inflation.

The Difference Matters for Policy

Is it a semantic dispute to distinguish between firms facing inflationary supply and demand conditions that produce increased profits, as opposed to businesses' pricing being the source of inflation? In some cases, it is hard to see what the different greedflation stories add above the supply-and-demand framework. But the distinction matters for the purposes of public policy responses.

If inflation is supply-driven or demand-driven, we can imagine direct policy responses to alleviate it. For example, if backlogs at shipping ports slow down supply chains, we may want to introduce a policy to increase port capacity. We have a precise prediction from the theory. Increasing port capacity will reduce inflation if this supply shock is the cause. It may also be the case that we want to leave higher prices in a sector to encourage market actors and entrepreneurs to bring forth new supply.

If the cause of inflation is the Fed printing too much money leading to too much spending, then we have a different policy recommendation. The Fed should use its policy tools to slow down the growth of money to slow down future inflation, which it has done with rising interest rates and falling money growth. Again, we have a prediction.

But if the cause is greed, profits, or concentration, what will be the effects of these policies? One possibility is that the policies will overcome the greed or market power dynamics, reducing inflation anyway. Another possibility is that the policy proposals (such as raising interest rates) will be ineffective because they do not address the fundamental cause of profits or concentration. Then what?

Policy is where the greedflationists most strongly departed from the supply-and-demand folks. Some economists, such as Weber, argued for implementing price controls and windfall profit taxes. This sounds intuitive if the cause of inflation was purely market power by some sellers with excess profits. In that case, price controls would not have had the usual inefficiencies that economists attribute to them. That is why Weber suggested using "tailored controls on carefully selected prices" to bring down inflation.[21]

Yet price controls as a means of reducing inflation more broadly are at best futile and at worst highly destructive, as economists have long recognized.[22] As demonstrated earlier, even if inflation would be somewhat lower with less market power, this has clearly not been the whole story of recent years. Supply-and-demand factors caused the bulk of inflation, and we know the inefficiencies of price controls in the supply-and-demand model. As a policy prescription, it's like cutting off a leg without changing one's diet and exercise habits to lose weight. It may show up in data as lower prices, but inflation will return without addressing the true underlying cause. The evidence simply isn't there to throw out decades of economic research on the inefficiency of price controls and the causes of inflation.

Our Recent Inflation Wasn't Wholly Driven by the COVID-19 Pandemic and the War in Ukraine

David Beckworth

The U.S. inflation surge of 2021–2023 was a big surprise to most Americans, including policymakers. After decades of low and stable inflation, prices began soaring and inflation hit almost double digits in mid-2022. Inflation became the public's top concern according to polls and was serious enough that it affected the outcome of the 2022 congressional elections.[1] Inflation did begin to ease in late 2022 and eventually returned close to its target value. But only after several years of above-target inflation.

This all raises an obvious question: What caused the inflation surge?

Many commentators, including Federal Reserve Chair Jerome Powell, initially attributed the inflation surge to "transitory" factors caused by the pandemic. President Joe Biden and others attributed the inflation to global forces that were outside his control, such as the war in Ukraine. The persistence of inflation, however, eventually caused most observers to acknowledge that there was more to inflation than pandemic disturbances and the Russia-Ukraine war. Specifically, the large amount of spending injected into the economy during the pandemic through fiscal and monetary policies became widely viewed by economists and policy-makers as the culprit for the lingering inflation.

This understanding did not come quickly or easily for a key reason: it is hard to know in real time the full causes of an inflationary episode.[2] The inflation rate can increase from economy-wide supply shocks like the pandemic-driven disruptions, demand shocks like the surge in federal spending, or some combination of both. All that can be directly observed, however, is inflation, as measured through price indexes, not its underlying causes. This drawback makes it hard to know in real time what is driving inflation and is why many observers only gradually changed their views on the reasons for the inflation surge.

The Causes of Inflation: Supply and Demand Shocks

"Inflation" is measured by the growth rate of the price level, which is a weighted average of all the individual prices in the economy. The price of oil, for example, is an individual price that can be affected by conflicts that reduce its supply and drive up its price, as we saw in the Russia-Ukraine war, or by new oil field discoveries that expand its supply and lower its price, such as the North American fracking industry in the 2010s. These shocks to oil are called relative price changes, since they cause oil prices to change while leaving most other prices unaffected.

Such idiosyncratic shocks are also called supply shocks because they affect the productive capacity or supply side of an economy. Many of the developments we saw during the COVID-19 pandemic—fewer people working, lower oil production, reduced global shipping—were examples of *negative* supply shocks. They reduced the availability of goods and services and, as a result, made them more costly. Positive supply shocks do the opposite; they facilitate production of more goods and services at a lower cost.

If supply shocks are big enough, they can temporarily affect the inflation rate. The flow of oil, as noted, was disrupted by the Russia-Ukraine war, which raised its price. This was a negative supply shock because more expensive energy can meaningfully impair the productive capacity of the whole economy, leading to higher inflation through a one-off jump in the price level. Most supply shocks, then, are temporary in nature and should not have a permanent effect on inflation. This appears to be case for most of the supply shocks coming from the pandemic and the Russia-Ukraine war.

Oil prices can also be affected by sudden changes in total dollar spending. Such demand shocks, however, affect all individual prices, not just the price of oil. For example, President Biden's American Recue Plan added $1.9 trillion to an economy in 2021 that was estimated to be producing output $400 billion below its output capacity. That meant most of this additional money, injected into the economy, would manifest itself in higher prices, including oil prices. Moreover, given the important role the dollar plays internationally, as a global reserve currency, this large demand shock spilled over into the global economy and contributed to the rise in global commodity prices.[3]

Rising inflation, then, can be caused by both negative supply shocks and positive demand shocks. Outside of inflation caused by these two shocks, there is also a trend path for inflation. For most advanced economies, it has been set via a central bank inflation target of 2 percent. The Federal Reserve, like many central banks, has been fairly successful over the past few decades in keeping inflation near its 2 percent target. It has done so by keeping total dollar spending on a stable growth path. Unsurprisingly, deviations from a stable growth path for total dollar spending are caused by demand shocks. This fact provides a workaround to the challenge of knowing what caused recent changes in inflation.

A Workaround for Understanding Inflation Movements

Macroeconomic policy—the combination of fiscal and monetary policy—shapes the growth path of total dollar spending. Most advanced economies, however, have chosen their central banks to be the final arbiter of total dollar spending; as a result, monetary authorities have typically determined the growth path of this spending over the medium run. That authority, in turn, allows them to implement their inflation target.

This understanding implies that a surge in inflation that coincides with a significant acceleration in total dollar spending above a stable growth path cannot be caused by negative supply shocks.[4] It must be caused by positive demand shocks. Alternatively, if total dollar spending growth is stable but inflation is surging, it must be because of negative supply shocks.

To see why, assume that the dollar size of the U.S. economy is $25 trillion, that the Fed is targeting 2 percent inflation, and that the potential real (inflation-adjusted) output growth of the economy is also 2 percent. Together, these assumptions imply that the Fed is implicitly targeting a total dollar spending growth path of 4 percent. In more technical terms, one would say the Fed is implicitly targeting a 4 percent growth path for nominal gross domestic product (NGDP). NGDP measures total current-price spending on final goods and services in the economy—it is the money economy we see in our everyday lives and has both real output growth and inflation embedded within it.

Using this setup and assuming the Fed can credibly hit its target, Table 4.1 illustrates what happens in various scenarios. First, as a baseline, the first column shows what happens if there are no supply shocks. NGDP grows 4 percent or $1 trillion and this spending is evenly split, as expected with a 2 percent inflation target, between higher prices and real economic growth.

TABLE 4.1

How supply shocks affect inflation and real growth

The impact of positive and negative supply shocks in a $25 trillion economy
with a 4% NGDP target

	No shocks		Negative supply shock		Positive supply shock	
	NGDP trillions	NGDP growth	NGDP trillions	NGDP growth	NGDP trillions	NGDP growth
Inflation	$0.50	2%	$0.75	3%	$0.25	1%
Real growth	$0.50	2%	$0.25	1%	$0.75	3%
Total growth	$1.00	4%	$1.00	4%	$1.00	4%

Source: Author's illustrative example.

Note: NGDP = nominal gross domestic product.

The second column shows what happens when there is a negative supply shock. The economy still grows by $1 trillion given the Fed's implicit NGDP target, but now three-fourths of that spending goes to higher prices and only one-fourth goes to real economic growth. That is because a negative supply shock reduces the economy's ability to produce goods and services. For a given level of spending, the price level thus rises, raising the inflation rate for that year. In this case, the negative supply shock leads to higher inflation—3 percent—but does not lead to higher total dollar spending.

A sure sign, then, that inflation is being driven by supply shocks is if total dollar spending stays on a stable growth path while inflation rises above its target. If instead, total dollar spending is rising sharply above its stable growth path and inflation is surging above 2 percent, then the higher inflation must be driven, in part, by positive demand shocks. This observation, combined with capacity constraints in the economy, implies that the larger the total dollar spending surge, the greater the amount of inflation caused by demand shocks. This is the workaround to the challenge of knowing what is causing movements in inflation.

To complete the story, the third column shows what happens with a positive supply shock. The economy, again, grows by $1 trillion, but now three-fourths of that spending goes to real economic growth and one-fourth to higher prices. In all scenarios, total dollar spending stays the same if macroeconomic policy controls the growth path of total dollar spending. Only the inflation rate temporarily moves around in response to supply shocks for a given NGDP target.

Applying the Workaround Insights to the Inflation Surge

If we apply this framework to the past few years, we can see the emerging consensus view in the data. Figures 4.1 and 4.2 show two breakdowns of total dollar spending data that help uncover what caused the inflation surge. Figures 4.1a, 4.1b, and 4.1c show the January 2020 Congressional Budget Office (CBO) forecast for NGDP, real GDP, and the GDP deflator (an inflation measure for all goods included in GDP), respectively, against the actual outturns. Figure 4.1a shows that total dollar spending, as measured by NGDP, dramatically overshot its CBO forecast by 7 percent or $2 trillion, as of the first quarter of 2023. A total dollar spending overshoot of this magnitude does not happen unless fiscal and monetary policy is overly expansionary and causes it to happen.

Since NGDP is the product of real GDP (RGDP) and the GDP deflator (i.e., NGDP = RGDP × GDP deflator), some have argued that the decrease in supply—a reduction in real GDP—during the COVID-19 pandemic pushed up prices and is responsible for the NGDP surge. It is true, as noted earlier, that for a given amount of NGDP, a reduction in RGDP will drive up prices. The problem with this claim, though, is that that total dollar spending is a policy choice. It could not have grown by 7 percent above the CBO forecast without macroeconomic policy—via stimulus checks, enhanced unemployment insurance, child tax credit, low interest rates, housing support policies—allowing it to happen.

FIGURE 4.1

Nominal GDP and inflation have been far above forecast

a. Nominal GDP versus CBO forecast, trillions of dollars

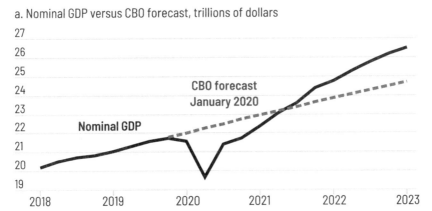

b. Real GDP versus CBO forecast, trillions of 2012 dollars

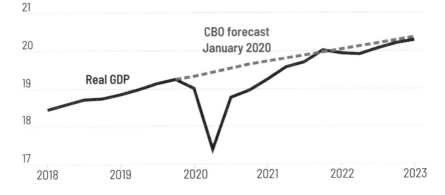

c. Nominal GDP versus CBO forecast, 2020 Q1 = 100

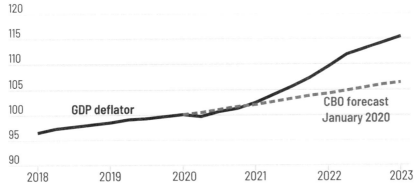

Sources: Congressional Budget Office, Bureau of Economic Analysis, and International Monetary Fund.[5]

FIGURE 4.2

Excess aggregate demand drove much of the inflation spike

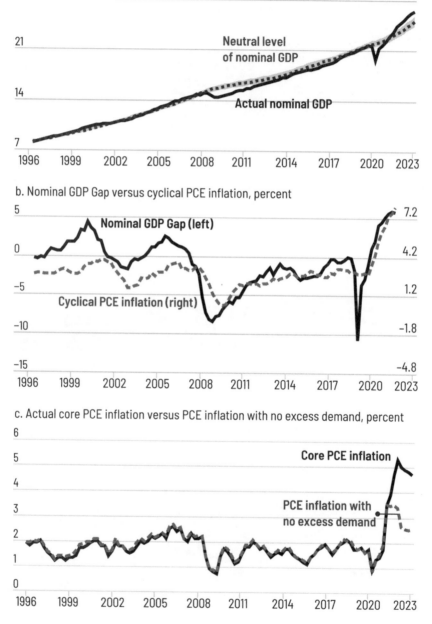

a. Actual versus neutral level of nominal GDP, trillions of dollars

b. Nominal GDP Gap versus cyclical PCE inflation, percent

c. Actual core PCE inflation versus PCE inflation with no excess demand, percent

Sources: The Mercatus Center's "Measuring Monetary Policy: The NGDP Gap," Federal Reserve Bank of San Francisco, and author's modeling.[6]

Note: PCE = Personal Consumption Expenditures Price Index.

As economist Jason Furman notes, a far more plausible story is that adding economic stimulus that was about 10 percent of GDP in the first quarter of 2020, when excess capacity in the economy was near 2 percent, was bound to quickly run up against capacity constraints. Real GDP could only grow by about 2 percent, whereas the remaining 8 percent of the dollar spending growth total would eventually find its way into the price level. Figure 4.1c confirms that projection. The GDP deflator was about 8 percent above the CBO forecast by the first quarter of 2023.[7]

Now the insights from Figure 4.1 are limited to the overall price level, which is the accumulation of past inflation rates. We are really interested in the period-by-period inflation rate. Figures 4.2a, 4.2b, and 4.2c provide it by using a measure called the NGDP gap. It comes from the Mercatus Center at George Mason University and is estimated as the difference between actual NGDP and the calculated "neutral" level of NGDP.[8] This latter measure is based on consensus forecasts from economists and allows for updating expectations about the future growth path of NGDP. The neutral level of NGDP, in other words, provides each period with an updated trend path for NGDP.

A positive NGDP gap can be viewed as total dollar spending that is high relative to expectations or, equivalently, is an indicator of excess aggregate demand. This measure, as seen in Figure 4.2b, turns out to be highly correlated with a separate measure from economist Adam Shapiro called "cyclical core PCE [Personal Consumption Expenditures] inflation." This is important because PCE inflation is the measure the Fed targets at 2 percent. The core PCE is a version of it that strips out volatile product categories, such as food and energy. Core PCE inflation can be seen, then, as a measure of the underlying or trend PCE inflation rate. It happens to be what many Fed officials watch closely. Cyclical core PCE inflation, therefore, is the part of core PCE inflation that is tied to swings in the business cycle.

The close relationship between the NGDP gap and cyclical core PCE inflation suggests that excess aggregate demand pressures were important drivers of the inflation. To see how important excess total dollar spending pressures have been to the inflation surge, I have estimated a statistical model that compared all parts of the PCE inflation rate with the NGDP gap. The estimated model was then run with the assumption that the NDGP gap returned to zero in the second quarter of 2021 and stayed at that value through the first quarter of 2023.[9]

Figure 4.2c shows the result of this counterfactual exercise. Interestingly, it reveals that core inflation would still have surged in 2021 but largely because of factors other than aggregate demand. These factors would have begun to start falling in 2022, whereas the aggregate demand pressures would have started to push up core inflation in 2022, keeping it elevated through the first quarter of 2023. This finding supports the emerging consensus view that the pandemic-related shocks initially drove the inflation surge in 2021, but by 2022 excess aggregate demand became the more important driver.

The U.S. inflation surge of 2021–2023 therefore provides a valuable learning experience. It shows that sudden swings in inflation can be hard to understand in real time. Fed officials and many economists saw the initial inflation surges as coming from large supply shocks due to the COVID-19 pandemic and then the war in Ukraine. Although these supply shocks did raise the price level, policymakers failed to see that starting in 2022 the persistence of inflation arose from the large amount of total dollar spending injected into the economy through fiscal and monetary policies during the pandemic. This chapter has shown that one way to avoid such confusion is to look at deviations of total dollar spending from its trend growth path. Doing so can help eliminate the confusion we've seen in the United States and Europe as to the underlying causes of the inflation surge.

CHAPTER 5

World War II Price Controls Were Not a "Total Success"

Ryan Bourne

As night follows day, high inflation will be met with calls for price controls. The inflation spike of 2021–2023 was a particularly ripe environment for such arguments. Skyrocketing natural gas prices following Russia's invasion of Ukraine had obviously contributed to a rising price level. Supply chains were still disrupted post-COVID-19. Central banks were citing both factors as evidence of inflation being "transitory"—at worst, a one-time jump in the price level. Given that the Federal Reserve couldn't control the global gas supply, produce computer chips, or unclog ports, the logic of the Fed's initial 2021 position was that a monetary tightening to reduce inflationary pressures would be counterproductive. Meeting a supply shock by squeezing aggregate demand as well would risk a deep recession.

Princeton historian Meg Jacobs and economist Isabella Weber therefore called instead for federal price caps on markets like fuel, food, and housing. Price increases in these sectors were not a symptom of a broader inflation but supply issues "driving inflation." "Congress," they explained, "can stabilize prices and reduce inflationary pressures through selective price caps combined with investments to increase the resilience of our economy."[1]

Jacobs and Weber acknowledged the poor track record of past price controls (see Chapter 7), but concluded that their success or failure this time hinged on political leadership, rather than economics. If President Joe Biden could articulate a clear rationale for them and so rally the country for the measures required, they thought history showed that using the force of law to prevent inflation could work.

Where did this confidence come from? President Franklin D. Roosevelt's price controls during World War II. Jacobs and Weber deemed America's wartime price caps a "total success" because (a) measured inflation fell during the time they were enforced, (b) the poor's living standards improved while they were implemented, and (c) inflation then surged again when those controls were lifted. If the price controls used today were well targeted, well monitored, and backed by FDR-style leadership, they concluded that setting price ceilings could mitigate our inflation at a far lower cost than tightening monetary conditions.

We have already seen, of course, that individual product prices do not "drive inflation" without accommodative monetary policy (Chapter 1) and that supply shocks cannot fully explain our recent inflation (Chapter 4). Strong eventual price pressure in sectors as diverse as "furniture, car and truck rentals, and hotels and motels" showed that this was a macroeconomic inflation and that using "targeted" controls to mitigate it was a chimera.[2]

Yet all that aside, the idea that American World War II price controls were a "total success" is itself a Panglossian take that deserves critiquing.

World War II Price Controls Brought Rationing and Bureaucracy

From 1941, President Franklin D. Roosevelt's administration began enforcing selective price controls, before freezing most prices across the economy at March 1942 levels under the General Maximum Price

Regulation. One rationale was to quell the inflationary pressures associated with monetary expansions alongside disruptions to the supply of goods. From 1943, a government bureaucracy determined specific product prices, prohibiting most increases.

Officials understood that shortages would be the inevitable consequence of disallowing price increases for products whose market prices would otherwise be rising. To ensure that customers could get essential goods, they therefore set up a comprehensive system of consumer rationing, limiting purchases of dairy, meat, sugar, tires, gas, and clothes. Large agencies, like the Office of Price Administration and its 64,500 staff members, were established to manage these price controls and to determine whether adjustments to prices were necessary. Public volunteer boards, totaling almost 108,000 people per year by the war's end, helped police the controls.[3] A range of other agencies played various roles in setting specific prices and rationing limits too, while businesses themselves had to engage in extensive compliance activity. These were huge and costly restrictions on economic and personal freedoms.

In wartime, however, price controls were considered the lesser of two evils. The government's focus had shifted to achieving military victory, with economic efficiency taking a back seat. Markets would struggle to respond to price signals with a government directing resources to the war effort anyway. Production of some consumer goods like refrigerators and cars was banned, whereas other items faced strict output limits. The collapse in production of household goods, coupled with the government having to create new money to fund the war effort—given the limits on its taxing and borrowing capacity—might risk household inflation really taking off.

Price controls and rationing were thus considered reasonable, despite their evident impositions. Not only might price ceilings help maintain national solidarity in wartime, but perhaps they might temporarily reduce the velocity of money—the frequency with which a unit of currency is exchanged to purchase goods and services. Price controls would make it possible for the government to purchase a given level of munitions or equipment without creating as much new money, thereby maybe even reducing the longer-term inflationary risks associated with the war.

None of the conditions we saw in the early 2020s would have justified such sacrifices. During the recent inflationary outburst, there was no reason government borrowing could not be financed through ordinary means; no larger societal ambition required sacrificing a functioning market economy; and reaching for price controls would have been rightly seen as an ex post decision that undermined the credibility of monetary policy.

What's more, given that inflation was a macroeconomic phenomenon, the sorts of "targeted price controls" Weber and Jacobs called for would have inevitably failed to stem the broader inflationary pressures we saw. Even the Roosevelt administration concluded that "selective" controls were hopeless to prevent broad-based inflation. At the very best you would get a waterbed effect, whereby holding down some prices would lead to greater price pressures for other substitute products elsewhere as consumers had more money to spend on them.

At that stage, there would have been calls for economy-wide price controls, as seen eventually in World War II and under President Richard Nixon. Such controls are obviously more damaging to the functioning of a market economy in peacetime. Even a low inflation rate is a weighted average of prices, made up of some soaring and others dropping significantly, due to changes in demand, supply, and the relative prices of individual goods. These movements in relative prices help guide economic activity. By freezing or restraining all prices, these price signals are muffled, leaving our economy directionless and inefficient, all without addressing the root causes of inflation.

Measured Wartime Inflation May Just Show Suppressed Inflation

Weber and Jacobs claim that the World War II price controls were successful because official prices increased more slowly when price controls were in place and then shot up when controls were lifted. And yes, it's true: economist Simon Kuznets's contemporary calculations for the Commerce Department estimate that the price index grew by just under 5 percent per year from 1942 to 1945, before jumping to an average of 10 percent per year from then to 1947—trends (but not magnitudes) corroborated by modern indexes of World War II–era wholesale and consumer prices.[4]

Yet as the economist Donald Boudreaux points out, this is no more evidence that price controls successfully control inflation than would readings of 120 pounds on a bathroom scale capped at 120 pounds show the scales help control body weight. Having outlawed price rises throughout the economy, it's no surprise that official inflation figures were lower during those controlled periods. What matters is whether those recorded prices just suppressed realities about the economy that were only revealed when the price controls were rescinded.

Most economists would start from the premise that inflation between two points in time is determined by changes in the money supply, real output, and the velocity of money. It's conceivable that price controls, by setting expectations of more price stability, might temporarily reduce the velocity of money, reducing the need for as much money creation to finance government spending, thereby reducing long-term inflationary pressure. It's also almost guaranteed that the inefficiencies created by price controls would reduce real output growth somewhat, thus increasing underlying inflationary pressure.

To a first approximation, however, we would expect any inflationary trends to be largely independent of price controls. Thus, when price controls are lifted, price increases previously concealed are suddenly revealed, just as if our weight cap had been removed from the scales.

As Milton Friedman and Anna Schwartz wrote about the experience with price controls during World War II:

> Price increases took indirect and concealed forms not recorded in the indexes. The large rise in price indexes when price control was repealed in 1946 consisted largely of an unveiling of the earlier concealed increases. Hence the recorded price indexes understate the price rise during the war and overstate the price rise after the war.[5]

Adjusting for what we might have expected to happen in the absence of controls, Friedman and Schwartz thought the effective price level increased by 27 percent during the regulated period, much higher than Kuznets's 15.6 percent.[6] Underlying prices, in other words, were really rising much more significantly during the 1942–1945 period than the official inflation statistics suggested.

Price Controls Had Quality and Time Costs

What were these "indirect and concealed forms" of price increases? Three spring to mind: quality deteriorations, time costs, and black markets.

When producers cannot increase prices to turn a profit, they are incentivized to reduce their product quality such that it more accurately reflects the suppressed price. A U.S. Bureau of Labor Statistics appraisal from 1943 concluded, "We believe that consumers' goods and services, in the aggregate, have since 1939 suffered some loss of quality that is not reflected in reported prices" under price controls.[7]

Contemporary wartime letters describe meat quality "that no amount of working can make tender," and a National Public Radio report documents how meatpackers "began filling sausages and hot dogs with soybeans, potatoes, or cracker meal," sold steaks with extra bone weight, or misrepresented the quality of meat cuts to circumvent price ceilings.[8] Coffee became mixed with roasted cereal, dried grass was sold as tea, and there was "shrinkflation" in candy bars (the practice of reducing the size of a product while maintaining its sticker price).

It wasn't just food products. Clothing was sold that economized on material. Soap manufacturers made greater use of the inferior linseed oil. Services usually provided alongside product sales were scaled back as some cheaper product lines were simply discontinued. To circumvent price controls, buyers and sellers often used "in-kind" favors too. During World War II, fringe benefits such as health insurance were expanded by employers to increase workers' remuneration as a means of circumventing wage controls, for example.

Regulators tried to adjust for these changes in setting price controls, but the sheer scale of these adaptations overwhelmed their efforts. Price increases in official wartime measures therefore substantially understated the actual price increases consumers faced, whereas inflation after decontrol was overstated in official records. Even in 1949, a Bureau of Labor Statistics retrospective estimated that the failure to account for quality deteriorations alone meant wartime inflation was a cumulative 5 percent higher than recorded.[9]

Another obvious result of price caps in World War II was shortages of certain products. That was expected, of course, and was why rationing was introduced. But the expansion of the gap between the quantity demanded and the quantity supplied meant shopping became more time-consuming in general.

The late economist Steven Horwitz described how a journalist in 1942, "Mr. Civilian," documented having to visit seven stores just to find soda.[10] Unsurprisingly, people eventually began to give up on buying their preferred goods, making more of their own clothes or growing produce in "victory gardens," keeping old refrigerators and stoves, and substituting available products for those they'd ordinarily prefer. Much of that entailed a greater time cost to obtain a given product or to keep it in good condition, increasing that product's effective price to consumers in ways inflation indexes would not detect. Official inflation data therefore reflected the changing prices of a different basket of goods that consumers would otherwise have spurned.[11]

Black markets were also a big issue. In markets with shortages, some buyers will be willing to pay more than the price cap, and some sellers will risk breaking the law to make a larger profit by selling above it. Those underground markets during World War II did not show up in official statistics, but they included goods smuggled across the border from Mexico into Texas and sellers evading official controls or rations. There were large shadow markets in gasoline and meat, for example, as well as zippers, liquor, used furniture, and tools.[12] The Office of Price Administration's Marshall Clinard later wrote that "such extensive conniving in the black market in illegal prices and rationed commodities" raises "serious questions . . . as to the strength of the moral fiber of the American people."[13]

Historian Hugh Rockoff has confirmed that price controls produced "extensive" evasion, generating "nearly as many civil [court] cases as the rest of the federal statutes combined."[14] These secondary markets mitigated the damage of price controls on economic efficiency, but, again, they made official inflation statistics less reliable.

Price Controls Didn't Make Americans Better Off

All these observations cast doubt on Jacobs and Weber's claim that price controls enhanced the poor's living standards. This assertion seems largely based on research by McMaster University historian Harvey Levenstein, which found that meat consumption for the poorest third of Americans increased during the war (by 17 percent), while falling for the top two-thirds.[15]

Government documents show a big per capita increase in meat consumption during the war for the average American civilian, with the 1935–1939 annual average of 126.2 pounds per capita consumed rising to 144.4 pounds by 1945.[16] But this observation requires broader context: it increased further to 155 pounds by 1947, when price controls and rationing had ended, suggesting a structural break in eating habits rather than price caps making people better off.

Reading through the general retrogression in economic life, it is unsurprisingly difficult to argue that the panoply of wartime controls were "good" for economic welfare. People often had to relocate to places with wartime production, working longer hours, more inconveniently, and at higher physical risk to then purchase fewer, lower-quality goods.

Holistic assessments of living standards during mass mobilization conflicts are difficult. The real gross national product per capita figures typically used as proxies for living standards during World War II are misleading. Given official inflation data understates true inflation, calculations of the real value of industrial output will tend to be overstated. Interpreting wartime output's value is itself difficult. Under the command and control of the government, American industries certainly churned out a lot of production. But much of that was not "final goods" that ordinary consumers desired. They were products bought by governments for warfighting efforts at administered, rather than market, prices.

Using the Friedman and Schwartz price index, historian Robert Higgs concludes that real—inflation-adjusted—consumption per capita over the wartime period would therefore be a better proxy for people's actual living standards than national output data.[17] Under this consumption measure, living standards declined between 1941 and

1945 and had increased by only 6.8 percent from 1939 through the end of the war—a relatively tardy growth. When controls ended in 1946, there was a boom in real consumption, which is all the more striking given that pent-up demand returned for products that required new industrial capacity to quickly start being produced again.

The success of the World War II price controls presented by Jacobs and Weber thus misrepresents the historical record. Yes, official statistics showed a slower growth in the price level during the period of price controls. But that masked the inevitable bureaucracy, dysfunctions, shortages, and quality deteriorations the price controls brought— understating true inflation and overstating gains in real living standards, both of which were revealed only when controls were removed.

In January 2022, the Initiative on Global Markets at the University of Chicago Booth School of Business (now the Clark Center Forum of the Kent A. Clark Center for Global Markets) asked a group of economists whether price controls could help tame inflation over the next 12 months.[18] Weighted by their confidence levels, most economists disagreed (65 percent), no doubt assuming the question referred to underlying inflation. Among the 24 percent who agreed, however, all clarified in their answers that price controls would nevertheless cause "huge distortions" and shortages, or would simply postpone measured inflation until later. Very few serious economists today believe price controls are an efficient way to tackle inflation. And yet every time inflation rears its head, this misleading history reappears.

CHAPTER 6

Modern Monetary Theory Has No Road Map for Dealing with Inflation

Stan Veuger

Just a few years ago, around 2018, a craze started sweeping the nation—or at least the economics community on Twitter—and received the endorsement of Rep. Alexandria Ocasio-Cortez (D-NY).[1] Modern monetary theory (MMT) would at long last bring us full employment and price stability by carefully navigating the actual constraints keeping us from a flawless macroeconomic policy.

These constraints, so we were told, were emphatically not budgetary in nature. There was no inherent limit to the federal government's ability to borrow to spend. Stony Brook University economics professor Stephanie Kelton, perhaps the theory's most prominent proponent, wrote a *New York Times* bestseller titled *The Deficit Myth: Modern Monetary Theory and the Birth of the People's Economy* that was published in the early months of the COVID-19 pandemic.[2]

As Kelton put it in a *New York Times* op-ed around the time of the book's release: "In 2020 Congress has been showing us—in practice if not in its rhetoric—exactly how M.M.T. works: It committed trillions of dollars this spring that in the conventional economic sense it did not 'have.' It didn't raise taxes or borrow from China to come up with dollars to support our ailing economy."[3] She wasn't entirely wrong: the Federal Reserve printed lots of money and the federal government did spend more than \$4 trillion through six pandemic relief bills, but even this spending was largely financed through borrowing from the public.[4] Of course, when that borrowing occurred, the federal government did "have" those trillions of dollars, even in the most conventional economic sense.

In any case, the MMT promise was that policymakers in countries like the United States, that have their own currency and issue sovereign debt denominated in it, do not have to worry about deficits and debt. Instead, the line goes, only real resources—the availability of idle labor, inputs, and capital goods—represent a potentially binding constraint on what the government can accomplish. What we would observe if we ever hit that constraint is increasing rates of inflation. And after a decade of stable inflation, during which mainstream economists were talking about secular stagnation and structurally low private demand, that constraint seemed unlikely to bind anytime soon.

MMT in Theory

Modern monetary theory is not quite what one might expect from contemporary economic theory. It is a movement—a group of people and the writings, speeches, and tweets they produce— more than a precise set of ideas, rigorously derived, with testable implications.

But some of the foundational elements are clear. First, there is the— trivially true—fact that governments can always meet their nominal obligations in their own currency. MMT proponents make a big deal out of this. Second, there is the technically true but misleading implication that this implies that governments do not need to raise tax revenue or issue bonds to finance their expenditures. Instead, they can simply create money to pay transfer recipients, suppliers, public-sector employees, and so forth.

On one level, MMT proponents take this to mean that the exact level of the deficit per se does not matter; only inflation does. Where money is needed, the government can simply create it. Fiscal policy (that is, taxation and government spending), not directly constrained by concerns over debt and deficits or financing, can then be oriented toward the implementation of social policy goals and the directed allocation of resources. Only if inflation becomes a threat does fiscal policy play a major macroeconomic role, whereas monetary policy as typically conceptualized is practically nonexistent within the MMT framework. Compared with the thinking of mainstream economists, this is almost a complete role reversal.[5]

On a different level, MMT departs from the idea that aggregate demand and output gaps, as conventionally considered, matter as much as mainstream economists believe they do. Instead, as long as specific capital goods or people sit idle, there is always room for additional spending and consumption. The most meaningful way in which MMT differs from conventional macroeconomic thinking, for policy purposes, is the idea that politicians can spend all they want on their social policy goals unless inflation arrives, and that they do not have to worry about aggregate indicators of overheating or labor markets tightening in ways that most economists do.

It is perhaps worth highlighting how this difference manifested itself in early 2021. While MMT advocates were celebrating the overly aggressive fiscal and monetary response to the COVID-19 pandemic, more mainstream macroeconomists—even those who had gone a bit overboard in their enthusiasm for loose fiscal policy in the years before the pandemic—started to get concerned.[6] Their concerns were based precisely on the kind of conventional output gap reasoning (that spending would be far too high relative to any spare capacity in the economy) dismissed by the MMT crowd.

Here is a sample of what MMT boosters, such as J. W. Mason, an associate professor of economics at John Jay College, City University of New York, were writing instead:

> What we need now is textbooks and theories that bring out, system-atize and generalize the reasoning that justifies a great expansion of public spending, unconstrained by conventional estimates of potential output, public debt or the need to preserve labor-market incentives. The circumstances of the past year are obviously exceptional, but that doesn't mean they can't be made the basis of a general rule.[7]

Economic thinking is defenestrated and replaced with standard big-government central planning, masquerading behind bizarro accounting logic.

When inflation does arrive, the idea is that we can simply turn to price controls or taxation or varying the salaries of people in government job guarantee programs or expanded supply—or really anything but conventional monetary policy. As Nathan Tankus, research director of the Modern Money Network, put it, "It would be kind of ridiculous, if you don't have much influence, to make the cookbooks of the future."[8] So MMT proponents have traditionally refused to be pinned down on which specific correct policy mix would be appropriate in which situation, although their initial instinct, at least until recently, had been to raise taxes when inflation is high to reduce the private sector's spending capacity.

Usually, however, what you get instead is a laundry list of things one might or might not do to address inflationary pressures. To the extent that they provide policy prescriptions to deal with inflation, they tend to lean into the idea that inflation is a sector- or region-specific problem more than a macroeconomic one. As an illustration, here are the inflation-fighting suggestions made by Tankus, University of Missouri economist Scott Fullwiler, and Cornell doctoral fellow Rohan Grey in a 2019 *Financial Times* article[9]:

- Cut Medicare and Medicaid prices
- Strengthen antitrust policy
- Hold public hearings
- Construct alternative price indexes
- Raise taxes
- Tighten financial and credit regulations
- Shrink the fossil fuel, real estate, defense, and financial industries
- Tighten environmental regulations
- Implement the Green New Deal
- Address bottlenecks in specific industries
- Prevent shortages
- Regulate big business more actively
- Reform the congressional budgeting process
- Have the Congressional Budget Office produce inflation scores
- Strengthen automatic stabilizers
- Introduce a Federal Jobs Guarantee
- Increase the availability of savings bonds
- Index tax brackets to an inflation target
- Raise payroll taxes
- Introduce more tax brackets

You may or may not like some of these policies, and I am certainly not opposed to using our current inflationary environment as justification for policy changes I have supported all along, but this approach is ineffective both because it scatters responsibility all over the federal government and because some of the proposed anti-inflation policies are either ineffective or counterproductive.

To take a few examples: Who in their right mind would look at recent congressional negotiations over raising the debt limit and say, "Sure, let's have Congress fine-tune inflation through tax policy as well?" How would intensifying environmental regulations conceivably place downward, as opposed to upward, pressure on inflation, when it would reduce economic output? How would shrinking industries increase supply? How would the myriad agencies involved in this process actually coordinate?

Frankly, it is a mess, one that highlights the value, whatever its weaknesses, of the rigor imposed by the academic peer review process.

The Inadequacy of MMT

Fast-forward two years, and the concerns expressed by some mainstream economists in 2021 are now generally considered to have been vindicated. The deficit myth encountered reality, and running large deficits without corresponding monetary tightening brought us persistently high rates of inflation, as shown in Figure 6.1. This undermined a strong version of MMT, the view, expressed by Mason, that the economy is "normally well short of supply constraints rather than at potential on average."[10]

But a generous reading is that the real test for MMT advocates was yet to come. They had consistently argued that inflation—and inflation alone—would indicate that policymakers should consider implementing new policies. Of course—and this was certainly not a phenomenon limited to the MMT-sphere—first came a lengthy period of inflation denial (it's "transitory"), anger (it's "greed"), and bargaining (what if COVID-19 hadn't happened, what if supply chain issues resolve, and how about the war in Ukraine?), characterized by the construction of increasingly more esoteric inflation measures to dismiss that a problem even existed.[11]

Before returning to MMT, it's worth noting that these more esoteric inflation measures were in a sense modeled on the idea of "core inflation" that the Federal Reserve uses to exclude particularly volatile

FIGURE 6.1

The inflation surge showed the United States didn't have lots of spare economic capacity

Annual Consumer Price Index inflation (excluding food and energy), percent change from one year ago

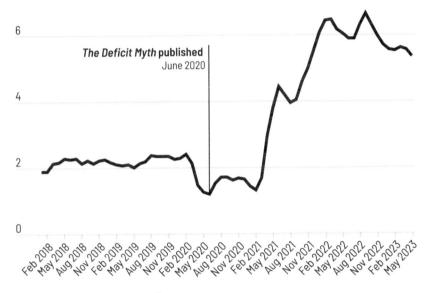

Source: Bureau of Labor Statistics.[12]

components of the consumption basket from its inflation measure. What observers were allegedly doing was excluding categories of goods and services that were particularly affected by temporary supply disruptions, and thus looking only at price increases in unaffected, nonvolatile categories of consumption as a proxy for true inflation.

This connects directly to the MMT thinking described earlier. MMT thinking dismisses to a significant extent the importance of aggregate demand-and-supply dynamics in favor of a focus on microeconomic and targeted interventions in particular subsectors to address rapid increases in the general price level. If only we could address the troublesome product categories with prices that are increasing the most!

It also connects to the broader theme of this book: by actively ignoring a subset of prices, policymakers who struggle to aggregate information in the best of worlds set themselves up for failure. Pointing repeatedly at categories of prices that are special—affected by the COVID-19 pandemic, or by the war in Ukraine, or by remote work—made it all too easy to ignore the one price that mattered: the overall rate of inflation. And of course, the whole inflation situation connects to it directly as well: deviations from stable price growth make it difficult for producers and consumers alike to interpret price signals.

What did not materialize were more focused policy prescriptions; instead, all we got was more of the laundry list–type content discussed earlier. Does anyone seriously believe a Federal Jobs Guarantee would have mitigated, rather than worsened, labor shortages? Would setting price controls for facemasks have made them less scarce? Wishful thinking about public-sector investment growing the supply side may make for good, catchy names for legislation (the Inflation Reduction Act), but reduce inflation it does not.

The Aftermath

Now, one may wonder: How have MMT's advocates adjusted their thinking in response to the broad-based surge in prices that materialized after some of their preferred policies were adopted? How did their advocacy adapt to the realization that there was far less slack in the economy than they suggested?

The short answer: not at all. Even though we did what they wanted on spending and soon discovered that it backfired, their positions remain unchanged. The only thing we hear less of is the call to increase payroll taxes to control inflation.

There is still a lot of pointing toward "concrete situations"—specific supply chain issues that should have been addressed, like inefficiencies at ports. A major advantage of the laundry list approach favored by MMT champions is that they can always point to items on the list that have not yet been tried.

To put it more clearly: generalized inflation will always manifest itself in increases of prices of specific goods and services first, so there are always specific product markets to point to as problematic. But it is an error to think that generalized inflation will manifest itself in all prices in the same way at the same time. Some prices are stickier than others, and some goods are more durable than others. It should perhaps not come as a surprise that folks who believe there is a money tree would miss the forest for the trees.

PART 2

Prices and Price Controls

Prices and Price Controls: An Introduction

Ryan Bourne

High inflation and supply shocks in certain sectors since 2021 have helped revive the policy allure of price controls.[1] After all, if rising prices are a problem, why not simply ban businesses from increasing them, particularly in "essential" sectors that are crucial to the well-being of the poor?

Governments have been interfering with prices for over 4,000 years.[2] Economists overwhelmingly reject the theory that a general system of price controls (as in the 1940s and 1970s) can mitigate inflation, at least without serious harm, as we saw in Chapter 5. But a time of rapidly rising prices has nevertheless seen an increased interest in market-specific price controls, purportedly to help those struggling most with rising living costs.

In Europe, that took the form of capping the price of domestic energy and, in some countries, food prices. Here in the United States, we have seen a fresh outbreak in rent control proposals. But, in truth, there are many individual sectors in which the federal, state, and local governments have controlled or continue to control market prices already, often bringing substantial economic harm.

What Are Market Prices?

Few elements of economics are as fundamental as the concept of prices. At its crudest, a price is just the monetary value assigned to a product or service by whoever sets it. A *market* price is more interesting: it's the amount of money that a buyer pays a seller in open exchange for a good or service.

Market prices are broadly determined by the supply and demand for the product in question—that is, they reflect the intersection of consumers' preferences and willingness to pay with producers' costs and willingness to supply. This distinguishes them from administered prices—those that are decreed by some authority, such as the government, or (theoretically) a monopoly with pricing power.

A lot of public discussion of prices takes place as if all prices are administered prices, in the sense of businesses having free rein to set them at whatever level they wish. In the real world, market prices rise and fall because of shifts in supply and demand. Firms can only profitably charge prices that (a) consumers are willing to pay and (b) competitors (current or potential) cannot easily undercut. A company may notionally set its own prices, but in anything other than the immediate term, the price it can sustainably charge is dictated by these broader forces.

Yet rather than see prices as the outcome of an ongoing market process, it's common for the public to recoil at high prices, blaming them on market actors and appealing to governments to control them. Public opinion often casts prices as roadblocks to people's dreams, deeming them "unreasonable" or "excessive." Consider wanting to rent a decent house in a safe Northern Virginia neighborhood. It's easy to label current rents as "ridiculous" and call for government intervention to cap them to make renting more affordable.

The perception of individual prices as "unfair" emerges partly from the very nature of market trades. Transactions occur when they benefit both parties—when the buyer values the product more than the money parted with, and the seller appreciates the cash more than the product relinquished. Each party to the transaction usually receives a surplus. The consumer's surplus is the difference between the maximum the buyer would be willing to pay and what the buyer ends up paying. The producer's surplus is the difference between the sale price and the minimum the seller would be willing to accept. The fact that both parties consider themselves better off means that, technically, the seller would also be willing to accept a slightly lower price, and the buyer a slightly higher price, than agreed. Both sides can thus feel they have sacrificed a bit more than they really needed to, even if each is better off overall.

What Economic Role Do Prices Play?

Market prices are crucial to solving "the economic problem." That is, they help us decide how to most effectively allocate scarce resources in a world of unlimited wants and needs.

Consider the myriad resources out there: my labor, copper, orange farms in Florida, homes in Milwaukee, tickets for a Taylor Swift concert, hospital beds, semiconductor factories, Walt Disney World hotels, and any other product or service you can think of. We could combine or use the labor, capital, land, and entrepreneurs available in trillions of different ways. We could, theoretically, place me in a hospital tomorrow to undergo coronary artery bypass surgery, surrounded by my Cato colleagues cosplaying doctors and nurses, under the management of Sen. Bernie Sanders (I-VT). The results would be disastrous.

Without resorting to random resource allocation, we need a more refined mechanism. For a time in the 20th century, "central planning" was considered the silver bullet. Governments would assess societal needs, and experts would coordinate who does what and how. Historical experiments like the Soviet Union demonstrated the disastrous inadequacy of this approach. Germany's split into a democratic capitalist state in the West and a communist one in the East provides a perfect example. Around the time of Germany's reunification, gross domestic product per capita in East Germany was less than half the level of that in West Germany.[3]

A key reason for this is that no planner can harness the knowledge necessary to effectively allocate goods and services to their highest-value uses. Would my next-door neighbor be most effective as a medic, an economist, or a plumber? Should the local factory make cars or aircraft parts? How about the farm: Would the land be better deployed for a housing project? What is the most effective way for managers to motivate an individual worker? This information is not just dispersed and difficult to gather, but often tacit, rooted in instinctive or particular knowledge and experience.

Unlike a central planner, a market economy, through its price mechanism, can harness this knowledge. That is because all that knowledge is expressed in decisions that are driving supply and demand and thus prices. Prices are therefore crucial in coordinating our activity toward productive ends. They help communicate vast amounts of information from millions and millions of transactions, which then helps guide our plans toward acts that add value for others.

How does this work? Market prices encourage us to use resources more efficiently by providing people with signals about which plans they should undertake without the need for costly information gathering. Prices capture the relative scarcity of different goods based on today's context-specific conditions and communicate that information to everyone else. You don't need to know that baby formula prices are rising because of a temporary factory closure. The higher price alone tells you it's not the best time to make bulk purchases of baby formula, helping ration goods for those who value them most. Similarly, unaffected producers can see from the higher price that it's more profitable to run overtime, fire up spare capacity, or run down inventories to provide more baby formula to the market now. The price increase therefore encourages an expansion of the quantity supplied, shifting us toward an efficient allocation of resources. Market prices thus help align the interests of buyers and sellers.

As George Mason University economist Alex Tabarrok puts it, "Prices are a signal wrapped up in an incentive."[4] That phrase captures prices' dual economic role. Price movements provide information (the "signal") about the broad state of the market that helps producers and consumers reassess their plans. Rising prices show that a good has seen either increased demand (perhaps because a substitute product has seen its price rise) or a fall in supply (perhaps because of a shortage of inputs or a natural disaster). Crucially, such movements provide an "incentive" that encourages buyers and sellers to use the scarce resource efficiently.

Not all market prices will be "correct" at any given time. In a market economy, we are all constantly involved in the trial-and-error process of trying to make better decisions. For companies, that means making myriad decisions at all times: Should we reorganize that team? Run a different advertising campaign? Sell those two products bundled together? Abandon this line of production entirely?

But prices themselves provide a crucial feedback mechanism for improving decisionmaking. That's because the wisdom of past decisions can be assessed by using prices to compute revenues that we can then compare with costs of production (also prices) to examine profit and loss. This profit and loss information provides evidence on whether the new good, or the new management technique, or whatever else has been tested, generates net value.

If a healthy profit results from a new form of product, it signals to other entrepreneurs "more of this please," attracting them into the market to offer similar goods at a higher quality or lower price. This ongoing process is what drives societal improvements in how we use resources, making us richer.

Market prices are thus crucial to economic well-being in three respects:

- They help guide us in what we should do given the ever-changing realities around us and our own preferences.
- When we do act, they help generate profit-and-loss information, which allows us to evaluate whether our decisions were good ones.
- Price movements, and then profit and loss, encourage experiments, entrepreneurialism, and market discoveries of better ways of doing things over time.

Market prices are therefore a crucial driver not just of economic efficiency, but of entrepreneurial economic growth.

What Are Price Controls?

Price controls are government-enforced restrictions on the rates sellers can charge for their goods or services. These rules often come dressed as two principal characters: price ceilings and price floors.

A price ceiling is a legally mandated maximum price that can be charged for a good or service. We are interested in price ceilings when they bind—that is, when they hold the legal price below the natural market price. Rent control in cities like New York serves as a classic case, where annual rent increases are kept in check with the aim of safeguarding affordable housing for the less affluent.

A price floor, on the other hand, is a legally set minimum price. It binds when set above the equilibrium market price. Minimum wage laws serve as an example. The federal government and many states and localities set a minimum hourly wage rate that employers can pay workers, notionally to eliminate exploitation and to protect poor families' living standards.

In truth, however, governments impose many other forms of price controls. These include bans on money transactions (a zero-dollar price control, as for kidney donations), regulations on differential pricing for diverse customers (as with health care premiums), constraints on specific fees or price structures (see President Joe Biden's "junk fees" agenda), and legal repercussions for rapid price hikes during emergencies (anti-price-gouging laws).

What Are the Major Effects of Price Controls?

Following the same reasoning for why market prices *encourage* economic efficiency, implementing government price controls tends to *discourage* it. By setting a mandated price that ill reflects market supply-and-demand realities, price controls usually provide faulty information to producers and consumers about a product's relative scarcity. This, in turn, affects our production and consumption decisions, which deviate from those seen under markets with freely floating prices. Crucially, putting a government floor or ceiling on prices eliminates mutually beneficial trades. It stops (at least legally) people from trading with others at a price that both would accept—a price that is indicative of both sides considering themselves better off.

An example helps illuminate this effect. Suppose the federal government imposed a crude price ceiling that said no landlords across the United States could increase rents for five years (see Figure P2.1a). The price of rental housing would be fixed below market rates. At that lower price, more people would seek rental accommodation than before—there would be an increase in the quantity demanded. But at the same time, landlords would now have less of an incentive to make their housing available for rent relative to, say, selling for owner occupation, living in it themselves, or selling the land for some other use. The quantity of rentable accommodation supplied would fall.

As Figure P2.1a shows, the primary impact would be an acute shortage of rental accommodation caused by that supply-and-demand mismatch. That means there would be potential tenants out there wishing

FIGURE P2.1

Price ceilings and price floors deliver shortages and surpluses, respectively

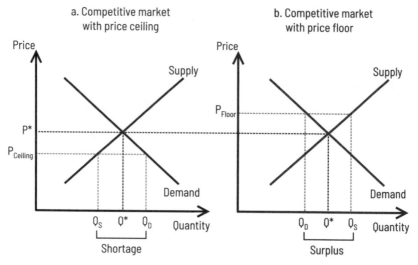

a. Competitive market
with price ceiling

b. Competitive market
with price floor

to rent, and willing to pay the price landlords would demand, but who could not form that agreement legally because of the price ceiling. This destroys value, even before we think about the longer-term perverse incentives that a sustained period of below-market rents would cause for the provision of new supply.

Price floors create the opposite problem but are similarly inefficient in competitive markets (Figure P2.1b). Fixing a price above the market rate reduces the quantity demanded, but it expands sellers' willingness to supply. So you end up with a surplus of the good. Some sellers who would be willing to sell at a lower price are legally unable to do so, despite there clearly being willing buyers at the lower price. This, again, destroys economic welfare.

The creation of these shortages and surpluses is the most obvious consequence of crude price controls in competitive markets. Yet there are many more subtle effects and adjustments to their imposition, especially when policymakers preempt the likelihood of shortages or surpluses by allowing exemptions or carveouts from the laws.

First, price controls can lead to the seller or buyer adjusting the quality of the controlled product or service, or else using other offsetting fees or compensation to protect their interests. Fixing rents below market rates, for example, can lead to landlords skimping on renovation or upkeep and thus allowing the apartment's quality to decline to reflect its new price. Setting a minimum wage above the market pay rate can likewise lead an employer to adjust other nonwage benefits or the quality of the work environment to save money to offset the cost of the higher hourly wage rate. Mandating a below-market price can similarly lead to imaginative new fees or charges such that the effective price consumers face is essentially unchanged.

Second, price controls are often associated with new, intrusive means of allocating goods or services. If goods aren't rationed by price, they must be rationed by first-come, first-served lines, by explicit rationing (e.g., one purchase per customer per visit), by more extensive consumer searching for the product, or through favoritism or nepotism. A lot of these means of allocation are socially wasteful, replacing market prices with extra search or time costs for customers that nobody captures. There are no guarantees that allocating goods this way will benefit the poor, in whose name many price controls are implemented. For example, rent controls can lead to situations where wealthier individuals end up benefiting from reduced rents, while poorer individuals struggle to find available housing because of the resulting shortage. In markets with shortages, some buyers will inevitably be willing to pay more than the price cap, and some sellers will risk breaking the law to make a larger profit by selling above it. Secondary illicit markets thus develop to help mitigate shortages or surpluses, but they bring crime and underground activity, with all their attendant costs.

Third, price controls can have ripple effects in other parts of the economy. For instance, those renters lucky enough to benefit from rent control policies face large financial disincentives against moving to better job opportunities and facing market rents again. This can lead to workers staying in jobs, areas, and apartments ill-suited to their needs, but better suited to others' needs, harming broader productivity. A price control on oil might likewise create shortages, leading to interruptions in steel production and thus delaying a range of construction and manufacturing projects. Interfering with the price system can therefore lead to broader discoordination across the economy.

Fourth, by artificially lowering potential returns, price controls can reduce the incentive for businesses to invest in new technologies or processes, slowing economic progress. Imagine that we capped home-use water prices, for example, but underlying market prices were rising as the population grew in the western United States, increasing water demand. This price control would reduce the incentive over time to invest in the exploration of new water sources or technologies to help conserve water, even though both reactions to higher prices could eventually have produced innovative breakthroughs that helped lower long-run market water prices by increasing supply or reducing demand.

Price controls can therefore become near-permanent features in a market, as their existence reduces the incentives to deliver entrepreneurial actions to lower costs and prices. In fact, price controls replace the market process with the political process, with vested interests lobbying governments for price controls' continuation or expansion.

What Do Economists Think about Price Controls?

Economists generally oppose price controls because of all the misallocations and negative consequences outlined herein.[5]

As we read in Chapter 5, economists agree that economy-wide price controls are not a credible means of curing inflation. In January 2022, a survey of top economists by the University of Chicago Booth School of Business (now the Clark Center Forum of the Kent A. Clark Center for Global Markets) asked whether 1970s-style price controls could successfully reduce U.S. inflation over the next year.[6] Weighed by respondents' confidence levels, 65 percent disagreed, 11 percent were uncertain, and 24 percent agreed. Even those who thought banning price hikes could reduce short-term *measured* inflation qualified their answers by saying that price controls would nevertheless produce negative consequences and so should be avoided. Economist David Autor summed up this sentiment by writing, "Price controls can of course control prices—but they're a terrible idea!"[7]

The microeconomic case for price controls in individual markets gets similarly weak support from economists. Since 2012, large majorities of the Chicago Booth survey cohort have provided answers that indicate the downsides of rent control and their opposition to anti-price-gouging legislation, for example.[8]

Overall, it's clear that economists usually oppose price controls because price controls reduce efficiency, while often not delivering the promised benefits to those they are designed to help. Politicians and the public tend to push price controls in the name of helping the poor. Economists would instead advocate for policies that expand the supply of essential goods and services, lowering their market price to customers. If certain households still find themselves in need, economists argue that it's better to transfer cash assistance to them directly through the tax-and-welfare system, while preserving market prices to better coordinate economic activity.

Yet despite all this, in the United States, the federal, state, and local governments have controlled, and continue to control, prices across numerous individual sectors. This policy front in the war on prices is explored in this part.

CHAPTER 7

Price Controls Have Been Disastrous throughout History

Eamonn Butler

Government attempts to curb rising prices and wage costs are as old as recorded history. Indeed, as we have seen over *Forty Centuries of Wage and Price Controls*, to quote the title of a book I coauthored with Robert L. Schuettinger, no economic policy has been tested so long, so often, among so many peoples, and in so many places. Nor does any have such a uniform record of failure.[1] The historical evidence is clear: wage and price controls do not stop price inflation, because they address only its symptoms, not its causes—causes such as governments' mismanagement of the currency. Instead, capping prices creates shortages, misallocations, black markets, and contempt for the law.

Yet even today, we find politicians, officials, and economists reaching for these failed weapons to combat price increases wherever and however they arise, often citing the impact of price increases on the poor to justify controls.

Following the surge in energy prices caused by the war in Ukraine, for example, lawmakers throughout Europe imposed caps on energy bills. Economists such as Isabella Weber have also argued for "targeted controls" on "fuel, food and housing" prices that she thinks were "driving" inflation in 2022.[2] The Roosevelt Institute's Todd N. Tucker has argued that companies took advantage of the post-COVID-19 reopening to raise prices, which should have been curbed.[3]

American presidents from George W. Bush to Joe Biden have sought to limit drug prices. Despite the dismal effects on the housing market every time they have been tried, rent controls are being reestablished in many American localities and in Scotland, while figures such as Bernie Sanders (I-VT) and the United Kingdom's Green Party advocate their national rollouts. The demands to control prices do not stop.

Price Controls through Ancient History

The remarkable thing is that anyone thinks such controls can work given their long experience in history. In *Forty Centuries of Wage and Price Controls,* Schuettinger and I charted over 100 examples of their failure through history, starting with the price controls on grain in Fifth Dynasty Egypt around 2800 BCE.

Grain was an essential commodity, and Egypt's rulers depended on it being affordable. Cruelly policed by an army of officials, they imposed such onerous controls on prices that farmers could not make a living and simply ran off, leaving Egypt with severe shortages—the exact opposite of the rulers' intention.[4] Five hundred years later, the wage and price controls imposed by the Sumerian ruler Urukagina produced similar results.[5] A document from the time records widespread evasion by the people and dismal abuses by the authorities. It appeals for *amargi* ("freedom")—the first time that the word appears in writing.[6]

About 1750 BCE, Hammurabi of Babylon, who fancied himself the "king of kings," had the legal prices of goods and services inscribed on dolomite tablets for public view.[7] They specified payment of eight *gur* of corn annually for laborers and six for herdsmen; five grains of silver a day for potters and tailors, four for carpenters and rope makers; and so on. The result? Merchants and workers upped and left, and the

Babylonian economy declined as trade suffered (though the output of official documents continued to increase).[8]

Three thousand miles away, the Official System of Chou (1122 BCE) aimed to micromanage China's economy, sending out a regulator called a "master of merchants" for every 20 shops to fix prices according to costs.[9] Merchants were not allowed to raise prices, even in the face of harvest failures, natural shortages, and other serious events. It did not take long for these forlorn ambitions to be abandoned.

In India around 320 BCE, the political thinker Kautilya wrote on the art of government. Among other things, he specified the rate of profit that merchants should be allowed to earn and the wages of workers, from musicians and artisans to prostitutes and scavengers.[10] He proposed appointing officials to determine and enforce these prices. Likewise, ancient Greece employed an army of inspectors, called *sitophylakes*, to set prices, particularly those of essentials such as grain and loaves. When (despite the death penalty) the controls proved ineffective and the artificially low prices created inevitable shortages, the state had to appoint corn buyers, called *sitonai*, to source grain from wherever they could.[11]

The Roman Republic's Law of the Twelve Tables in 449 BCE fixed the maximum rate of interest on loans.[12] A law of 367 BCE even ruled that interest paid had to be deducted from the principal (an effective interest rate of zero).[13] Unsurprisingly, these efforts did not last. But other attempts to fix prices continued. In 122 BCE, the tribune Gaius Gracchus's *lex frumentaria* allowed Roman citizens to buy a certain quantity of grain at below-market prices.[14] Again, the idea was to ensure that the poor had sufficient food. But then farmers outside Rome, unable to make a profit, stopped working and moved to find other jobs in the city.[15]

Roman emperors commonly tried to ease their economic problems by debasing the coinage. By the time Diocletian ascended the throne in 284 CE, the silver *denarius* had been replaced by tin-plated copper coins, still called *denarii*.[16] People subsequently hoarded their more valuable silver currency and demanded many more of these low-value coins in payment for their goods. It was a classic episode of inflation, which Diocletian blamed on the "greed" of the hoarders rather than any government failure. In 301 CE, he sent an edict throughout the empire, fixing the wages of professions from laborers to academics, and setting the maximum prices at which meat, barley, beer, eggs, clothing, and even male lions could be sold—on pain of death for both buyers and sellers.[17] The result, according to a contemporary account, was that "people stopped bringing provisions to market because they could not get a reasonable price for them." There were food riots, and "much blood was spilled."[18] Diocletian abdicated four years later.

Price Controls from Medieval Markets to Revolutionary Regimes

In medieval Europe, the ruler Charlemagne published tables of prices and in 806 CE declared that those hoarding grain or wine in the hope of getting higher prices later were guilty of dishonesty.[19] Authorities in England tried much the same.[20] In 1199, the London city government tried to control the price of wine. It proved impossible to enforce. In 1202, King Henry III fixed exact prices for different weights of grain.[21] That failed too. By 1330, a new law ordered merchants to sell wine at "reasonable" prices based on their costs, but prices still soared.[22]

Wages soared too after the Black Death of 1348, when high mortality led to a shortage of laborers, bidding up workers' pay.[23] A statute designed to limit the increases saw about 9,000 cases come to court, almost all being found in the employers' favor—whereupon laborers either refused to take on work or moved into places or occupations where they could earn more.[24]

English authorities also attempted to control interest rates. In 1364, the City of London passed a law against usury, an idea extended nationwide in 1390.[25] But lenders and borrowers found loopholes. An even more stringent law in 1487 proved no more effective and was abandoned nine years later.[26] Nevertheless, local authorities continued trying to regulate the prices of essentials such as food, drink, wood, coal, tallow, and candles.[27] After 1485, the Tudor kings extended such controls into other commodities with little effect.[28] Prices of most goods and services soared in the "great inflation" caused by the Tudors' debasement of the coinage.

Across the English Channel, Spanish forces in 1584–1585 besieged Antwerp, in what is now Belgium. Food became scarce and prices escalated, whereupon the city government set maximum prices for each food item.[29] That regulation reduced the incentive for merchants to risk smuggling food into the city, and, given the low prices of food, citizens felt little pressure to cut back their consumption. Predictably, the food all ran out.

An even worse disaster befell Bengal after the 1770 failure of the rice crop. The government strove to keep down the price of rice, which only fueled the quantity demanded, leading to a shortage in which a third of the population died. Ninety-six years later, the province suffered a similar crop failure, but this time the authorities allowed prices to rise, helping curb consumption, encourage imports, and avoid disastrous shortages.[30]

On the other side of the world, in 1630, the New England colonists set limits of 2 shillings a day on the wages of thatchers, carpenters, bricklayers, and others, with a fine of 10 shillings on anyone paid more, while another law declared that no commodity could be sold above a third more than it cost in England.[31] These regulations lasted only six months before being abandoned.[32] Much later, in 1774, the

Continental Congress decreed that sellers should not "take advantage of the scarcity of goods" but should sell at the previous year's prices.[33] Its issuance of paper money—the infamous "continentals"—did not help these efforts.[34] Over the next two years, in various parts of the colonies, further price laws followed.[35]

Price regulation nearly did in George Washington's revolutionary army. The legislature of Pennsylvania, where Washington was based, decided to control the prices of food and other commodities the army needed.[36] Their hope was to reduce the cost of the war, but farmers simply refused to sell their produce at such low prices. Some even took their produce to the British, who paid market prices in gold.[37] In the harsh Valley Forge winter of 1776, Washington's army nearly starved.[38] John Adams complained that the "improvident act" of price controls had "done great injury" and unless repealed, would "ruin the state and introduce a civil war."[39]

Further north, in present-day Canada but then part of New France, legislators imposed a set price for codfish, and—learning from previous price-fixing failures—forbade fishers from refusing to sell at that price. Nevertheless, the result was a decline in this crucially important industry, as fishers and merchants simply moved elsewhere.[40]

Back in old France, the revolutionary government that deposed Louis XVI similarly adopted price controls. In May 1793, with inflation rising, it passed the Law of the Maximum, ruling that grain and flour in each district should remain at the current price—and that farmers had to accept the government's paper assignats at face value, just as if they were silver coin.[41] Once again, farmers refused to bring goods to market for low prices paid in worthless paper, and by August, the "Dirty Maximum" (as it became known) was mostly ignored. By September, the revolutionaries adopted a new plan, setting national prices for a long list of goods. Within a month, this too had failed. Undaunted, they introduced a more precise and better-enforced plan in November. But then, instead of selling in the markets, farmers sold their produce discreetly, door-to-door. And, of course, they sold mainly to those who could pay more—the exact opposite of the purpose of the Maximum, which was to ensure that food remained affordable to the poor.[42]

Price Controls through the 20th Century

Wage and price controls have been no less prevalent in modern times. Nor have they proved any more effective. During and between the two world wars, the New Zealand government fixed the prices of gasoline, milk, wheat, and sugar.[43] The controls did not stop the price of sugar from doubling, leading to the government then taking over the whole industry.[44]

This failure of price controls leading to wider intervention was far from unique. Back in Europe, Adolf Hitler's 1936 "Price Stop" policy (backed up by about 7,000 decrees on individual prices) proved extremely effective, not in stopping price increases, but in destroying markets and consequently helping the Nazis take over the central direction of the economy. Across the Atlantic, as we've read in Ryan Bourne's Chapter 5, World War II saw the wide adoption of wage and price controls in the United States. Those price controls resulted in lower-quality products, shortages, and black markets.

Attempts to fix the prices of world currencies with regard to gold after World War II were no less destructive. Intended to produce monetary stability, they instead encouraged speculation against weaker currencies, leading to sudden, dramatic, and often highly damaging devaluations. In 1971, President Richard Nixon yielded to the pressures and took the dollar off the gold standard; but he went on to institute a comprehensive system of wage and price controls to try to curb inflation. This policy was mirrored, almost precisely, by the UK government of Edward Heath, though this still did not prevent UK inflation peaking at nearly 25 percent.

Rent controls in the United Kingdom (starting in 1915) and in the United States (starting in 1943) had their own predictable effects. Property owners who could no longer make reasonable earnings from their rentals simply took those properties off the market or allowed the buildings to deteriorate to reflect the lower price they could obtain. Rental accommodation, as intended, became affordable—but also increasingly squalid and very hard to find, especially for the poor. In Britain, the private rented sector collapsed from nine-tenths of the housing stock when controls were introduced to just one-tenth when abandoned in 1989.[45] Efforts to correct these problems (making it harder to evict tenants, for example) further raised risks for landlords, compounding shortages.

Despite this long history of failure, price control enthusiasm shows no sign of abating. In the early 2000s, California suffered a series of rolling electricity blackouts. Why? In part because legislators capped the price at which power could be sold to consumers, while the cost of the gas and oil used to generate electricity rose in line with world prices. Power companies could only sell their product at a loss or shut down—as they did.[46] Consumers faced no incentive to curb their energy use. Federal efforts to control pharmaceutical prices have produced similar results—a fall in U.S.-based medicines research and innovation, leading to slower development and, undoubtedly, greater loss of life.[47]

Yet the lesson of history goes unlearned. Supply shortages, due to natural events such as crop failures or to human actions such as wars, protectionism, and prohibitions, push up the market prices of products. Government abuse of the currency devalues the money in our pockets. Wage and price controls cannot change these underlying pressures. They simply make market prices lie about the relative availability of goods or the strength of the currency. History shows us the inevitable results: shortages, black markets, economic disruption, and misery for many of those whom the controls most seek to help.

Today, wage and price controls have come full circle. In 2022, four millennia after the pharaohs fatefully regulated the price of grain, the Egyptian government responded to shortages caused by the Russia-Ukraine war by again legislating the price of bread. Will we ever learn? In another 4,000 years, will somebody be writing *Eighty Centuries of Wage and Price Controls*?

CHAPTER 8

Under Rent Controls, Everyone Pays

Jeffrey Miron and Pedro Aldighieri

Some bad policy ideas refuse to die. Rent controls, once viewed as relics of the past, are making a comeback across the United States. A harbinger of the Zeitgeist, Sen. Bernie Sanders (I-VT) championed the cause during his 2020 presidential campaign. He proposed restricting rent increases nationwide to the higher of 3 percent or 1.5 times inflation per year, putting rent affordability as his central policy goal.[1] Recently, a group of 32 left-leaning economists signed a letter to the federal government advocating federal rent controls too.[2]

At the state level, Oregon led the charge in 2019, capping rent increases at 7 percent plus inflation for units in older buildings and introducing "just cause" eviction requirements after one year of tenancy.[3] California followed suit in 2020, with a 5 percent plus inflation annual cap, limited to a maximum of 10 percent.[4] Colorado, Florida, Illinois, and Massachusetts are considering similar moves.[5]

In 2021, Michelle Wu, now the mayor of Boston, campaigned on restoring rent controls in the city, despite Massachusetts's statewide ban on the practice.[6] That same year, Minneapolis voters approved a ballot initiative giving the city council authorization to restore rent controls. At the city level, at least 14 local governments have enacted some form of rent controls since 2018.[7]

Rent control or rent stabilization policies regulate prices of rental housing. Their main stated goal is to make housing more affordable for disadvantaged groups, by keeping rents below market prices. In most recent cases, rent stabilization policies limit the increase in rents, rather than establish an absolute dollar price ceiling. To provide tenants with greater security, these rent stabilization policies are typically implemented alongside other regulations, including those restricting evictions to "just causes," such as nonpayment of rent or other contract breaches.

Rent control in the United States dates to the two world wars, when huge migration inflows to certain cities created perceived short-term housing emergencies. New York City did not relinquish its wartime rent controls completely and has had variants of rent control ever since.[8] As of 2019, in fact, 182 U.S. municipalities and cities had some form of rent control, including large cities such as Los Angeles, San Francisco, and Washington, DC.[9]

Interfering with prices is seldom good policy, and rent controls are no exception. Economists overwhelmingly agree that they have destructive consequences in both theory and practice.[10] Theory predicts that, by capping prices, binding rent controls discourage upkeep and improvements on rent-controlled units, resulting in lower property values. To avoid controls, landlords convert rental units to condos and sell them, reducing the quantity of rent-controlled housing and creating rental housing shortages. Tenants in rent-controlled units tend to become fixed in place to avoid losing access to below-market rents. Just eviction clauses make it more difficult to get rid of bad tenants, leading landlords to impose costly screening on all prospective renters and charge all tenants more to compensate for the risk of bad ones. By and large, empirical evidence confirms all these predictions.

Theory and Evidence on Rent Controls

A core prediction of supply-and-demand models is that if government restricts prices below the market-clearing level—that is, the price at which quantity demanded matches quantity supplied—a shortage ensues.

Shortages do not happen overnight. Market outcomes result from transactions among people, and people take time to adjust. If a government were to cap rent increases, some landlords would realize over time that renting is less profitable. Selling might become a better option if real estate prices go up (since rents are not allowed to keep up) or evicting bad tenants becomes too much of a headache. This result reduces the rent-controlled housing stock.

At the same time, cheaper rents incentivize more prospective tenants to seek rental accommodation. For example, some individuals who would previously prefer to buy a house might rather become tenants when rent controls are introduced. The shortage results from these two opposing forces—more tenants demanding and fewer landlords supplying.

The evidence is consistent with these predictions. Unsurprisingly, rental prices are lower for rent-controlled units.[11] A 2014 study of Cambridge, Massachusetts, by three Massachusetts Institute of Technology economists found that before the city repealed its regulations, rents for controlled units were 25 to 40 percent lower than those for uncontrolled units.[12] The same patterns can be seen internationally. The Catalonia region of Spain has seen a 20 percent price difference between regulated and unregulated rents in recent years.[13]

The quantity of rent-controlled apartments demanded thus becomes enormous. In New York City, some old rent-controlled units have become family heirlooms. A woman went viral on TikTok in 2021 after showcasing her redecorated $1,300 a month rent-controlled two-bedroom apartment on the Upper West Side, after inheriting the lease from her parents—a unit that would rent for three to five times as much on the open market.[14] In Stockholm, Sweden, where strict controls have been enforced for decades, the average wait time for a rent-controlled unit was 9 years by 2021 and may now exceed 20 years.[15]

The supply-side response is also consistent with economic theory. In 1994, San Francisco expanded rent control to small multifamily housing, which was previously exempt. One study shows that the supply of rental accommodation from affected landlords fell by 15 percent, with the number of renters living in such units falling by a quarter.[16] The lower profitability of rental units saw many landlords sell such units as owner-occupied condos instead. A 2007 study of the Boston metropolitan area by economist David P. Sims found the flip side: *ending rent controls increased the supply of rental housing.*[17]

The effects of rent controls on new housing development are more ambiguous. Under stringent controls that bind quickly, new building of rental accommodation can collapse. In 2021, the City of Saint Paul, Minnesota, approved a stringent rent stabilization ballot measure that capped rent increases at 3 percent per year, regardless of inflation. Following adoption, new multifamily building permits plummeted by 80 percent, while increasing almost by 70 percent in neighboring Minneapolis.[18] In late 2022, the Saint Paul City Council amended the ordinance to exempt new units from controls for 20 years.[19]

To avoid a collapse in building new apartments, most modern rent regulations exempt new housing from controls.[20] Such exemptions might, perhaps counterintuitively, boost construction of new market-rate rental housing. This effect can happen because rental prices are allowed to fluctuate in one segment of the market but not the other.

In the rent-controlled part of the market, the lower mandated prices can attract new prospective tenants who were not willing to rent at market prices. Some of them might get rent-controlled units even though others would be willing to pay more to rent, because prices cannot adjust.[21] But prices can adjust in the unregulated part of the market. Renters who are willing to pay a premium but were left out of the rent-controlled housing segment can bid up the price in the unregulated market, and this higher price can incentivize more construction of market-rate rental housing.[22] By encouraging landlords to convert rental apartments into owner-occupied condominiums, rent control pushes even more tenants to the uncontrolled rental market.

However, this construction-boosting effect assumes that landlords won't perceive the possibility of the government expanding controls to cover the unregulated properties. But given that the aim of rent control policies is to make rental accommodation affordable, developers will likely worry about this expansion in the scope of rent control, which could discourage new development anyway.

Germany offers evidence consistent with both these effects. On the one hand, rent ceilings affecting part of the housing market in some German regions led to an increase in the price of land, which suggests that it increased the demand for new housing development.[23] On the other hand, when, in 2020, Berlin froze rents at 2019 levels for apartments built before 2014, the law led to a swift and large supply reduction in rental units, relative to the reduction in rents.[24] The measure was repealed by the German Constitutional Court in 2021.[25]

By creating excess demand because of lower prices, rent controls induce misallocation. Nat Sherman, the late tobacco industry tycoon, used to brag about a six-room Central Park West luxury apartment he rented for $355 a month in 1979. In an interview, Sherman said the price was fair given how little he used the apartment.[26] Or consider the case of a former actress who died in her $28-a-month rent-controlled apartment without hot water or heating after a decades-long tenancy.[27] These examples portray misallocation costs starkly: artificially low rents mean tenants stick to apartments unreflective of their needs or that others would value more. The accommodation can be too big or too small, have or lack other features, or be in the wrong location, and so may not reflect tenants' true willingness to pay.

Misallocation costs are not mere anecdotes. A 2003 paper on the New York City housing market by economists Edward L. Glaeser of Harvard and Erzo F. P. Luttmer of Dartmouth found that 21 percent of tenants in rent-controlled units had more or fewer rooms than similar tenants in a free market.[28] A 2019 study of the San Francisco housing market by three Stanford economists found that rent-controlled tenants are 19 percent less likely to move.[29]

Rent controls also affect housing quality. A landlord who is unable to make a profit from increased rent may hesitate to invest in home improvements or even basic maintenance, allowing the quality of the dwelling to fall to reflect the lower rent. This consequence creates a situation where tenants might be willing to pay extra for better living space, but regulations deter it. Renters can make improvements themselves—and many do—but they have little incentive to invest in upgrades that outlast their stay, and regulations prevent landlords from sharing those costs with future renters.

Rent-controlled units in New York City, for example, tend to have worse overall building conditions, older appliances and fixtures, and more maintenance problems than their open-market counterparts.[30] The opposite is also true: annual investment in housing units more than doubled in Cambridge, Massachusetts, after it abolished rent control.[31]

Rent control therefore affects property values and, in turn, property tax revenues. Rent-controlled units become less valuable because of restricted market pricing, inadequate maintenance, and forgone improvements. This reduction in quality can often lower the value of neighboring properties.

For example, the 2014 Cambridge study revealed an 18 to 25 percent increase in decontrolled unit valuations and a 12 percent spillover effect on nearby properties after rent controls were abolished. This outcome boosted the value of Cambridge's housing stock by $1.8 billion.[32] Similarly, a 2022 paper found that Saint Paul's rent controls reduced property values by 6 to 7 percent, leading to an aggregate loss of $1.6 billion in value and a 4 percent decline in property tax revenues.[33]

Many cities worldwide acknowledge the drawbacks of rigid rent controls or rent stabilization and so have turned to tenancy rent controls, allowing landlords to set rents freely between fixed extended tenancies but not within them.[34] This approach aims to offer tenants increased short-term economic security, without the long-term destruction of supply. But security still comes at a cost. In markets where demand is expected to push up market rents, landlords might front-load rent increases or deliberately favor more mobile tenants to allow themselves greater flexibility in setting rents. Given that tenancy rent controls don't improve affordability, landlords might then anticipate tighter controls in the future, with some opting to leave the market altogether. Their fears are well founded: in Scotland, rent adjustment between tenancies was quickly deemed a "loophole" that was abolished as rents continued to rise.[35]

The Distributional Effects of Rent Control Policies

The most common argument for rent controls is that they benefit low-income and minority tenants who would otherwise be displaced by surging rents. The argument goes that rent controls transfer wealth from rich landlords to disadvantaged tenants, preserving socioeconomic diversity in neighborhoods and regions that would otherwise be "gentrified" or taken over by richer households.

Such arguments are far from convincing and not the full story. Prices are just one way to allocate scarce resources. When rent controls suppress prices, other allocation mechanisms operate instead: long queues form, quality degrades, and searching for rent-controlled units becomes more cumbersome. These mechanisms are less efficient than price allocation. Time spent in queues or hunting for apartments is unproductive, whereas higher rental prices could incentivize housing development.

More to the point, these other mechanisms might not even benefit the poor. Queues and waitlists can breed cronyism and bribes, favoring those with political connections rather than the disadvantaged. Owners of rent-controlled units who find themselves overwhelmed by countless applications may impose extra hurdles to discriminate against less affluent tenants, such as higher security deposits, written statements, or other screening measures. Landlords might also opt to sell their properties, with wealthier tenants less susceptible to this fall in supply, as they can more readily afford large down payments to purchase properties.

The evidence suggests that rent controls and regulations are inadequate tools to transfer wealth and prevent gentrification. In Saint Paul, researchers found that tenants who gained the most from rent control were white and more affluent, with barely any wealth transfer from wealthier landlords to poorer tenants.[36]

In San Francisco, landlords responded to rent controls by converting rental units into upscale condos, and the resulting redeveloped housing attracted residents with incomes at least 18 percent higher relative to buildings unaffected by rent controls in the same ZIP code.[37] Instead of stopping gentrification, rent controls seem to have accelerated it. Legally removing tenants in rent-controlled units is costly but possible. Landlords have a stronger incentive to legally remove such tenants in areas where market prices are particularly high relative to regulated prices, even though the tenants, for the same reason, might be especially reluctant to let those units go. Such activity helps explain why redevelopment and evictions would likely happen more in upscale neighborhoods and condos, leading to gentrification.

Similar evidence comes from San Jose, California, where in 2013, middle- and high-income households occupied 62 percent of rent-controlled units.[38] Rent controls' distributional impact is therefore nuanced, at best. Those looking for policies to improve housing affordability would be advised to look elsewhere.

Policy Implications

A review of theory and evidence indicates that rent controls not only are inefficient but also fall short in redistributing wealth from richer to poorer households. In fact, the more rent controls succeed at suppressing prices and improving affordability, the greater the economic distortions they cause. Exempting new buildings or permitting price increases between tenancies are policy improvements precisely because they reduce the controls' ability to suppress rents below market rates.

The most sustainable and effective way to promote affordable rental housing is to enable new construction through the deregulation of zoning, land use, and building requirements. Such policies can make development cheaper, resulting in lower rents, including for low-income units. A flexible rental housing supply also ensures that surges in demand—perhaps because of income or population growth—will lead to more new housing development, rather than rising prices. With an ample supply of apartments in desirable locations, landlords must then compete for tenants, offering better amenities at lower costs.[39]

If low-income households still struggle with housing affordability in lightly regulated land-use and zoning regimes, better targeted approaches exist to help them financially than rent control. A leaner, more cost-effective alternative would be to transfer income for rent directly to poor households, using housing vouchers. Vouchers alone may drive up rental costs for others if the housing stock cannot expand readily to this subsidy-induced demand—shifting who lives where. However, in a deregulated market, vouchers will mainly encourage a housing stock expansion.

Price movements serve as a signal that creates incentives, but rent controls prevent prices from performing this important role. Government-suppressed rental prices instead signal to developers and landlords that more rental housing is not needed, and that the overall quality of the extant housing stock is too high for the prices they are allowed to charge. The rent-controlled housing stock dwindles and decays as a result.

As we have seen, the effects don't stop there. Artificially low rents encourage tenants to seek and retain housing unreflective of their needs. Rent control discourages mobility, with tenants forgoing more productive work opportunities elsewhere just to maintain cheap housing. Controls also lead to resources being wasted on queues, waitlists, and apartment searches. The broader economy suffers.

Crucially, however, rent controls often fall short in achieving their primary goal: to specifically benefit poor and disadvantaged households. The theory and evidence against their use are devastating.

CHAPTER 9

Oil and Natural Gas Price Controls in the 1970s: Shortages and Redistribution

Peter Van Doren

Gasoline consumption has been basically flat since 2006. Expenditures on gasoline are a small percentage of gross domestic product (1.7 percent in 2019) that has been declining over time (2.1 percent in 1990).[1] But when gasoline prices increase rapidly, Americans really notice—and so do elected officials, who often propose price controls.

For example, in response to the price shock induced by the war in Ukraine, a bill was introduced by Rep. Kim Schrier (D-WA) that would grant the president the power to declare an "energy emergency," during which large price increases would be unlawful.[2] Instead of directly setting energy prices, this bill, as well as the congressional response to the 2005 gasoline price increases, would have tasked the Federal Trade Commission with investigating mischief in the price-setting process (e.g., price gouging, as explored in Chapter 13).[3] That's because Congress has eschewed direct energy price controls since the United States' negative experience with them in the 1970s.

To understand actual energy price controls in the United States, we therefore need to reexamine that period, when an array of price controls and allocation regulations were imposed on crude oil and refined petroleum products.[4] For the most part, the price controls were not complete—that is, they covered part of the oil sold in the United States but let market prices function in some segments of the market—so prices cleared markets, instead of creating shortages. But price controls did create genuine shortages in the 1972–1973 winter for heating oil, as well as in the 1973–1974 winter and early 1979 for other refined products, including gasoline. The result was the infamous gas station lines that are now emblematic of the 1970s.[5]

After 1974, the main effect of the price control program was to transfer economic rents from domestic crude oil producers to domestic refineries and consumers. There was also political competition to obtain access to valuable price-controlled domestic oil when market prices were rising.

Although petroleum price controls were imposed consciously, natural gas price controls were accidental.[6] And they applied only to interstate commerce. The result was shortages during the 1970s, except in Louisiana and Texas, where natural gas did not cross state lines and so was not price controlled.

Price controls on both petroleum and natural gas, as implemented, created complex layers of rules, with exemptions and varying prices for different classes of products, producers, and consumers. The political micromanagement was numbing in its complexity. Deregulation of petroleum took place over three years, from 1979 to 1981. Natural gas deregulation started in 1978 but wasn't completed until 1989.

Nixon's Price Controls

President Richard Nixon launched America's most recent grand experiment with price controls using the broad powers Congress gave him to control inflation in the Economic Stabilization Act of 1970. His price control regime had four phases.[7]

Phase I, which lasted from August through November 1971, applied to all wages and prices throughout the economy. Fortunately, global oil prices were not increasing during those three months, so Phase I had only a minor effect on U.S. oil supplies.

Phase II, which lasted from November 1971 through January 1973, allowed all firms, except those in the oil or gas sectors, to increase prices above Phase I ceilings to reflect higher production costs. Gasoline, heating oil, and crude oil prices were thus effectively frozen at Phase I levels. This freeze created heating oil shortages during the winter of 1972–1973 in areas far from the coasts that did not have access to imported, decontrolled product.[8]

Phase III, which lasted from January 1973 through August 1973, initially made Phase II price controls voluntary. The heating oil shortages of the winter of 1972–1973 dissipated as heating oil prices rose. In March 1973, the Nixon administration issued Special Rule No. 1, which reimposed strict price controls on the largest oil companies, accounting for 95 percent of the industry's sales. Smaller oil firms, however, were exempt. Thus, market-clearing prices were not controlled. The differential treatment of large and small oil companies created very bad political optics, because the large companies (which reduced imports in response to the price controls) appeared to be conspiring to hold back supplies from numerous independent distributors and retailers that normally received product from the large companies.

The price increases from the 5 percent of firms not under price controls led President Nixon to reimpose price controls for the entire economy for 60 days on June 14, 1973. This Phase III freeze was followed by Phase IV, which started in August 1973 and was later incorporated in the Emergency Petroleum Allocation Act (EPAA) in November 1973.

During the Yom Kippur War in October 1973 between Israel and a coalition of Arab countries, Saudi Arabia declared an embargo on crude oil exports to countries that supported Israel, including the

Netherlands and the United States. Popular culture often attributes the gas lines of 1973–1974 to that embargo rather than to price controls. But economists say the embargo had no effect.[9] As the book *Energy Aftermath* concludes: "It was no more possible for OPEC [Organization of Petroleum Exporting Countries] to keep its oil out of U.S. supply lines than it was for the United States to keep its embargoed grain out of Soviet silos several years later. Simple rerouting through the international system circumvented the embargo. The significance of the embargo lies in its symbolism."[10]

The EPAA and the Entitlements Program

The EPAA froze the price of oil at about $5 a barrel for the level of well production that occurred in 1972—so-called "old" oil.[11] But "new" oil (oil produced above the 1972 level), oil from "stripper wells" (wells that produced fewer than 10 barrels of oil per day), and imported oil were not subject to price controls.[12] The rationale for "old" oil price controls was that producers should receive pre-oil-shock prices for their pre-oil-shock production levels and current market prices only for their incremental post-oil-shock production amount.

Even though price controls existed for most of the 1970s, they caused shortages only in the winter of 1972–1973 for heating oil and other products like gasoline in the winter of 1973–1974 and early 1979. The reason is that retailers, although technically subject to price controls, were allowed to pass through all input cost increases to their customers in the form of higher prices. In his 1981 book on the economics of oil price controls, economist Joseph Kalt argues:

> Refined product price controls have apparently been window dressing, allowing policymakers to show relevant constituents concrete measures that (appear to) prevent oil company "rip-offs" while avoiding the economic, bureaucratic, and political havoc of actual shortages.[13]

Market prices reflect the marginal rather than the average cost of raw materials. So the price of gasoline reflected the price of "new" rather than "old" oil. That meant refiners who had access to "old" oil made much larger profits on their gasoline sales than refiners who depended on market-priced crude oil.

To equalize profits across refiners, the Federal Energy Administration adopted an "old oil entitlements" program in December 1974.[14] Refineries that used more price-controlled oil on a percentage basis than the industry average had to pay for the right to buy that "old" oil at the controlled price from refineries that used less than the average amount of controlled oil.

This entitlements program created incentives to import oil because the average use of "old" oil decreased as imports increased. The incentive to increase imports continued until the total value of entitlements equaled the value of the "old" oil (the difference between the market and controlled prices multiplied by the fixed volume of "old" oil).

Although the purpose of the original entitlements program was to equalize profits across refineries, subsequent amendments favored some refineries at the expense of others. The most important was the Small Refiner Bias regulation, which gave small refineries extra entitlements to "old" oil.[15]

The Energy Policy and Conservation Act of 1975

The Energy Policy and Conservation Act (EPCA) amended the EPAA and took effect in February 1976.[16] The law expanded price controls to the "new" oil produced from domestic fields established after the EPAA was introduced. "Old" oil became "lower tier" (less expensive), formerly "new" oil became "upper tier" (more expensive), and so-called stripper oil and imported oil remained decontrolled.

The average price for lower- and upper-tier oil could not exceed $7.66 per barrel, a figure that was permitted to increase up to 10 percent annually to account for inflation and various incentive payments.[17] In September 1976, the EPCA was amended to allow average domestic prices to rise by 10 percent a year without regard to the inflation rate or regulatory incentive adjustments.

This new three-tier regime required changes in the "old" oil entitlements program because there were now two categories of "old" oil— lower tier and upper tier. Accordingly, each barrel of upper-tier oil was granted a fraction of the entitlement given to lower-tier oil.

Special exemptions to the "old" oil entitlement program continued. Beginning in April 1976, residual fuel imports into the East Coast were eligible for partial entitlements, and middle distillates (industry jargon for jet fuel, diesel fuel, home heating oil, and kerosene) were granted similar partial entitlements in February and March of 1977 in response to the severe winter that year. Salable partial entitlements were granted to middle distillate imports from May through September of 1979. Special allocations of entitlements to refiners were also granted for the use of low-quality California crude oil, certain uses of nonpetroleum fuels, and Puerto Rican petrochemicals. The federal government also received marketable entitlements for purchases of crude oil for the Strategic Petroleum Reserve.

The EPCA gave the president authority to place the petroleum price controls on standby status any time after May 1979. The Carter administration largely dismantled the price control regime through administrative action, and President Ronald Reagan abolished all remaining controls in January 1981. Congress made no effort to reauthorize the program, and the EPCA formally expired in September 1981. The price control regime had lasted about 10 years.

The Economic Cost of Price Controls

During the EPAA and EPCA regimes, roughly 60 to 70 percent of domestic oil output was subject to federal price controls.[18] As a result, average domestic oil prices were reduced by \$3 to \$5 per barrel below market levels.[19] The oil price increases in 1979, however, greatly increased the gap between regulated and market prices. In 1980, lower-tier oil sold for about \$6 per barrel, whereas imported oil prices averaged \$33.89.[20]

Because the price control system was incomplete in that it didn't cover every part of the U.S. oil market, the price controls were rarely binding. When they were, in the winter of 1972–1973, winter of 1973–1974, and early 1979, shortages occurred. During the rest of the 10 years, the price controls and entitlements program mainly acted like a tax and transfer system. Economist Joseph Kalt found that from 1974 to 1980, federal oil price controls (primarily through the old oil entitlements program) transferred \$43–\$153 billion annually (in 2023 dollars) from domestic crude producers to refiners.[21] Because this lowered the marginal cost of production of refined products, some of the transfer reduced product prices and benefited consumers. Kalt estimated that 60 percent of the transfer stayed with refiners and 40 percent was passed through to customers.[22]

The price controls and the incentive to import created by the entitlements program reduced domestic production by 0.3–1.4 million barrels per day.[23] And the wealth losses of crude oil producers exceeded the gains obtained by refineries and crude oil consumers. The difference between the two figures is the economic value that price controls destroy—what economists call "deadweight loss"—which Kalt estimated to be between \$3 billion and\$15 billion annually (in 2023 dollars) from 1975 to 1980.[24]

Kalt's analysis assumed that world oil prices were unaffected by U.S. controls. But economist Rodney T. Smith calculated that EPCA price controls *increased* world crude oil prices by 13.35 percent.[25] And economist Robert Rogers, who incorporated Smith's findings into an econometric model, found that the EPCA increased domestic oil prices.[26]

Natural Gas

In 1938, Congress passed the Natural Gas Act, which authorized the Federal Power Commission (FPC) to regulate interstate pipeline construction and the rates the pipelines charged. Congress exempted "production and gathering" from federal regulation.[27]

However, the Supreme Court ruled in 1947 that this congressional exemption applied only to regulation of the physical processes of production. The exemption did not apply to regulation of the sale prices of natural gas.

In response, Congress passed legislation to explicitly exempt natural gas producer prices from regulation, but President Harry S. Truman vetoed the bill in 1950. In 1954, the Supreme Court ruled in *Phillips Petroleum v. Wisconsin* that the FPC must regulate natural gas prices at the wellhead. In 1956, Congress passed legislation exempting independent producers from price controls. Before President Dwight D. Eisenhower could sign the legislation, South Dakota Sen. Francis Case reported that he had been offered a bribe for his favorable vote. President Eisenhower vetoed the legislation to avoid a scandal. Subsequent deregulation bills never left committee. The FPC essentially froze interstate prices at 1959 levels until 1974.[28]

Federal price controls applied only to natural gas sold in interstate commerce. Intrastate gas was exempt. As the gap between the low controlled interstate prices and market intrastate prices grew, producers sold their product within states and withheld supplies from interstate pipelines.

The result was that consumers in states that did not produce natural gas experienced shortages during the 1970s that grew more severe over time. Congress increased prices in 1974 and 1976, but not by enough to eliminate the incentive for producers to avoid interstate sales.

In 1976 and 1977, many factories and institutions, such as schools, were forced to close occasionally from lack of natural gas.[29]

Presidents Nixon and Gerald Ford, and candidate Jimmy Carter, recommended an end to price controls for "new" gas, but Democrats in northeastern consuming states favored continued controls because they feared constituents' reaction to price increases.[30]

Eventually, in 1978, Congress passed the Natural Gas Policy Act, which phased out natural gas price controls by 1985 through a complex compromise scheme of temporary price regulations. The compromise kept price controls on "old" gas but decontrolled "new" gas, creating numerous market distortions during the 1980s. The act mandated that prices for residential customers must be based solely on "old" gas prices. Industrial and commercial users were charged "new" gas prices. But shortages were avoided only if "new" gas prices exceeded spot prices (the daily price of natural gas on commodities exchanges).[31]

The resulting average price of overpriced "new" gas and underpriced "old" gas cleared the market initially, but industrial users switched to oil or coal to avoid high costs. Pipeline companies had signed contracts for "new" gas that required payment regardless of whether the gas was consumed, so pipelines increased their rates in response to reduced industrial consumption. Additional legislation was needed in 1989 to complete the job of fully deregulating wellhead prices.

The 1970s' experience with energy price controls was so negative that recent congressional responses to constituent anger over energy prices have consisted of calls for the Federal Trade Commission to investigate the usual suspects to justify any enforcement action, rather than just enacting actual price controls.

Price controls are simple to apply in theory, but the U.S. experience with oil and natural gas price controls shows they are extremely complicated exercises in practice. Price-controlled oil and natural gas were valuable. Thus, intense political competition developed to gain access, which was provided to important constituencies. In periods when price controls were incomplete, shortages were avoided. But transfers from producers to refiners and consumers took place, and these gains were less than the producer losses, resulting in a net loss of economic efficiency.

CHAPTER 10

Interest Rate Caps Do Not Protect Vulnerable Consumers

Nicholas Anthony

Across the United States, state legislators have drafted and passed restrictions on the rate of interest that can be applied to loans of as little as a few hundred dollars (Figure 10.1). These restrictions most commonly impose a 36 percent interest rate cap on short-term loans that low-income consumers are likely to take either in a moment of crisis or until their next paycheck. In Washington, DC, federal legislators have tried to extend these restrictions nationwide.[1]

These interest rate caps are regularly touted as a lifeline for low-income Americans. By restricting the amount of interest that may be charged on a loan, proponents argue that loan repayments become more affordable. Sen. Dick Durbin (D-IL), for example, has said that interest rate caps "would eliminate high-cost payday loans and other costly forms of credit that trap vulnerable consumers in endless debt cycles."[2]

Often, these arguments are made under the cloak of paternalism. Proponents argue that high-interest-rate loans are not in the best interest of consumers and, therefore, consumers shouldn't have the option. For example, Sen. Elizabeth Warren (D-MA) has said

FIGURE 10.1

Many states have adopted interest rate caps of 36% or lower on small-dollar loans

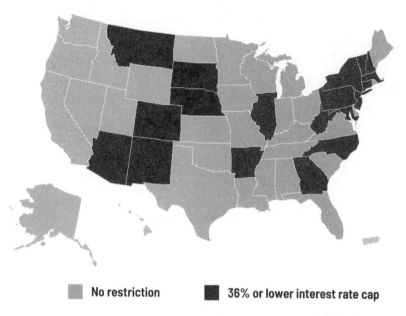

No restriction   36% or lower interest rate cap

Source: Data compiled by author, mainly from Justia.[3]

that interest rates need to be capped "to help states protect their citizens from high interest rates that families can't afford,"[4] while Sen. Sherrod Brown (D-OH) has claimed, "[Payday lender] profits depend on tricking Americans out of their money."[5] Titles of laws, including the Predatory Loan Prevention Act or the Protecting Consumers from Unreasonable Credit Rates Act, make it clear that policymakers present the case for interest rate caps as one of protecting constituents from harm (Table 10.1).[6]

For others, the argument for interest rate caps is about leveling the playing field between financial institutions and individual consumers. For example, Rep. Alexandria Ocasio-Cortez (D-NY) and

TABLE 10.1

Legislative proposals for interest rate caps display clear paternalism

Title	Year introduced or enacted	State or federal
Predatory Loan Prevention Act	2022	State
Protecting Consumers from Unreasonable Credit Rates Act	2019	Federal
Loan Shark Prevention Act	2019	Federal
Veterans and Consumers Fair Credit Act	2021	Federal
Payday Borrower Protection Act	2005	Federal
Predatory Lending Sunset Act	2010	Federal

Source: Data compiled by author.

Sen. Bernie Sanders (I-VT) have argued that interest rate caps will help end the practice of banks borrowing money from the Federal Reserve at just a few percent and then charging people double-digit interest rates.[7]

Expanding affordable access to financial services, looking out for the best interest of others, and creating a level playing field for competition are all worthy ideals. The problem is that, as a type of price control, interest rate caps achieve the opposite of these intended effects. A payday loan with a high interest rate may not be everyone's first choice, but evidence shows that consumers benefit from having the opportunity to smooth their consumption amid unexpected costs, changes in income, or even just as they wait for their next paycheck.[8] By restricting the price of credit, interest rate caps reduce—and even eliminate—the profitability of providing that service to the riskiest of borrowers. In other words, the viability of lending is reduced or eliminated, and that means borrowers are left with few, if any, options for credit.

Price Controls Restrict Access to Credit

Diego Zuluaga, former associate director for financial regulation studies at the Cato Institute, described interest rate caps as "financial inclusion without finance."[9] Like other price controls, interest rate caps create artificial shortages, resulting in fewer people having access to loans.[10]

Consider a situation where the market has found some interest rate to be the appropriate price to satisfy both borrowers and lenders (see P^* in Figure 10.2). The problem occurs when policymakers decide that the market rate is too high and impose an interest rate cap, or price ceiling (P_{PC}). Economic theory predicts that if the imposed price ceiling is below the equilibrium price $(P_{PC} < P^*)$, there will be a shortage of credit because the quantity demanded (Q_D) will be greater than the quantity supplied (Q_S).

This revelation is not novel. Many economists have warned over the years that interest rate caps, like price controls broadly, create shortages.[11]

FIGURE 10.2

Price ceilings risk creating a shortage of loans

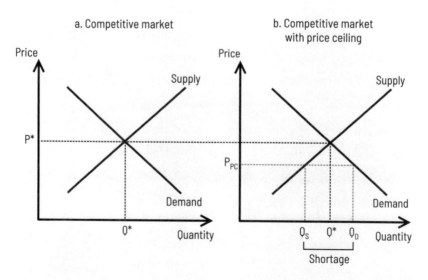

Paul A. Samuelson—the first American to win the Nobel Prize in Economics—explained in 1969 that the shortages created by interest rate caps "result in drying up legitimate funds to the poor who need it most and will send them into the hands of the illegal loan sharks."[12]

Why do we see the supply of loans dry up? First, interest rates are used to recover the fixed costs of providing loans, and many of the costs that exist on a $100,000 loan also exist on a $100 loan. Restricting the ability to at least cover those costs is to make small loans economically impossible to offer. Second, interest rates are also determined in response to the risk a borrower presents. Although it is unfortunate to label large swaths of the population as "high risk," people with lower incomes are more likely to pose a higher credit risk because they have an increased likelihood of being unable to repay.[13] However, being a higher credit risk should not make someone an outcast or bar them from the financial system. Rather, it just means that businesses should be able to use tools, such as higher interest rates, to mitigate that risk. Capping rates is to deny lenders that tool and, in turn, to deny borrowers access to financial services.

The experience in the states, on the federal level, and even across countries demonstrates that capping interest rates reduces the supply of financial services. One study looked at the effect of the 36 percent interest rate cap in Illinois and found, as economic theory predicts, that both the availability of small-dollar loans and the status of consumers' financial well-being had decreased in the two years after the enactment of the restriction.[14] Most notably, the number of loans that were issued to the financially vulnerable fell by 44 percent in the six months after the rate cap was enacted.

In South Dakota, another study documented that the enactment of a 36 percent interest rate cap drove payday lenders out of business.[15] These findings carry over to the experience in other states, where researchers found residents of Arkansas and North Carolina regularly travel across state lines to take out small-dollar loans because of the lack of access created by interest rate caps in their home states.[16] In fact, in Georgia and North Carolina, researchers also found that households bounced more checks and filed for Chapter 7 bankruptcy at a higher rate relative to people living in states that permit payday lending.[17]

On the federal level, the Military Lending Act of 2007 prohibited members of the military from having access to loans with interest rates over 36 percent. Yet research since then has found that members of the military are not affected negatively by having access to payday loans—what the law was purportedly "protecting" them from.[18] In fact, it's possible that the law is actually hurting members of the military by pushing them to alternative sources of funds like overdrawing accounts, forgoing bill payments, and turning to informal lenders, such as loan sharks, pawnshops, family members, and coworkers.[19] For these reasons, finance experts Thomas W. Miller Jr. and Todd Zywicki have described the Military Lending Act as "a cautionary tale—not a model—for consumer credit regulation."[20]

Internationally, interest rate caps have led to similar issues.[21] One study from the International Monetary Fund in 2021 found that "despite their intended objective of broadening financial inclusion, [interest rate caps] can have undesirable effects on financial inclusion under certain conditions."[22] For example, restrictions in Cambodia led to an increase in fees charged on loans in lieu of interest, a decline in the number of borrowers, and a shift in lenders' business models. Similar issues have been found in the Caribbean and Latin America, where interest rate caps have resulted in a reduction in financial outreach to the poor, women, and people living in rural areas.[23]

Although this history is only a small sampling of the experience with interest rate caps, it paints a dim picture for the policy. Across nations, levels of government, and time, it seems that Zuluaga was right: interest rate caps create financial inclusion without finance.[24]

Paternalist Policy Fails in Practice

Interest rate caps are often justified by paternalistic arguments that certain consumers are irrational or do not know what's in their best financial interest. The idea that government can step in to correct these errors, however, assumes that the government knows what's best for any given individual and what's best overall.[25]

It's all too common for government officials to assert that they know what is best for individuals.[26] For example, in a 2021 report, the Department of Defense acknowledged that interest rate caps would likely harm members of the military, but it said that the ends justified the means:

> [If] adopted, these [price controls] may have the result of limiting the availability of certain types of credit to Service members, but . . . such measures were necessary to ensure they resolve financial issues through more responsible means, such as available financial counseling or less costly financial products and prevent such harmful practices from undermining military readiness.[27]

Yet every individual using payday loans or short-term credit has different needs. For some, it can be extremely helpful to bridge the gap until anticipated income arrives. For others, the need to cover part of an essential, unexpected expense can make such credit attractive. The Department of Defense's suggestion to seek financial counseling is unlikely to help someone suddenly short on rent and facing eviction—something an emergency small-dollar loan might help avoid.

Likewise, the suggestion to seek less costly financial products fails to recognize that approximately 18.7 million U.S. households have a bank account, but still choose to use alternatives like payday loans.[28] Across the country, people choose these products despite their cost because they need money quickly or they don't have enough credit (or collateral) to get a loan elsewhere.[29] No doubt some borrowers get into debt spirals; however, interest rate caps act as sweeping bans that restrict access to credit for everyone, regardless of their situation or prospects.

The other problem is that the government might simply be wrong about the ideas it seeks to mandate. Proposals for interest rate caps showcase this issue all too well. For example, Rep. Glenn Grothman (R-WI) said:

> It's hard to imagine who would want to take out a loan with an interest rate of 150 or 200% a year. There is no way that is in anybody's best interest at all, and taking advantage of people who are either in desperate straits or more likely just plain financially illiterate is immoral.[30]

Representative Grothman is not alone in making this misleading comparison, but it is still misleading nonetheless.[31] Put simply, using an annual percentage rate (APR) exaggerates the cost of these loans, which are typically used for short-term finance. In other words, using an APR to characterize a fixed two-week loan is like referring to the cost of staying at a hotel as $45,625 per year when most people are only going to spend $125 to stay a single night.[32] Even if one avoids that mistake, it's wrong to think that there is some objectively correct price for a loan. Whether it is $18 for a sandwich or $85 for a haircut, there will always be prices that are high for some but just right for others. Value, after all, is subjective.[33] As circumstances change, prices must change alongside them to reflect those market forces. Interest rate caps prevent those signals from operating.

It Is Misleading to Compare Interest Rates Paid by Banks and Consumers

Comparing the interest rates that banks are charged by the Federal Reserve with interest rates that consumers are charged by banks is also extremely misleading.[34] Both types of transactions involve one party receiving a loan from another, but ending the story there fails to understand the purpose of interest rates and the differences between the two loans.

Interest rates are typically calculated by considering the conditions of both the market and the borrower. In other words, lenders ask themselves whether the money could be better used elsewhere and whether there is a risk that the borrower might not pay off the loan. Asking these two questions makes it clear that lending to a bank and lending to an individual are two very different actions.

First, banks often have thousands of loans on their books to verify their credibility. In contrast, individuals likely to face high interest rates may ask for varying loan terms and come to the institution on a one-off basis with bad or even nonexistent credit.[35]

Second, banks that have access to the Federal Reserve also have access to vastly more assets than the average American. For example, a bank is considered "small" if it has less than $1.5 billion in assets, but the median low-income American has only $810 in his or her checking account.[36] Taken together, the risks of a loan being paid late or going unpaid entirely are significantly smaller for a financial institution relative to an individual consumer.

Yet the problem goes deeper. Setting aside the fact that interest rates are used to mitigate risks, there's another reason that loans are more expensive for a bank lending to individual customers: they are providing a consumer-tailored service. From compliance checks to underwriting and physical locations to digital services, banks incur costs to provide these services and cannot remain viable without covering their costs. For example, complying with the requirements of the Bank Secrecy Act alone cost the U.S. financial system an estimated $45.9 billion in 2022.[37]

Moving Forward

Policymakers are right to want to help the financially vulnerable, but capping interest rates would restrict the financial access to services on which many of those same people rely. Time and time again, price controls have been shown to hurt consumers. There are better solutions at hand.

Policymakers could start by addressing the costs financial institutions incur to provide credit. Although compliance costs U.S. financial institutions tens of billions of dollars a year, there is little evidence to suggest that the Bank Secrecy Act, for example, is successful in fighting crime.[38] Repealing, or at least significantly reforming, that legislation would reduce costs that financial institutions pass on to customers and allow law enforcement to better focus on catching criminals.

Next, if policymakers want to see financial service providers innovate further, they should remove the laws and regulations that have imposed existing restrictions on the supply of credit and that curb financial innovation.[39] For example, state interest rate caps across the country, the Durbin Amendment, and Regulation Z under the Credit CARD Act all restrict prices of financial services and, therefore, restrict access.[40] Likewise, the barriers to offering financial services writ large have severely limited competition by creating entry barriers to new competitors. Removing such barriers would be a step forward to expanding the financial system for everyone.

Interest rate caps may be intended to make credit more affordable for the financially vulnerable, but economic theory and experience both show that price ceilings harm many consumers in practice. If policymakers truly want to help expand the reach of financial services at lower cost, they should turn toward freeing, not restricting, the financial system.

CHAPTER 11

Abolishing "Junk Fees" Would Be Junk Policy

Ryan Bourne

On September 26, 2022, President Joe Biden announced plans to crack down on hidden and deceptive fees, charges, and add-ons he believed were "weighing down" Americans families' budgets.[1] He labeled such charges "junk fees," later citing early termination fees for communications services, hotel resort fees, large bank overdraft charges, and airlines charges for families' seat selections as examples.[2]

The White House defines "junk fees" as charges "designed either to confuse or deceive consumers or to take advantage of lock-in or other forms of situational market power," including fraud, undisclosed mandatory fees, surprise charges, and predatory costs.[3] Economically, such fees are said to harm competition by making comparison shopping difficult, creating financial barriers to customers switching providers, and exploiting vulnerable and myopic consumers.

In March 2023, the president thus urged Congress to pass the Junk Fee Prevention Act.[4] The bill would introduce government regulation of various fees:

- Mandating that hotels, travel agencies, and online ticketing sites "clearly and conspicuously display" the *total* price of their services;
- Prohibiting "excessive or deceptive" mandatory fees;

- Eliminating early termination fees and family airline seating charges; and
- Granting the Federal Trade Commission sweeping authority to promulgate new rules over entities it deems are using "mandatory or deceptive fees."

The federal government should not micromanage businesses' pricing structures in this way. Yet the president views this as an important issue, even mentioning it in his 2023 State of the Union address. That raises some important economic questions: Would eliminating these charges really save American households substantial sums of money? Are these pricing structures really evidence of uncompetitive markets and exploitation? And what unintended consequences might restricting such charges bring?

Huge Effects on Households' Budgets?

The administration talks as if junk fees cost households tens of billions annually, referencing revenue from credit card late payments, hotel resort fees, airline fees, and "hidden" cable fees.[5] Invoking these huge numbers implies that the government regulating fees could save consumers large sums.

Yet this is highly misleading. As Figure 11.1 shows, these charges are a drop in the ocean relative to revenues in these industries.

More importantly, the primary effect of banning additional fees in competitive markets would be higher basic prices. Shifting to that kind of price structure might redistribute money between types of customers, but the total amount spent by American households would be largely unchanged. Even in sectors where firms have market power, in fact, policing one part of a firm's price doesn't change the fundamental industry power dynamics, so the total price consumers face would be largely unaffected.

The administration argues that better pricing transparency from regulating fees will itself make switching suppliers easier and

FIGURE 11.1

Supposed junk fee revenues are relatively small

Total versus "junk fee" revenues by industry, billions of dollars

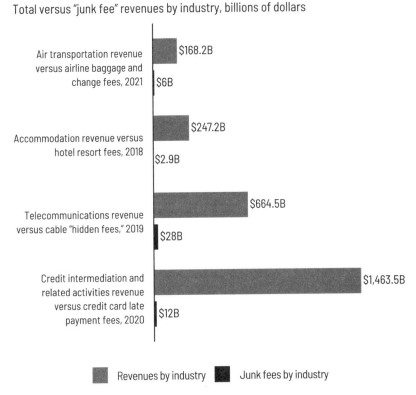

Sources: Census Bureau and the White House.[6]

encourage firms to compete more vigorously on cost and quality, indirectly benefiting consumers through lower prices arising from more robust competition.[7] Yet the administration presents scant evidence for such assertions—and certainly not enough to justify the proposed extension of executive authority.

Use of Fees Can Bring Significant Economic Benefits

In his junk fees narrative, Joe Biden seems to think unbundling (where businesses charge separately for certain options), price partitioning (where businesses display nonnegotiable prices in separate components), and contract early termination fees are inherently undesirable.

Yet these normal pricing practices can bestow significant benefits on consumers. Banning or restricting their use could have important unintended consequences.

Preventing unbundling could reduce access to services

Charging extra for specific preferences, such as a seat selection on a flight, enables lower basic prices, increasing access to no-frills options for lower-income customers, while allowing businesses to customize their services to individual customers' preferences. Airlines unbundle in-flight food and checked bags, for example, leading to more profit opportunities and lower base fares. Yes, "price discrimination"—charging various customers different amounts for the same product—can sometimes be harmful to customers on net. But banning such unbundling when consumers put wildly different values on certain services can price out poorer consumers and compel others to pay for services they neither want nor need.

Banning partitioned fees can sometimes reduce information to customers

Whether it is regulations imposed by governments, pricing disputes with suppliers, or price increases due to supply shocks, partitioning prices into line items on bills can sometimes provide customers with important contextual information. Consumers often have little idea of the costs of providing goods and services. Itemizing a bill, even if the total price remains the same, may provide crucial transparency. For example, restaurants sometimes include surcharges on bills to reflect large local minimum wage rises.[8] Such actions help explain to customers the underlying reason for price increases, dispelling false accusations of "greed" or the abuse of monopoly power. Banning partitioned pricing can therefore actually hide information from customers.

Banning early termination or overdraft fees would hurt certain consumers

Early termination telecom and cable fees deter consumers from leaving contracts early, which enables companies to offer discounted promotional prices and gives them greater certainty over revenue in making large investment decisions—including upgrading and building out infrastructure to serve more customers.[9] There are one-off costs to acquiring new customers, setting up accounts, and providing and installing equipment. These must be recovered, even if customers opt to end their services early. Banning early termination fees would therefore lead to higher monthly prices, fewer promotional rates, higher installation charges, or shifts toward more unbundled, "pay-as-you-go," or on-demand services within cable TV packages. There's no inherent reason to think this would be better for consumers.

Likewise, overdraft fees from banks help disincentivize costly behavior. Banks incur costs and face heightened risks when customers overdraw their accounts. Overdraft charges help deter this behavior in a well-targeted way, by imposing charges on those customers whose accounts become overdrawn. Capping or constraining overdraft fees doesn't eliminate these costs and risks; it just means someone else must be charged for them in a different way. Banning overdraft charges thus means higher prices for some other subset of a bank's customers.

Markets Provide Incentives to Eliminate Deception

Customers shouldn't be charged for products without their consent, and businesses should disclose fees clearly. But markets provide strong incentives against businesses using unpopular deceptive or surprise fees, undermining the idea that these are a huge economic issue.

Online reviews are one important feedback mechanism. A 2019 *Consumer Reports* survey found that 16 percent of consumers had posted comments or reviews on social media about their experience with "hidden fees," deterring other customers from using the offending service.[10]

As transparency is valued by many consumers, intermediaries have emerged to provide that information. Google Flights, for example, lets customers tailor their itinerary search by specifying their baggage requirements, ensuring like-for-like pricing comparisons and mitigating the risk of surprise fees.

More generally, in repeat markets, a company's success hinges on its reputation. Otherwise, entrepreneurs will enter and compete. This fact disciplines firms to be transparent. The ticketing website StubHub, for example, began giving users the option to see the all-in ticketing price at the start or end of a sale process.[11] Several financial institutions, such as Citibank, offer credit cards with no late fees, while many small banks and credit unions offer lower fees than the major players.[12]

A business that engages in practices that consumers dislike or regard as deceptive will not be successful for long. Given consumers' instinctive biases against fees, then, why do some businesses charge them? Two case studies of charges that President Biden wants to eliminate may shed some light.

Case Study 1: Airline Seating Charges

President Biden rails against fees charged for "sitting next to your child on an air flight."[13] No airline explicitly charges for this, but if families want seats together, they typically must buy tickets with advance seat selection, pay for seat selection separately, or hope adjacent seats are still available around check-in. Given that the very cheapest fare categories typically do not allow advance seat selection, Biden's complaint is really that customers holding cheap tickets with kids under 14 years old should obtain grouped seating for free, despite other passengers having to pay to ensure that they will have it.

The president's rhetoric implies that such airline fees simply extract revenue from unwitting customers. Yet seat selection is really another form of unbundling. People often have strong seat preferences, with middle seats perceived worse than aisle or window seats. It is logical that those with strong seating preferences pay more than those who would accept random assignment. Structuring prices like this grants airlines more profit opportunities, given passengers' different willingness to pay. It allows them to run more routes at lower basic fares—which surveys show is what passengers most care about.[14]

A policy of eliminating airlines "charging" for family seating, then, is really a social mandate to compel other passengers to subsidize families with cheap tickets traveling with kids. To pressure airlines to adopt this policy, the Department of Transportation began running a dashboard showing which airlines allowed "free" seat selection for passengers with children.[15] The Junk Fee Prevention Act proposes explicit regulation, under threat of civil penalties. Air carriers would have to provide adults and children adjacent seats, offering a full refund or a week's wait period if they are unavailable. If nothing crops up, they must allow passengers to rebook or waive their new right. For carriers with open seating, airlines must board passengers to ensure that all children under 14 years old can be seated with adults.

As noted earlier, the main effect of this policy would be higher basic fares or other ancillary charges. It would also cause significant practical issues with airlines' business models. Southwest Airlines is known for its family-friendly policies, offering two pieces of free checked baggage, flexible cancellations, and early boarding for families with children under age seven. Yet the airline currently generates revenue through EarlyBird Check-In and Upgraded Boarding services, which allow paying customers to obtain earlier boarding positions that give them better seat options in Southwest's open seating system. A regulation guaranteeing that all families with children under 14 years old also get propelled up the line would diminish the benefit to other passengers of these pay-for services. So fewer would use them, leaving Southwest needing to make up revenue through higher prices or charging more for other services.

All airlines will face similar conundrums, as well as new difficulties with reservation systems. Updating them for new assignment rules and additional notices for families rebooking or requiring refunds will add costs. Dealing with last-minute family bookings would be especially problematic. Airlines would need new systems to rearrange positions of fee-paying passengers, to waive family seating rights, or to warn families about booking when flights are near full.

This enforced cross-subsidy will thus reduce airlines' abilities to tinker with boarding and seat allocation practices. In doing so, it will increase headline ticket prices marginally, reduce the revenue viability of other ancillary services, and reduce airline profitability. And for what? Customers can already book using multiple airlines that offer different boarding policies and fee structures that better fit their seating needs. In rare cases where parent and child are separated after check-in, flight staff and other passengers typically find ways to bargain or trade to allow them to sit together anyway.

Case Study 2: Hotel Resort Fees

Hotel resort fees are nonnegotiable charges for hotel services and amenities that supplement advertised room rates.[16] In effect, a resort fee is just a line item on the customer's bill—part of the overall price of staying at the hotel. President Biden describes them as deceptive junk fees, hindering hotel cost comparison and surprising unassuming customers. The Junk Fee Prevention Act would compel hotels to only display or advertise a "total price" for stays that include resort fees, so as to try to reduce their use.[17]

Though seen by many consumer advocates and customers as a "total scam," only about 6 percent of hotels charge resort fees, mainly in tourist hot spots like Orlando, Las Vegas, and major city centers.[18] These hotels do tend to provide significantly more amenities, including pools, gyms, tour services, parking, and water sport rentals.[19]

The overwhelming effect of banning resort fees outright would be hotels charging higher nightly room rates, leaving most customers' wallets largely unaffected. Yet hotels' use of resort fees suggests they must improve their profitability somehow, at least relative to either (a) charging customers for individual amenity use (unbundling services) or (b) rolling everything into higher nightly room rates.

There are obvious downsides to unbundling services entirely. Monitoring access to pools and gyms can be expensive for hotels and inconvenient for vacationers. When guests have diverse preferences over amenities, bundling them at a lower total price can simply be more profitable for hotels, as not every guest will use every facility.[20] Charging a fixed fee also avoids revenue uncertainty. In fact, the mystery is why all hotels don't just bundle even more explicitly and charge higher nightly rates to reflect these amenities. Biden thinks they are acting fraudulently, luring certain customers through lower advertised prices. Yet this explanation seems inadequate in competitive hotel markets.

The American Hotel and Lodging Association argues that hotels would be financially worse off if resort fees were banned.[21] Online travel agents' commissions are often based on basic room rate charges. By using resort fees, hotels can therefore save money compared with charging higher nightly room rates. We would expect at least some of these savings to be shared with customers through lower prices.

Third-party websites often rank hotels by room rates in search results, which suggests that there are clear competitive incentives to use this partitioned pricing and itemize the resort charge.

Yet the bargaining power between hotels and online travel agents is independent of resort fees, so any additional profits from using them are likely short-lived. Booking.com started charging commissions on resort fees in 2019, eliminating any financial benefit for hotels. At best, hotels may be in a cat-and-mouse game of trying to exploit travel agents' commission and search listings, generating some temporary modest savings for customers.

Another theory for the use of resort fees is that hotels use them to reduce their own tax bills. A 2018 analysis showed that resort fees were exempt from Hawaii's "transient accommodations tax," meaning they lowered hotels' tax liability compared with higher room rates, a windfall again shared between the state's hoteliers and consumers.[22] Both New York City and Los Angeles do not include resort fees in their tax bases, indicating why hotels in these cities might charge them.[23] Yet this explanation clearly cannot explain their use in Orlando or Las Vegas, and would be easily remedied by states' revising their tax bases, as Hawaii eventually did.

Behavioral economists have developed the most sophisticated theory for why deceptive resort fees might endure even in competitive markets.[24] If two hotels (A and B) charge the same total price and face the same cost structure, then B educating customers that A adds a resort fee (whereas B transparently advertises a total nightly cost) still provides no *financial* incentive for customers to give up A for B. In fact, where customers can use loyalty schemes to reduce resort fees, as some chains allow, providing this information could even harm B's profitability by driving customers to stay at A.

This consumer-shrouding conspiracy of silence perhaps might explain why we see resort fees entrenched in highly touristy areas. But online travel agents and third-party booking sites—which are ignored in this theoretical model—have much stronger incentives to provide the information. In fact, Expedia, Kayak, and Booking.com have already factored resort fees into their price-comparison sites, catering to consumers' demands for clarity on prices.

In short, banning resort fees or restricting the ability to advertise them as a partitioned charge wouldn't be an obvious boon for customers. Yes, some ill-informed customers would avoid making reservations they later regret, but price-comparison websites and online travel agents increasingly help customers in that regard anyway.

Some customers would likely be worse off. Any new tax or commission liabilities will be borne in part by customers, while groups who currently escape resort fees using loyalty points or late cancellations may find themselves hit if hotels don't set up equivalent discount schemes in a world of higher room rates.

The economics of President Biden's anti-junk-fees agenda is therefore pretty baffling. There are key theoretical benefits to unbundling pricing for services, partitioning pricing, or using fees to compensate for contract termination. Competitive markets already provide incentives to mitigate deception. What's more, the law the president is pushing would primarily raise headline prices and reduce firms' abilities to cater to low-income and credit-constrained customers.

CHAPTER 12

Government Price Fixing Is the Rule in U.S. Health Care

Michael F. Cannon

The United States, reports *The Economist*, is "one of the only developed countries where health care is left mostly to the free market."[1] The *Los Angeles Times* reports the U.S. health sector has "largely unregulated prices."[2] These myths cannot withstand even a cursory glance at the processes that determine the prices that govern U.S. health care.

Direct government price setting, price floors, and price ceilings determine prices for more than half of all U.S. health spending, including practically all health insurance premiums. Government indirectly distorts all medical prices and health insurance premiums further upward by mandating excessive levels of health insurance. Excessive health insurance reduces both price sensitivity among consumers (i.e., willingness to shop around for lower prices) and price competition among producers.[3]

Government distortion of health care prices sometimes leads to below-market prices, shortages, and low quality. Government sets a price ceiling of zero dollars on transplantable organs, for example. More often, it manages to combine *excessive* prices and consumption with low quality. Either way, as former Clinton and Obama

administration health economist Sherry Glied writes, "There is no reason to believe that current prices provide incentives that reflect either
underlying costs or consumer preferences"—that is, market prices.[4]

Government Purchasing Means Government Pricing

When government is the buyer, political rather than market forces
determine prices. Medicare, Medicaid, and other government programs account for 49 percent of U.S. health spending.[5] Out-of-pocket
spending subject to Medicare price setting accounts for another few
percentage points.[6] Right off the bat, government-set prices control
more than half of U.S. health spending.

Former Medicare and Medicaid Services administrator Tom Scully
described the $1 trillion Medicare program as "a big, dumb price-
fixer."[7] In dollars, the traditional "fee-for-service" part of Medicare is
the single-largest purchaser of medical care in the world.[8] Each year,
its physician-price-setting scheme divines prices for 10,000 distinct
physician services across 112 distinct "payment localities," whose
borders government also sets.[9] Traditional Medicare has 21 such
price-setting schemes for different types of facilities and suppliers.[10] In
the $800 billion Medicaid program, each state sets its own prices for
as many distinct services.

When government programs aren't directly purchasing medical care,
they purchase health insurance on enrollees' behalf. More than 50 percent of eligible Medicare enrollees,[11] 69 percent of Medicaid enrollees,[12]
and all Obamacare enrollees have heavily subsidized "private" coverage. In these cases, government controls two prices: a premium for each
enrollee and the total price the insurer receives for that enrollee.

Traditional Medicare's pricing errors are as ubiquitous as they are
intractable. One among many indications of widespread mispric-
ing is that Medicare routinely sets different prices for identical items

depending solely on who owns the facility. As law professors Charles
Silver and David Hyman note:

> In 2012, Medicare paid an average of $1,300 for colonoscopies per-
> formed in doctors' offices, but it shelled out $1,805—39 percent
> more—when these procedures were delivered at hospitals. . . . When
> a hospital gives a lung cancer patient a dose of Alimta, its fee is about
> $4,300 larger than a doctor with an independent practice would
> receive. For Herceptin, a drug given to women with breast cancer,
> the site-of-service differential is about $2,600. And for Avastin, when
> used to treat colon cancer, it is $7,500.[13]

Medicare pays ambulatory surgical centers $1,000 per cataract sur-
gery with intraocular lens insertion but pays hospitals $2,000.[14] The
list continues.[15]

Differences in quality, consumers, convenience, and cost cannot
explain why Medicare sets different prices for the same service. In
2014, Medicare paid long-term-care hospitals 3.1 times as much
as skilled nursing facilities—$1,400 per day versus $450 per day,
a per-admission difference of about $30,000—to provide simi-
lar services to similar patients, without any evidence of additional
benefit.[16] It pays more for evaluation and management appoint-
ments in hospitals than at physician offices (see Figure 12.1), even
though such patients do not need hospital-level care nearby.[17] When
a hospital purchases a physician practice or other facility, Medicare
increases the prices it pays for the same people to provide the same
services to the same patients in the same office.[18] Medicare sometimes sets *higher* prices for facilities that have *lower* input costs and
less costly patients.[19]

As these examples suggest, Medicare routinely sets prices well above
cost. As a 2018 report from the U.S. Department of Health and Human
Service admits, "The Medicare program pays nearly twice as much as
it would pay for the same or similar drugs in other countries."[20]

FIGURE 12.1

Medicare pays hospitals more than physician practices for the same services

Total Medicare payment to physician offices and hospitals by billing (CPT) codes for evaluation and management services in 2013 dollars

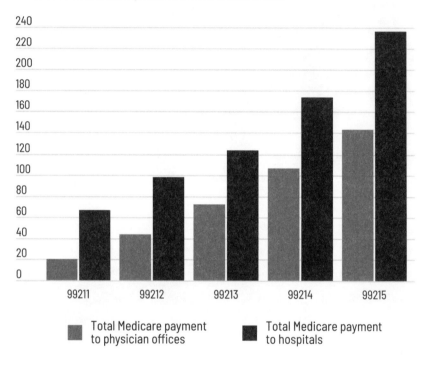

Legend: Total Medicare payment to physician offices / Total Medicare payment to hospitals

Source: Worth (2014).[21]

Note: CPT = Current Procedural Terminology.

Gundersen Health System in Wisconsin offers an illustration. Its all-inclusive input cost for knee replacements in 2016 was "at most" $10,550.[22] The average Medicare price was higher in all states.[23] Figure 12.2 shows average Medicare prices in 2016 and 2018— excluding surgeon and anesthesiologist fees—for Wisconsin, nationwide, Maryland, and Alaska. By 2018, Gundersen reduced its input costs 18 percent to $8,700.[24] In a competitive market, prices would likewise fall. The average Medicare price rose in Wisconsin, Maryland, and nationwide. It did fall in Alaska—by a negligible 0.3 percent.[25]

FIGURE 12.2

Medicare prices for knee replacements rose even as input costs fell

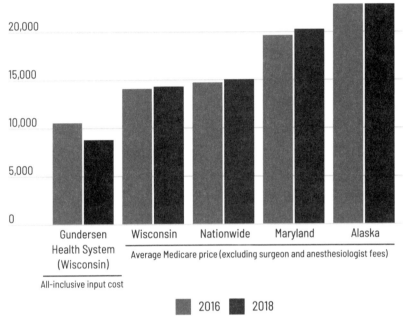

Average price, dollars

Sources: Evans (2018) and U.S. Centers for Medicare & Medicaid Services.[26]

Scully explains how to spot excessive Medicare prices: "All of a sudden you start seeing [ambulatory surgical centers] pop up all over the place to do colonoscopies or to do outpatient surgery."[27] The proliferation of physician-owned specialty hospitals is due largely to entrepreneurial physicians trying to capture the excessive prices Medicare sets for many procedures. (Congress's subsequent ban on Medicare subsidies to new physician-owned hospitals is a consequence of general hospitals' lobbying to keep those excessive payments for themselves.) Hospitals have no incentive to admit that "studies conducted in the USA generally conclude that price setting by a regulator . . . improved hospital financial stability."[28]

As if traditional Medicare's prices weren't excessive enough, the prices Congress sets for "private" Medicare Advantage plans leave taxpayers paying an average of 6 percent *more* per enrollee than if the enrollee remained in traditional Medicare.[29] The larger resulting subsidies explain why more than half of enrollees now choose Medicare Advantage over traditional Medicare.

Despite general acknowledgment of the problem by researchers, Medicare's pricing errors often exhibit greater longevity than Medicare enrollees. The U.S. Federal Trade Commission and Department of Justice have complained about Medicare's site-of-service pricing errors for at least two decades.[30] In 2018, Medicare's price control advisory commission—officially, "the U.S. Medicare Payment Advisory Commission"—confessed its "long-standing concern" that Medicare sets prices for procedure-based specialists and radiologists too high relative to primary care physicians.[31]

Price setting by government programs even results in excessive *private* prices. Medicare and Medicaid often set the prices they pay for drugs at a percentage of whatever manufacturers charge private payers.[32] These price-setting mechanisms create incentives for manufacturers to increase private-sector prices, because doing so means they get more money from taxpayers. One study estimated that Medicaid's drug-pricing scheme increased private-sector prices 15 percent.[33] The way Medicare sets prices for physician-administered drugs creates the same incentives.[34]

On top of those incentives, government programs encourage higher private prices by making enrollees less price sensitive. When providers raise prices, they lose private patients. The resulting revenue loss discourages price increases. Medicare and Medicaid create large pools of price-insensitive patients on whom providers can draw to replace that lost revenue. When providers have market power, which is increasingly the case,[35] Medicare and Medicaid encourage them to raise prices more than they otherwise would because those programs reduce the resulting revenue loss.[36]

The higher Medicare and Medicaid set their prices, the more those programs encourage providers to increase private prices. Higher government prices enable providers to replace even more revenue loss from increasing private prices. One study from 2015 estimates "a $1.00 increase in Medicare's fees increases corresponding private prices by $1.16." The study estimates that if Medicare were to increase physician prices by 1 percent, private-sector spending would increase by three times as much as Medicare spending ($3.5 billion versus $1.3 billion annually).[37]

Excessive private-sector prices are thus due in no small part to government price setting and subsidies. It is a testament to how wildly government distorts U.S. health care prices that Medicare's prices can be excessive and still 40 percent lower than private prices.[38]

Government Controls Health Insurance Prices

As of 2014, practically all health insurance in the United States is subject to federal price controls that restrict or eliminate the ability of insurers to vary premiums according to an individual's health risk.[39] Rather than allow markets to set premiums according to risk, "community rating" price controls impose a price floor on premiums for the healthy (at whatever the insurer charges the sick) and a price ceiling on premiums for the sick (at whatever the insurer charges the healthy).

When government increases premiums for the healthy in this manner, it makes insurers eager to sell to them but makes healthy consumers less eager to buy. Government "solves" this problem with subsidies that force taxpayers to shoulder the excessive premiums. Medicaid covers the full premium for all enrollees. Medicare and the Affordable Care Act (Obamacare) provide subsidies that vary with income and often cover the full premium.[40] Insurers and brokers then compete to capture the excessive prices government pays for healthy patients.[41] Medicare Advantage programs differentially attract the healthiest seniors—and thus capture those excessive prices—by offering gym memberships.

Conversely, community-rating price controls reduce premiums for the sick, which makes those consumers extremely eager to buy but forces insurers to avoid them. Since all sicker-than-average enrollees cost more in claims than they pay in premiums, community rating effectively penalizes insurers who offer coverage that sick patients find attractive. Insurers must therefore "avoid enrolling people who are in worse health" by designing insurance policies to be "unattractive to people with expensive health conditions."[42]

This is not theoretical. Community rating required insurers providing employee coverage to Harvard University, Stanford University, the Massachusetts Institute of Technology, and the state of Minnesota to compete to avoid the sick through such means as eliminating comprehensive plans.[43] It led insurers in the Federal Employees Health Benefits Program and New York's small-employer health insurance market to compete to avoid the sick by dropping coverage for 24-hour nursing care—not because such care is expensive but because the patients who use it are.[44]

Congress tries to mitigate these unintended consequences with—you guessed it—more government price setting. "Risk adjustment" programs provide additional subsidies to community-rated "private" health plans that attract sicker-than-average individuals. In 2018, Congress paid Medicare Advantage plans $5,707 to cover a typical 84-year-old male. If he had diabetes or vascular disease, the plan would receive additional risk-adjustment payments of $1,058 or $3,031, respectively. Some diagnoses trigger payments of $10,000 or more.[45]

The purpose of risk-adjustment subsidies is to mimic actuarially fair-market prices for health insurance—that is, to bring the total premium an insurer receives for an enrollee in line with the enrollee's expected medical expenses. This is key: risk-adjustment programs attempt to mimic the risk-based premiums that would naturally occur in markets because *market prices minimize insurers' incentives to avoid or shortchange the sick*. In a sense, risk adjustment is the homage market enemies pay to market prices.[46]

The trouble is, it works no better than other forms of government price setting. Even after risk-adjustment subsidies, Obamacare's community-rating price controls still penalize insurers for offering attractive coverage for infertility (penalty: $15,000 per patient), multiple sclerosis ($14,000), substance abuse disorders ($6,000), diabetes insipidus ($5,000), hemophilia A ($5,000), severe acne ($4,000), nerve pain ($3,000), and other conditions.[47]

The result has been a race to the bottom. Obamacare's community-rating price controls have caused individual-market provider networks to narrow significantly since 2013, when network breadth reflected consumer preferences.[48] They have eroded coverage at a cost to chronically ill patients of thousands of dollars per year.[49] Obamacare plans:

- Offer "poor coverage for the medications demanded by these patients";[50]
- Increase deductibles and copayments;
- Exclude top specialists,[51] "star" hospitals,[52] and leading cancer centers[53] from their networks;
- Mandate drug substitutions;
- Exclude coverage for certain drugs;
- Impose frequent and tight preauthorization requirements;

- Require highly variable coinsurance instead of predictable copayments;
- Issue inaccurate provider directories;[54] and generally
- Make coverage as unpleasant as possible for sick patients.

Even healthy consumers suffer because "currently healthy consumers cannot be adequately insured against the negative shock of transitioning to one of the poorly covered chronic disease states."[55] A coalition of 150 patient groups complains that this dynamic "completely undermines the goal of the [Affordable Care Act]."[56] Risk-adjustment subsidies likewise fail to offset similar unintended consequences of community rating in Medicare Advantage.[57]

The damage does not stop there. Community rating encourages adverse selection, where high-risk consumers are more eager to buy insurance and low-risk consumers are less eager to buy. Both dynamics lead to increasingly higher premiums over time. Obamacare doubled or even tripled premiums for many healthy consumers.[58] Premiums have risen so dramatically that in 2021, Congress began subsidizing premiums for households with annual incomes of up to $600,000.[59] One study estimates that community rating is the primary cause of Obamacare's rapid premium growth.[60]

Adverse selection also introduces volatility that favors larger insurers and insurance market concentration. As a result, it has led to fewer health plan choices for Obamacare enrollees (see Figure 12.3).[61]

Community rating causes premiums to rise so dramatically that insurance markets often shrink or outright collapse.[62] Obamacare's community-rating price controls have had that effect in its own long-term care entitlement and in the market for child-only health insurance.[63] Lavish taxpayer subsidies appear to be the only thing preventing Obamacare's health insurance Exchanges from imploding.

FIGURE 12.3

The number of health plan choices for Obamacare enrollees has fallen

Median number of issuers per state, 2011–2020

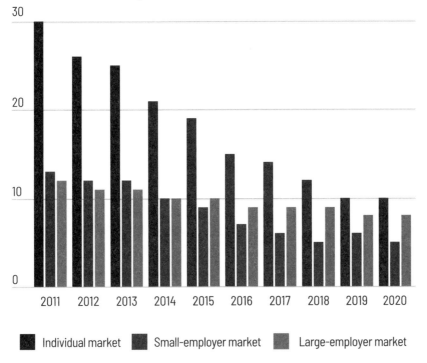

Source: Government Accountability Office.[64]

More Ways Government Distorts Health Prices

Health care subsidies, health insurance mandates,[65] and sweeping tax incentives for employer-sponsored health insurance[66] further distort prices upward by reducing price sensitivity among consumers and price competition among producers. Figure 12.4 shows that as such policies caused the share of medical spending that consumers pay out of pocket to fall, prices for medical goods and services rose increasingly faster than general inflation.[67]

Correlation is not causation. Yet one can also observe correlations between price sensitivity and prices for specific products.

FIGURE 12.4

As the out-of-pocket share of health expenditure has fallen, medical prices have soared

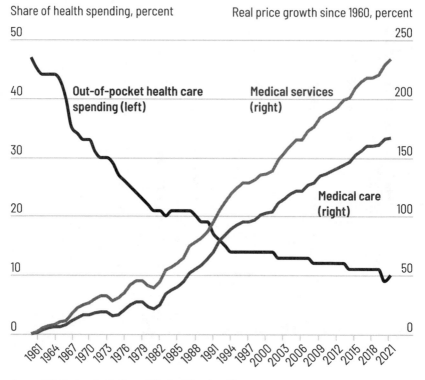

Source: U.S. Centers for Medicare & Medicaid Services.[68]

Figure 12.5 shows that before Obamacare mandated that consumers purchase 100 percent coverage for prescription contraceptives, real prices for hormones and oral contraceptives had been falling. Once the mandate made consumers less price sensitive, prices for hormones and oral contraceptives skyrocketed.[69]

Conversely, Figure 12.6 shows that, in a series of experiments where enrollees became price conscious when purchasing various services, prices for those services fell quickly and dramatically.

Finally, Figure 12.7 shows that, consistent with multiple randomized experiments,[70] falling price sensitivity correlates with higher per

FIGURE 12.5

After an Obamacare mandate to cover contraceptives, real prices soared

Change in real price relative to December 2009, percent

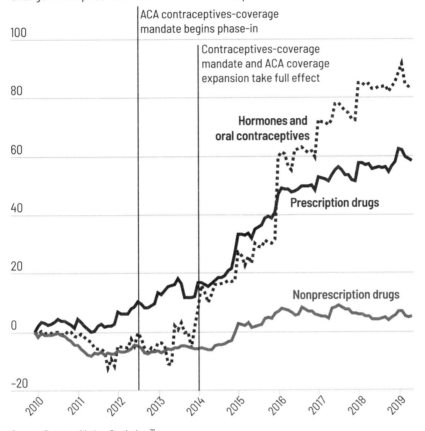

Source: Bureau of Labor Statistics.[71]
Note: ACA = Affordable Care Act, 2010.

capita health spending, which of course increases health insurance premiums.

The foregoing examples scarcely exhaust all the ways government controls or distorts U.S. health care prices. One state, Maryland, has explicitly controlled prices for all hospital services, including private transactions, for nearly 50 years.[72] For 30 years, so did West Virginia.[73] More than 30 states impose "payment parity" price controls that impose either ceilings on what providers may charge patients or

FIGURE 12.6

More price-conscious consumers led to falling prices

Average price reductions within two years of patients becoming cost-conscious, 2008–2014, percent

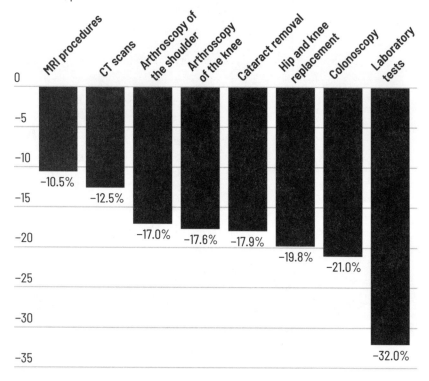

Source: Robinson, Brown, and Whaley (2017).[74]

(more often) price floors that increase what insurers pay providers.[75] As of 2018, 35 states had some form of "any willing provider" regulation, which distorts prices upward by preventing insurers from negotiating volume-based discounts from providers.[76] Congress and more than 30 states have enacted "surprise billing" laws that limit how much out-of-network providers can charge patients and their insurers.[77]

Government indirectly increases prices via regulations that restrict supply. States increase prices by barring competent clinicians from

FIGURE 12.7

As price sensitivity falls, per capita health spending increases

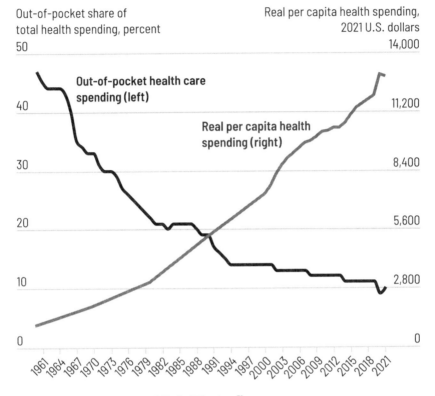

Out-of-pocket share of total health spending, percent

Real per capita health spending, 2021 U.S. dollars

Out-of-pocket health care spending (left)

Real per capita health spending (right)

Source: U.S. Centers for Medicare & Medicaid Services.[78]

providing certain services;[79] barring quality, affordable insurance from out-of-state carriers; and in many cases, barring market entry by new medical facilities. Congress puts upward pressure on prices by barring entry of new medical goods[80] and lower-priced health insurance. The express purpose of government-issued patents is to encourage innovation—by increasing prices.[81]

Health wonks of all political stripes believe government price controls necessarily push prices lower. If U.S. medical prices are high, it must mean government isn't controlling prices. In the real world, U.S. medical prices are often high *because* government controls them.

Medicare alone has allowed pharmaceutical manufacturers "to increase prices and capture far more value than they could when facing a market with less insurance and more flexibility," to the point where the program "might have allowed firms to capture more value than their products created."[82]

The ability of freely moving market prices to improve human lives is nothing short of a marvel.[83] For U.S. patients to enjoy those benefits, government must eliminate tax and regulatory distortions of health care prices—and get out of the business of purchasing health care.[84]

CHAPTER 13

Anti-Price-Gouging Laws Entrench Shortages

Ryan Bourne

Hurricane Harvey hit the Texas coast near Port Aransas on August 25, 2017.[1] It was the second-costliest hurricane on record, resulting in over 100 deaths and $125 billion worth of damage to hundreds of thousands of buildings and cars.

Days later, Texas attorney general Ken Paxton told CNBC that his office had received 500 complaints about "price gouging"—instances of sellers charging prices for goods and services at levels so high they are deemed neither reasonable nor fair. Some businesses were charging $99 for a case of water; hotels had tripled or quadrupled their rates; and gas prices had soared from $4 to $10 a gallon. "These are things you can't do in Texas," Paxton said, reminding viewers of the state's emergency law against what many deemed "greedy profiteering."[2]

Disasters completely disrupt the supply-and-demand patterns for goods and services. Hundreds of southeast Texas communities had no safe drinking water, which sent the demand for bottled water soaring. Damaged homes led to a surge in hotel bookings and the need for more tools and building materials. Impassable roads and bridges hampered the delivery of groceries and other retail products, while the total shutdown of oil refineries directly limited fuel production.

Prices thus become highly volatile after natural disasters. Consumers, however, resent paying more for essential goods, particularly when they have been triggered by soaring demand (as with bottled water), as opposed to businesses' costs rising because of the disaster. As a result, 37 states and Washington, DC, have anti-price-gouging laws (APGLs) that use government power to prevent or limit large price increases during emergencies.[3]

Texas's APGL kicks in when a disaster is declared by the governor or the country's president. Under the law, merchants are not allowed to sell or lease fuel, food, medicine, lodging, building materials, construction tools, or other necessities at "exorbitant" or "excessive" prices, with those caught facing civil penalties of up to $10,000 per violation, rising to $250,000 if elderly consumers are affected.[4]

APGLs like this are often extremely popular. After Hurricane Harvey, 67 percent of polled Americans thought there should be a *federal* APGL, with just 3 percent saying no such laws should exist at any government level.[5]

Concerns about price gouging during the COVID-19 pandemic and the recent inflation crisis encouraged federal legislative proposals in Congress. Sen. Elizabeth Warren's Price Gouging Prevention Act of 2022 would, for example, have made it unlawful "to sell or offer for sale a good or service at an unconscionably excessive price" during "exceptional market shocks" like natural disasters, power outages, strikes, civil disorder, war, or public health emergencies. The proposed fines were huge, at 5 percent of parent company revenue for very large and important companies. Firms would only be able to avoid them if they could demonstrate price increases were a direct result of rising costs outside their control.[6]

The Basic Economics of APGLs

In a free-market economy, prices serve as a vital mechanism to balance supply and demand, with price movements signaling changes in underlying market conditions. Consider a hurricane that significantly increases the demand for bottled water, due to disruptions to public water supplies and electricity outages. This shock creates a relative scarcity of water at the old price, leading to a situation where the quantity demanded exceeds the quantity supplied.

In response to this unmet demand of more dollars chasing dwindling stocks, the price of bottled water begins to rise. This rising price sends a loud message of a relative scarcity in the market—of supply not satisfying now-higher demand—at the old price. Yet that price increase brings useful incentives for suppliers and consumers to adjust their behavior to avoid these shortages.

First, the higher price acts as a financial rationing device. Consumers, facing an increased cost of purchasing, reassess their needs, prioritizing buying only what is necessary, rather than what is nice to have. This behavior helps ensure that those who value water the most at that time—and are willing to pay higher prices—can still obtain it.

Second, the rising price compensates suppliers and merchants for bringing more bottled water to market. The higher price justifies the costs and risks associated with opening stores in damaged areas, transporting bottled water from surrounding states, paying overtime to workers and truckers, or ramping up production or transportation through acquiring new inputs and storage space.

The higher price thus increases the quantity supplied to meet the higher demand, which means that more water is sold, albeit at higher prices, than before the hurricane. In fact, the potential for prices to rise in areas where hurricanes could hit grants retailers the incentive to invest in option-ready supply or contingency arrangements for that eventuality in the future.

Yes, we'd obviously see some charity and relief efforts to ship in water from other states when disaster strikes, even if prices were capped. As Nobel Prize–winning economist Richard Thaler and others have observed, big drugstore chains and big-box retailers face large reputational risk from being seen to raise prices significantly in emergencies.[7] To protect perceptions about their brand, and so longer-term profits, they often decide not to hike prices significantly anyway, accepting some shortages or non–price rationing in their stores, or else bear the cost of developing systems to transport supply from nonaffected areas.

Yet with price increases, other small sellers, independent stores, and newer individual suppliers, without major brands to worry about, face stronger incentives to open stores, and release stocks of bottled water, transport it from elsewhere, or reorient their production facilities to increase the supply. Their efforts help mitigate the immediate shortage.

A binding anti-price-gouging law alters this dynamic. True, these APGLs vary significantly across states, typically applying to cleanup products, medical supplies, home heating oil, housing, transportation, storage, and motor fuels once emergencies are triggered. Some laws are prescriptive, with California's limiting price increases to less than 10 percent above their precrisis level, unless the business can validate that it now faces higher costs.[8] Other laws are more opaque: Virginia bans "unconscionable prices" for covered goods, loosely defined as a price "grossly" exceeding that charged for the same or similar goods in the 10 days before the emergency.[9]

All these laws, however, can act like price ceilings when they bind— and distort prices in a way that sends out the wrong signals about the relative scarcity of products. In California's case, that price control is explicit when demand really surges, so the law holds prices below market rates. For most other states, the laws create uncertainty. Vague definitions like "unconscionable" or "excessive" create an unwillingness to raise prices because of the lack of clarity about the legality of any such action or requirements to prove that cost increases—which are often broader than specific product costs, such as for labor and transportation—are driving those pricing decisions.

In short, we'd expect APGLs to worsen shortages by disincentivizing the closure of the gap between the quantity demanded and the quantity supplied. With prices capped below market rates, consumers wouldn't feel the same urgency to conserve bottled water and would overbuy to be on the safe side, quickly depleting stocks. From a seller's perspective, fewer merchants would find it profitable to bring goods to market, including from out of state, while those holding stocks in cupboards or warehouses would be more likely to hoard supply in the hope of selling in the higher-priced black market. This situation would leave some customers unable to find water at any price.

Such a law might discourage businesses from making necessary contingency investments, increasing market susceptibility to future demand shocks too. High-profile advocates, such as the economist Isabella Weber, implicitly admit this, arguing that APGLs must be supplemented by "buffer stock systems" and "monitoring capacity" to be effective.[10] This acknowledges that APGLs cause shortages. Such planning schemes essentially attempt to mimic market outcomes for these goods through corrective government action.

APGLs during COVID-19

After COVID-19 struck, the national state of emergency saw many state APGLs triggered, covering personal protective equipment, hand sanitizer, and various drugs and medicines.

These laws proved more damaging during a pandemic. Unlike natural disasters that affect specific regions for a short time, COVID-19 was a long-lasting crisis across the entire country. There was no "outside" area from which major stores could bring in extra supplies, and the elevated demand for, say, hand sanitizer and facemasks endured much longer given the protracted nature of the pandemic.

So APGLs prolonged shortages. Hand sanitizer shelves at major chains such as CVS were barren right through May 2020. CEOs helping access facemasks from abroad said business worry about accusations of price gouging prevented their importation. Economists Rik Chakraborti and Gavin Roberts found that states imposing APGLs saw "significant increases in online searches for hand sanitizer," implying people were having to search more aggressively to find it.[11]

This problem was worse in states that had APGLs before the COVID-19 pandemic, implying that people's experience with APGLs led to expectations of shortages, which in turn led to more hoarding and panic buying early on.[12] Interestingly, APGLs might have even worsened the virus's spread in March and April 2020.[13] Those economists' later research found that states with APGLs saw more people visiting stores (perhaps having to search more extensively for out-of-stock items), alongside higher COVID-19 case rates and deaths.

Of course, not all sellers would have raised prices aggressively, even absent these laws. Economists Luis Cabral and Lei Xu found that facemask prices on Amazon Marketplace rose 270 percent in March 2020 compared with 2019. But those who had sold them pre-pandemic only charged 63 percent of new sellers' prices—indicating that it's harder to hike prices as an established firm.[14] Amazon itself was critical of price gouging, and stores such as CVS and Walmart appeared to react as they would with localized disasters through fear of the public reaction.

What APGLs did, however, was create new legal uncertainties for smaller convenience stores and online merchants willing to sell at higher market prices. That diminished the incentives for the economy to produce more of these goods that were in sustained high demand. It also deterred firms from making investments to build up capacity that could help during future pandemics.

The Economic Arguments for APGLs

Proponents of APGLs claim that large price increases during emergencies merely reflect companies' exploitation of customers—a greed for profiteering from disasters. "People are outraged at 'vultures' who prey on the desperation of others and want them punished—not rewarded with windfall profits," says philosopher Michael Sandel.[15]

The laws of economics, however, don't stop functioning just because a hurricane hits. Companies are disciplined when setting prices by customers' willingness to pay and competitors' ability to undercut them. The question is whether quasi–price controls lead to worse or better outcomes for allocating goods and ensuring people's needs are met when disasters strike.

Two seductive economic objections are held up for APGLs. First, if prices rise too much, Pulitzer Prize–winning journalist Michael Hiltzik has written, then the poor suffer disproportionately. It is understandable, he says, that the public consider a first-come, first-served approach more reflective of need, in such situations, than a "most-money-best-served advantage."[16]

Why assume, though, that lines, rationing, or black markets help the poor? When shortages arise (as with COVID-19 tests in the spring of 2020), lots of nonprice forms of allocation occur instead that have extremely regressive effects. Merchants can sell to those who are well connected, at higher black-market prices, or give preference to their own family and friends. Richer people, who are less likely to have suffered catastrophic damage to vehicles or homes after hurricanes, given their greater resources, are better placed to pay people to go stand in line and buy up goods when available. The poor, whose lives may be less resilient to damage—meaning the lack of availability of goods to repair their home or to get their vehicle working has far graver consequences—may be willing to pay more to ensure quick access to goods for which APGLs create shortages.

A second, more sophisticated critique comes from economists Jeff Ely and Sandeep Baliga.[17] They argue that after natural disasters, supply often cannot respond effectively and quickly to meet spikes in demand, so price increases are inevitable. In these extreme circumstances, when we are deciding how to allocate a fixed quantity of goods, policymakers should try to maximize "consumer surplus" and ignore "producer surplus." The benefits to consumers from keeping prices low will exceed the efficiency gains of allocating goods to those who most value them.

But their assumption determines their conclusion. A high price really does affect marginal decisions to supply goods. The South Carolina attorney general's office found that after Hurricanes Gustav and Ike, some "station owners reported that to avoid bad publicity they simply shut their doors instead of purchasing gasoline at elevated prices."[18] Small independent stores, when deciding whether to risk opening or transporting product in from out of state, are influenced by prices. In fact, free-market pricing affects supplier expectations about acting on an elevated willingness to pay when crises hit, encouraging them to store more product and mitigating shortages even before natural disasters strike.

The Morality of APGLs

Economists therefore generally object to APGLs. Asked whether they backed Senator Warren's APGL proposal, just 3 percent of 40 top economists in the Initiative on Global Market's survey agreed, whereas 84 percent disagreed.[19] A 2012 poll over a proposed anti-price-gouging law in Connecticut saw the same result.[20] That's because economists see prices as reflective of supply and demand, rather than business whims. Firms are constrained in what they can charge by customers' willingness to pay and by competition from other businesses at all times. Price movements provide crucial incentives to act on market realities.

The public clearly disagrees with economists, reacting with moral revulsion to large price hikes during emergencies, even when informed that experts believe APGLs deliver shortages and store closures.[21] Philosopher Michael Sandel speaks for many in saying that "a society in which people exploit their neighbors for financial advantage in times of crisis is not a good society."[22] As economist Dwight R. Lee concludes, it's as if we collectively demand a "magnanimous morality" of business during crises—an active sacrifice for the greater good, just as we hope someone jumps into a frozen lake to save a drowning child.[23]

This sort of small group moral instinct is not invoked consistently, of course. During the spring of 2020, few accused traveling nurses earning $10,000 per week in New York, with free accommodation, car rentals, and covered travel, of "wage gouging."[24] Companies are treated differently.

More importantly, this instinct fails a consequentialist morality test. The disaster, and its effects on demand and supply, cannot be wished away. The question is how best to deal with it. Yes, donations of money, goods, or services, such as help providing water and tools, are welcome. But if such relief efforts were sufficient to overcome the destruction, firms wouldn't even be able to raise prices significantly and we'd see no shortages, black markets, or rationing with APGLs. That we do shows charity is insufficient. What's more, only a freely operating price system, not relief agencies or charities, can coordinate action across large populations and sectors, including resolving tradeoffs over how much victims value the supply of, say, bottled water compared with plywood or medicines.

Some have argued that economists' opposition to APGLs is over-blown. Given the limited scope and duration of these laws, the often extensive carveouts if firms can prove that price increases are caused by cost increases, and the fact that major firms often avoid raising prices anyway, due to the reputational effects, some economists, such as Josh Hendrickson of the University of Mississippi, have argued that APGLs "aren't so bad." [25]

But as the COVID-19 pandemic showed, they can still undermine our resilience and recovery from major shocks. And the sort of mis-guided economic thinking that gives rise to their adoption is even more troublesome.

Recent debates suggest much of the public considers it illegiti-mate for firms to raise prices significantly if they are being driven by demand increases, for example. Companies were blamed for high inflation, despite the role of excessive stimulus driving demand. There has even been some pushback against dynamic pricing as it has been rolled out beyond ridesharing companies to bowling alleys and other entertainment centers (see Chapter 24).[26] If such impulses, which underpin APGLs too, become law in "normal times," these sorts of price regulations could do much more damage.

CHAPTER 14

The West Needs Water Markets, but Achieving That Is Tough

Peter Van Doren

The American West is dry. Average rainfall is about 15 inches per year in Los Angeles, 4 inches in Las Vegas, and 8 inches in Phoenix. And the population is growing, especially in Nevada and Arizona.[1]

What should be done about the limited supply of water and increasing demand for it? The focus of the press is often on imposing water use restrictions on farmers, especially when droughts hit.[2] During the mid-2010s, Governor Jerry Brown of California imposed restrictions and incentives to micromanage who could use water through usage limits on golf courses and campuses, mandates on new housing developments, and rebates to encourage replacement of old appliances with water-efficient ones.[3] Economists (and sometimes enlightened public officials), though, reject regulatory restrictions and advocate the use of market prices.[4]

When demand increases relative to supply in a normal market, prices of tradable goods increase. This price signal has two crucial benefits when it comes to water. First, the rising price reduces the quantity of water demanded—the price effectively rations the use of this now more valuable resource. Per capita water use is approximately 300 gallons per day in Fresno, California, where water use is not metered, and 50 percent lower in nearby Clovis, where consumers face actual prices for use.[5]

Second, market prices encourage the transfer of resources to those who value the water the most. In the context of the West, this would often see farmers send their water to urban users willing to pay more.

The farmers who arrived first in the West have rights to the water in rivers through the first possession doctrine—a similar principle to land and mineral rights.[6] Under this doctrine, historical patterns of water use give rise to de facto property rights. Specifically, whoever historically has diverted water and put it to beneficial use gains a legal right to continue diverting water for beneficial use in the future. Farmers diverted flows from rivers and streams through dams and irrigation ditch networks. Projects by the Bureau of Reclamation, part of the U.S. Department of the Interior, augmented these systems and after 1926 would contract only with irrigation districts for water delivery.

The fact that farmers have rights to and use vast quantities of water in an arid region is not a problem, in theory, if those water rights could then be traded to urban users who might value them more. But the history of water trading in the West offers a cautionary history about how difficult it can be, in practice, to facilitate true markets and arrange trades through property rights.

Groundwater provides over half the water used in the West. Unlike surface water from rivers where rights have existed for some time, underground water has been a common pooled resource with access for all who drill wells. The result has been unsustainable use and, in extreme cases, land subsidence. The development of rights for underground water, along with pricing that allows sustainable use, has proved slow and difficult to achieve, but it is no less important.

Los Angeles and the Myth of Owens Valley

For those who oppose water markets and pricing, the original sin is the project that developed the Los Angeles Aqueduct in the early 1900s to transfer water from agricultural uses in the Owens Valley.[7]

The Los Angeles Aqueduct was constructed from 1907 to 1913, and the city's population grew from 250,000 in 1900 to over 2.2 million in 1930. If you have wondered why the city of Los Angeles is so large in area and oddly shaped, the reason is that the Water Board provided Owens Valley water only to land that was annexed by the city.[8]

Popular culture has not been kind to the transfer of water from farmers to Los Angeles. The most prominent version of the story is the 1974 movie *Chinatown* starring Jack Nicholson and Faye Dunaway. According to environmental economist Gary Libecap, "The allegations are that Owens Valley water was stolen from farmers by a rapacious Los Angeles and, once it was shipped out of the valley through the Los Angeles Aqueduct, the agricultural economy was ruined, and the valley was left a wasteland."[9]

To obtain Owens Valley water for the aqueduct, the Los Angeles Water Board purchased over 800 farms and the water rights that came with them. Negotiations were difficult because of bilateral monopoly. The board was the only buyer and was under pressure to buy because Los Angeles was in a drought in the early 1920s. Large farmers formed pools to collude as sellers. Sellers wanted the surplus from the increased land values in Los Angeles arising from the water availability. The city's board offered compensation based on agricultural revenue from the farms.

Some farmers resorted to violence to increase their compensation. From 1924 through 1931, the aqueduct was repeatedly attacked with explosives. The board responded by increasing its offers. Up to 1934, the Water Board paid $19 million for agricultural properties, which was more than the value of the land in agricultural use. From 1900 to 1930, land values in Inyo County, where Owens Valley was located, increased by a factor of 11, whereas land values in nearby Lassen County only doubled. This very much suggests that Los Angeles did not steal the water.[10]

An additional complication arose when owners of property in the five towns in the Owens Valley demanded reparations for their lost property values as the surrounding farms stopped producing. The California legislature enacted legislation requiring compensation to businesses and village property owners, which was upheld by the California Supreme Court in 1929. Los Angeles paid about $6 million in compensation.[11]

So why the negative portrayal of the trade, which has poisoned support for water markets? Environmental economist Gary Libecap argues that the hostility arose from the distribution of the gains from trade. From 1920 to 1930, the value of agricultural land and buildings in Inyo County increased by $12 million, whereas that of *agricultural land* in Los Angeles County—the San Fernando Valley—increased by over $400 million. In other words, landowners who sold in the Owens Valley did better than neighboring agricultural counties, but the gains of Los Angeles *agricultural* landowners were almost 40 times larger.[12]

One hundred years after the events of Owens Valley, the public understanding of the water history of Los Angeles continues to stigmatize water rights trading as a concept.

The Public Trust Doctrine

So the farmers have initial rights, and the infrastructure that facilitates their access to water to enable agriculture in the West has been subsidized by federal taxpayers. None of that technically prevents water flowing from farmers to more valuable urban uses through trades.

To be sure, cultural understanding of the trading of rights from Owens Valley farmers to the Los Angeles Aqueduct continues to cast a negative cloud over proposed water rights trades even today. Another important impediment to trading, however, is the public trust doctrine.[13] Its origins lay in the right of the public to access navigable waterways and limit the rights of landowners that border rivers and streams. The idea was expanded in environmental law journals in the 1970s.[14]

The intellectual arguments of the public trust doctrine became the basis for a lawsuit brought by environmental groups against Los Angeles Aqueduct's use of water. In 1983, the California Supreme Court ruled in *National Audubon Society v. Superior Court* that the "core of the public trust doctrine is the state's authority as sovereign to exercise a continuous supervision and control over" the waters of the state to protect ecological and recreational values.[15] The ruling allowed the reallocation of water rights without compensation and gave citizens standing to raise a claim of harm under the public trust against private water users. The net effect was to transform clearly defined water rights into a common pool in which many parties— primarily environmental groups—could litigate settlements arranged by any subset. Settlement of this particular dispute took nearly 20 more years.[16]

Groundwater Use

Recent coverage of the allocation agreement among states for Colorado River water ignores the importance of underground water in the West.[17] Groundwater often accounts for 50 percent or more of the annual water supply in states such as Arizona, California, New Mexico, and Texas.[18] Limits on the use of groundwater have been more the exception than the rule. Surface property owners in Texas, for example, have the right to drill for water under their property regardless of the consequences for other surface owners who tap the same underground aquifer. In California, the San Joaquin Valley farming town of Corcoran has sunk as much as 11.5 feet over the past 14 years because of excessive aquifer water use that has resulted in land subsidence.[19]

The Mojave groundwater aquifer is in Southern California, just north of the growing urban areas in the Los Angeles Basin. In the early 1990s, local groundwater users began a process to settle and quantify ground-water claims.[20] These quantified pumping rights became tradable, lay-ing the foundation for a functioning groundwater market administered by a third-party legal entity called a "watermaster" that administers rights and trading. Pumpers received initial allocations that entitled them to pump quantities in line with their historical use, and these have been progressively ramped down over time to achieve sustainable use of the aquifer. Water users trade both annual pumping allowances and permanent rights to pump.

The groundwater rights system does not cover the entire valley. Land values are much higher (by about $400 million) just within the adjudicated area than in a comparison (control) group along the fringe.[21] In part, this difference arises because of the ability to transfer water to high-value uses in urban settings.

You would think that designing institutions that result in land value gains of $400 million would be easy. Unfortunately, it is not. The cre-ation of a pumping rights system started in the 1960s, failed, and was not restarted until the 1990s, when lawsuits resulted in more than a decade of negotiation and litigation that took some parties to the state supreme court. Among all California groundwater adjudications, the average time from initial court filing to judgment has been eight years, with delays reflecting a mix of disputes over the basis of exist-ing groundwater claims, measurement and allocation approaches, and other points of contention.[22]

An examination of both successful and failed attempts at ground-water rights development in California suggests that negotiations between farmers and urban users (as in the Owens Valley case decades earlier) often result in stalemates because the valuation differences are so large. Once more land is urbanized, the remaining resid-ual farmers are more willing to trade because the wealth gains are so large.

But the large wealth gains also cause another negotiation problem: how to evaluate dormant groundwater claims of landowners who have not pumped in the past but own land over an aquifer. A recent adjudication in Antelope Valley resolved this question successfully through negotiated settlement, but the process took 15 years.[23]

Idaho Case Also Illustrates Large Transaction Costs

A large increase in aquifer use in Idaho reduced groundwater seepage downstream back into the Snake River, which, in turn, reduced flows to downstream hydroelectric generators at Hells Canyon owned by public utility Idaho Power.[24] The utility's surface water rights were senior to upstream groundwater users' because the utility began pumping water earlier. In 1977, an interest group representing utility customers successfully sued Idaho Power, arguing that it had failed to protect the public interest by not enforcing its senior water rights against upstream groundwater users with junior rights. In 1983, the Idaho Supreme Court found that Idaho Power had a public duty to protect its water rights. Idaho Power filed curtailment notices against every upstream groundwater user in the state, including over 7,500 farmers. In 1987, the state settled the case. It purchased some of Idaho Power's water rights and required that the water rights in the entire Snake River Basin be adjudicated to prevent future conflicts.[25]

Over the subsequent 27 years, the state of Idaho conducted the most complex water rights adjudication ever undertaken in the United States. Between 1987 and 2014, the Snake River Basin Adjudication determined who had legal rights to use water and what trades would be hydrologically permissible, involving 139,000 water rights and 90 percent of Idaho's water use. The adjudication cost $94 million but has increased the value of Idaho's agricultural output by $250 million per year.[26]

Conventional accounts of water problems in the West often blame farmers and their excessive use of water. And public officials then often implement water use restrictions when demand exceeds supply, rather than allowing water market prices to work their magic. But the initial entitlements of farmers would not be a problem if farmers could trade their water rights to urban users for more than they would earn in agricultural production.

Economic welfare could be improved significantly, in other words, if water markets and trading were expanded across the West. But their development has been transaction cost filled, making it a slow process. The struggles and violence over the economic surplus associated with the development of the Los Angeles water system 100 years ago continue to inform rural-to-urban water trades today.

Although the public trust doctrine impeded the development of clear rights and trading in California, even conservative market-oriented Idaho took 27 years to formalize groundwater rights. The formalization and trading of water rights in the West are thus a tough, slow slog, but a worthy one.

CHAPTER 15

Minimum Wage Hikes Bring Tradeoffs beyond Pay and Jobs

Jeffrey Clemens

In public debate, the pros and cons of the minimum wage are frequently boiled down to a supposedly simple tradeoff between earnings gains and job losses. On the benefit side of the ledger, a higher minimum wage can translate into higher earnings for workers because of higher hourly wage rates. On the cost side, some workers might lose their jobs as firms find it more expensive to employ them. In this frame, the calculus appears deceptively simple: if evidence shows few jobs are lost and many workers receive wage gains, a minimum wage hike is deemed effective. As a result, analyses of the minimum wage's employment effects will appear to have outsized stakes for policy.

An emphasis on the minimum wage's employment effects therefore pervades analyses from government agencies and advocacy organizations alike. In 2019, for example, the Congressional Budget Office (CBO) released a widely discussed report titled "The Effects on Employment and Family Income of Increasing the Federal Minimum Wage."[1] The report's content delivered on its title, as did the accompanying interactive tool; forecasts of earnings and employment effects were front and center.[2]

Reports from progressive labor advocacy organizations, including the Economic Policy Institute and the National Employment

Law Project, have had similar emphases, though with a reading of the evidence that casts the minimum wage in a more positive light.[3] Indeed, minimum wage advocates sought to discredit the CBO's analysis by impugning its assessment of research on the employment effects of high minimum wages. Berkeley economist Michael Reich, for example, told the *Washington Post* that the CBO's summary of academic studies "reveals an unwillingness to recognize the major differences in scientific quality among studies."[4] In an op-ed in *The Hill*, economists Jesse Rothstein and Heidi Shierholz laid claim to the mantle of "modern scientific evidence" and wrote that the CBO was simply "wrong" in its assessment of the minimum wage's costs.[5]

In their attacks on the CBO's credibility, advocates' insistence that minimum wage increases have no effects on employment, even when those wage increases are large, is puzzling. A 2022 review of the empirical literature by economists David Neumark and Peter Shirley found the CBO's conclusions to be in line with the full body of evidence.[6] And indeed, studies of large minimum wage increases regularly find evidence that those increases result in substantial job losses, especially for the least-skilled, least-experienced, and least-productive workers.[7]

In focusing on the rightness or wrongness of minimum wage advocates' claims, however, we risk entrenching a conceptual framework about the tradeoffs that is too narrow. The broad point is that firms can make myriad adjustments to blunt the minimum wage's impact on their costs. These adjustments can often be described as entailing reductions in the quality of the job from a worker's perspective. It is thus crucial to appreciate that these adjustments will tend to mitigate, if not reverse, the minimum wage's effect on workers' well-being. Furthermore, job quality will tend to adjust more seamlessly than the quantity of jobs. As a result, an absence of adverse effects on employment is far from dispositive as an argument over a minimum wage hike's attractiveness.

Appreciating the varied aspects of job quality along which adjust-ments might occur in the wake of a mandated wage increase can require some imagination. Among the channels through which declines in job quality can emerge, some are intuitive, whereas others are less obvious despite their having high practical relevance. A fuller appreciation of these margins is essential for us to reliably evaluate the effects of min-imum wages and other price controls in their totality.[8]

Minimum Wage Increases Can Be Offset through Adjustments to Fringe Benefits

As implemented in the United States, the minimum wage imposes a floor on the hourly wage rate an employer can pay its workers. When the legislated wage floor exceeds what a worker would otherwise have been paid, we describe that floor as binding.

How might a firm's working conditions respond to a binding mini-mum wage? A straightforward starting point is to recognize that cash wage payments are not the only aspect of compensation. To be sure, wages and salaries account for a majority of employers' labor costs. Bureau of Labor Statistics data show, however, that firms' spending on "fringe benefits" like health insurance, paid leave, and pensions accounts, on average, for nearly one-third of total compensation.[9]

When a firm hires a new worker, it considers the worker's impact on its bottom line. The firm's benefit from hiring the worker is the result-ing increase in production. Compensation sits on the opposite side of the ledger. Because compensation includes both wages and benefits, a firm can react to the imposition of a higher hourly wage floor by reduc-ing fringe benefits.

In some cases, these adjustments might fully neutralize the impact of the higher wage on total costs. Yet if benefit reduc-tions fully offset an increase in the minimum wage, neither the firm nor even the worker is necessarily made worse or better off by the policy. Having seen wages rise and employees be retained, however, an analyst who looked no further than earnings would declare the increased minimum wage a success. Focusing narrowly on wage and employment impacts can therefore mislead about the true economic effect.

How important are adjustments to fringe benefits in practice? Across several data sources, recent analyses have consistently found negative effects of minimum wage increases on a worker's likelihood of having employer-provided health insurance (EPHI). RAND Corporation economists Michael Dworsky and others, for example, found evidence of a negative relationship between minimum wage increases and EPHI in data from the Current Population Survey.[10] Economists Mark Meiselbach and Jean Abraham found complementary results in the Medical Expenditure Panel Survey.[11] My own research with economists Jonathan Meer and Lisa Kahn finds similar results in data from the American Community Survey.[12] A back-of-the-envelope calculation based on estimates from my own work suggests that offsetting declines in EPHI led the value of compensation for retained employees to rise roughly 15 percent less than it otherwise would have because of minimum wage increases that took effect in several U.S. states between 2014 and 2016. Evidence from earlier papers on this topic tended to arrive at mixed results.[13]

Unfortunately, data on fringe benefits are far less complete or readily available than those on employment. Health insurance, as discussed, is the primary benefit tracked in standard data sets. Even employer-provided health insurance, however, tends to be measured on the basis of *whether or not* an individual has an insurance benefit, rather than the value of that benefit. Consequently, the data tend not to tell us about a health insurance plan's deductibles and other cost-sharing arrangements, let alone the expansiveness of its networks of hospitals and physicians. This is important because moderate declines in generosity in these margins may be sufficient to offset the cost of small increases in the minimum wage.

We know less still about the effects of minimum wages on miscellaneous benefits like employee discounts, which are common at the sorts of food service and retail establishments that regularly hire minimum wage workers.[14] Through its national employee discount, for example, McDonald's has offered its employees 30 percent discounts on meal orders at participating McDonald's restaurants in recent years.[15] Employee discounts provide a mundane but practically important example of an aspect of employment that it is essential to account for in order to fully evaluate the minimum wage, but on which data are sparse.

Firms Can Recoup Higher Costs by Changing Other Aspects of Employment

The aspects of jobs that an employer can adjust in response to changes in minimum wages extend far beyond fringe benefits. Additional margins of interest include performance requirements, schedule flexibility, training opportunities, and safety provisions. In economics jargon, these aspects of jobs are called "amenities" (meaning "desirable features") and "disamenities" (meaning "undesirable features").

Firms can spend money, for example, to improve workers' experiences on the job by creating a more comfortable workplace environment or improving mentorship. Because these positive job features are costly to firms, workers may have to choose between these amenities and higher wages.

Similarly, firms can save money by skimping on investments targeted at further reducing workplace risks of injury, on worker training, or on improving the aesthetics of the workplace. Ugly decor, poor mentorship, and marginal safety deteriorations are classic disamenities. Here again, there is a tradeoff. Workers will demand higher wages to work at firms that are known to be undesirable along dimensions such as these. The key point is that if jobs become less pleasant, less safe, or more taxing, workers are made worse off. Whether a minimum wage increase leaves workers better or worse off overall depends on how they value these features of their work environments relative to the wage gains an increase in the minimum wage might deliver.

Additionally, there is widespread evidence that increases in minimum wages lead to declines in compliance with the minimum wage itself.[16] In one recent paper, economist Michael Strain and I found that increased incidences of underpayment eroded roughly one-sixth of the wage gains that were mandated by minimum wage increases enacted over the past decade by U.S. states. In an analysis of 10 central and eastern European countries, economists Karolina Goraus-Tańska and Piotr Lewandowski provide complementary evidence that underpayment becomes more prevalent when wage floors are high relative to average wages. Economists Uma Rani and others develop a similar finding in an analysis of 11 developing countries. These results, which span labor markets around the world, highlight an underappreciated tradeoff between price controls and respect for the rule of law.

Some of the best recent research to consider the effects of minimum wages on amenities has focused on the intensity of work. One way that employers might seek to make up for rising wage costs is to demand more output from their workers, through tighter productivity tracking, reduced break times, or more stringent work targets. Recent economics research by Hyejin Ku and by Decio Coviello, Erika Deserranno, and Nicola Persico has found that low-productivity workers in agricultural and retail sales settings increase their work effort in the wake of minimum wage increases. Furthermore, both papers find large effects in the sense that increases in output offset a large fraction of the wage bill increase firms faced because of the uplift in the minimum wage.[17] A key point in this discussion is that a job's physical and mental toll are among its costs. An increase in those costs will thus tend, like a decline in a job's fringe benefits, to reduce a worker's well-being even as the associated increase in wages augments it. Put differently, workers "pay" in part for a higher minimum wage by enduring more intense, or otherwise less pleasant, working conditions.

Research on the responsiveness of other job features to minimum wage changes is sparse. One dimension of potential interest involves scheduling. Michael Strain and I, for example, developed a hypothetical example to illustrate how a shift away from worker-driven schedules toward employer-driven ones may help firms offset the costs of an increase in the minimum wage. We suppose that employer-driven schedules increase hourly output by enabling a manager to send workers home when there are few customers. By increasing hourly output, a shift to such scheduling practices can restore the balance between wages and output in the wake of a minimum wage increase. This shift may be costly for workers, however, as it makes their schedules and incomes less dependable.[18]

As with adjustments to fringe benefits, such a change would thus tend to nullify both the benefits to workers and the costs to firms of a higher minimum wage. In the United Kingdom, the increasing use of "zero hour" contracts, through which workers are effectively on call, illustrates concretely how increasing minimum wages can lead to these scheduling practices becoming more prominent.[19]

Adjustments to Whom Firms Employ and How Much They Employ Them

An additional point of interest is that data on industry-wide wage bills and employment counts can hide changes in the types of workers that are actually employed. If the least-skilled are replaced by higher-skilled workers, industry employment counts may mask job losses for the minimum wage's intended beneficiaries.

Several recent studies have found evidence that minimum wage increases change hiring patterns, as higher-skilled workers tend to replace lower-skilled workers. A notable study in this vein involved an actual randomized experiment conducted on the Amazon Mechanical Turk marketplace (an online labor market) by the MIT Sloan School of Management economist John Horton.[20] Horton's study finds strong and clear evidence that higher minimum wage rates lead firms to shift their hiring away from low-productivity workers toward higher-productivity ones.

In a study focused on data from the early to mid-2010s, economists Lisa Kahn, Jonathan Meer, and I analyzed both the types of workers employed in low-wage occupations and the skill sets requested by vacancy postings for workers in those roles. Our analysis found that increases in minimum wages predict increases in the average age and education of workers in low-wage jobs, as well as increases in the likelihood that vacancy postings for these jobs require a high school diploma.[21] A number of additional papers have found evidence consistent with worker substitution along these lines.[22] A high minimum wage may thus increase the wages and employment prospects of some; however, the workers at whose expense these gains come will tend to be those starting at the lowest level of skills.

Firms might also adjust by altering workers' hours. In their analysis of the City of Seattle's large increases in the minimum wage, for example, economists Ekaterina Jardim and others found evidence that work hours in low-wage jobs shifted away from new hires and inexperienced workers toward workers who had accumulated at least moderate levels of experience in low-wage jobs.[23] More experienced workers realized earnings gains, whereas inexperienced workers lost earnings because of reductions in hours. Recent work by economists Radhakrishnan

Gopalan and others provides additional evidence that incumbent workers tend to benefit from minimum wage increases, whereas the fresh hiring of low-skilled workers tends to slow.[24]

The Minimum Wage Is a Price Floor

A lack of imagination therefore regularly confounds efforts to analyze and appreciate the distortionary consequences of price controls. At a high level, the key point is that price controls will also tend to influence the quality of the good or service in question. Controls on rent, for example, may lead landlords to skimp on maintenance or forgo renovations. Controls on premiums may lead health insurance plans to increase cost-sharing provisions or shrink their networks of physicians and hospitals. These changes in quality may either supplement or occur in lieu of changes in quantities, whether in the quantity of housing units supplied, the number of insurance plans marketed, or the number of low-wage workers demanded.

As this chapter highlights, discussions of minimum wages are replete with this common yet pernicious conceptual error of ignoring these other aspects. The tradeoffs associated with minimum wages involve much more than whether pay raises reduce the number of jobs. Increases in minimum wages can influence benefit offerings, employee discounts, effort requirements, and other aspects of jobs, as well as who holds those jobs. These adjustments, which can undermine the minimum wage's goals in ways that are difficult to detect, can be crucial for appreciating the limits of what is known about the effects of high minimum wages.

CHAPTER 16

Minimum Wages Are an Ineffective and Inefficient Anti-Poverty Tool

Joseph J. Sabia

Throughout the 19th and early 20th centuries, state and federal courts largely ruled that the right to freely contract one's labor was protected under the Fourteenth Amendment to the U.S. Constitution and could only be limited on narrow grounds.[1] Evolving theories of constitutional law later concluded that states could have a "compelling interest" in setting laws for maximum work hours (*Muller v. Oregon* (1908)) and minimum wages (*West Coast Hotel Co. v. Parrish* (1937)).[2]

Poverty reduction was deemed one such compelling interest. In *West Coast Hotel Co. v. Parrish* (1937), the U.S. Supreme Court upheld a minimum wage law in Washington State to "reduce the evils of the 'sweating system,' the exploiting of workers at wages so low as to be insufficient to meet the bare cost of living."[3] Since that landmark decision, poverty alleviation has remained at the heart of political arguments in support of minimum wages.

President Franklin D. Roosevelt introduced the first national minimum wage—$0.25 per hour—on October 24, 1938, as part of the Fair Labor Standards Act, to alleviate deprivation among the one-third of Americans that were "ill clad, ill-housed, and ill-nourished."[4] In later years, Presidents John F. Kennedy, Lyndon B. Johnson, Bill Clinton, and

Barack Obama all reiterated the supposed link between minimum wages and poverty alleviation.[5] In making the case for a $15 federal minimum wage in 2021, for example, President Joe Biden said: "No one should work 40 hours a week and live below the poverty wage. And if you're making less than $15 an hour, you're living below the poverty wage."[6]

The potential poverty-reducing effects of minimum wages remain central to advocacy for increasing local, state, and federal minimum wage rates today. In 2021 and 2022, two bills were introduced in Congress to raise the federal minimum wage from $7.25 per hour to $15 per hour: the Living Wage Now Act and the Raise the Wage Act.[7] In 2023, Sen. Bernie Sanders (I-VT) introduced new legislation to raise the federal minimum wage to $17 per hour.[8] Proponents of these bills have regularly cited the Congressional Budget Office's prediction that nearly 900,000 individuals would be lifted out of poverty if the legislation was passed.[9]

These claims raise three crucial policy questions:

- Does the most credible empirical evidence suggest that modern minimum wage increases have been effective in alleviating poverty?
- Do employer responses to these laws undermine their poverty-alleviating ambitions?
- Are there more effective, efficient, and better-targeted means of delivering income to the working poor than raising a mandated wage floor?

In this chapter, readers will find that the answers to these questions are no, yes, and yes.

Minimum Wages and Poverty in Theory

The effect of minimum wage increases on poverty is theoretically ambiguous. For instance, a government-mandated hourly wage floor could reduce poverty by raising the total wages paid to low-skilled workers living in poor families, thereby raising family incomes and lifting those workers and their families out of poverty.[10]

Moreover, in theory, if low-skilled labor markets are characterized by search-related frictions or monopsony power by firms—firms acting as a single buyer of labor in a market—an optimally set minimum wage increase could increase employment among individuals living in poor families, raise their incomes, and thereby reduce poverty.[11]

More speculatively, some proponents claim that minimum wage increases redistribute income from those with a lower marginal propensity to consume (MPC) with each additional dollar earned—firm owners—to those with a higher MPC—low-skilled workers. This, they say, generates higher consumer spending, which will stimulate aggregate demand and will reduce poverty by boosting gross domestic product (GDP).[12]

On the other hand, if low-skilled labor markets are competitive, minimum wage increases could reduce employment and hours worked among low-skilled workers by reducing firms' demand for their now-costlier labor.[13] This might mean layoffs or reduced hiring of low-skilled individuals, particularly for entry-level job opportunities, which could have serious longer-term consequences for income and poverty trajectories. The same is true even in monopsony labor markets if the government sets the minimum wage too high. If employment losses are felt by workers living in poor and near-poor families, their incomes could fall, thereby plunging some low-skilled workers deeper into poverty.

Therefore, minimum wage increases might *redistribute* poverty rather than reduce it. Although poor workers who see a wage boost, with no employment or substantial loss in hours, may be lifted out of poverty, poor or near-poor workers who are laid off, are not hired, or have their hours substantially cut are likely to be plunged into poverty—or deeper poverty. Thus, the net impact of minimum wage increases on net poverty rates is uncertain. Additionally, if very few individuals living in poor (or near-poor) families are minimum wage workers, raising the minimum wage is unlikely to affect poverty much at all.[14]

Furthermore, most economists believe it is unlikely that minimum wage hikes will spur substantial economic growth.[15] Standard macroeconomic theories do not suggest that a price or wage control would boost aggregate demand.[16] A wage floor across competitive labor markets will typically reduce efficiency and employment, shrinking GDP. In fact, my panel study of U.S. states found that minimum wage increases affected state GDP negatively, especially in industries with relatively higher shares of low-skilled workers, such as retail, wholesale trade, and manufacturing.[17] Thus, the growth effects of minimum wage hikes are as likely (if not more so) to increase poverty as they are to reduce it.

Measuring Worker and Family Well-Being

As Jeffrey Clemens indicates in Chapter 15, minimum wage increases can affect worker well-being and living standards through other mechanisms beside their impacts on earnings or employment.[18] For example, increases in the wages of low-skilled workers in some markets are likely to result in higher prices of the products they produce. From a distributional perspective, if minimum wage hikes increase the prices of goods and services that poor individuals are more likely to purchase, then their effects may be significantly more regressive than the direct effects on workers' earnings alone would suggest.[19]

Employers may also respond to minimum wage increases by reducing nonwage compensation, including vacation days, sick days, the generosity of health insurance benefits, or non-compensation-related amenities, such as the quality of food or furniture provided in the break room. These would make workers lives' poorer, even if they do not directly affect measured poverty.

This likelihood raises an important debate on how best to measure poverty in the first place, which could influence the estimated effectiveness of minimum wage increases in reducing it.

Most studies examining the effects of minimum wage increases on poverty have used the official poverty measure (OPM) to determine economic need. The OPM is based on the family as the resource-sharing unit. It calculates *total family income* as the sum of market income—labor earnings, rents, pensions, Social Security payments, dividends, and interest—and cash transfers received by each person living in the family. It then compares this with a family size- and age-adjusted federal poverty threshold to determine whether that family is in poverty.[20]

Other researchers prefer the Census Bureau's supplemental poverty measure (SPM), which also includes the value of in-kind benefits, such as the Supplemental Nutritional Assistance Program, and excludes necessary expenditures, such as work-related transportation costs and taxes, in calculating total family resources. To the extent that minimum wage increases affect participation in such means-tested programs, the SPM will capture these effects (though it too has its critics).[21]

Alternative measures of economic deprivation may also be informative. Some of my own research uses measures of financial deprivation (i.e., being unable to pay rent or other bills on time), health deprivation (i.e., not seeing a doctor when needed), or food insecurity (i.e., being unable to afford meals when hungry) for a broader conception of how the income effects of minimum wage increases influence material hardship.[22]

In summary, the net impact of minimum wage increases on poverty largely depends on

- The effects of minimum wage increases on wages, employment, and work hours among low-skilled individuals in poor and near-poor families;

- The distribution of earnings gains and losses for poor and near-poor workers; and
- Spillover effects of the minimum wage on output prices, non-wage compensation, means-tested public program receipt, and material hardship.

Empirical Evidence of Minimum Wages' Impact on Poverty

The wage, employment, and hours effects of minimum wage increases—and the distribution of these impacts—are key to understanding their effects on poverty. There is robust and uncontroversial evidence that minimum wage hikes raise the average hourly wage rates of employed low-skilled individuals, with the strongest effects among the least-experienced, least-educated, least-skilled workers, and those who earn wages between the old and new minimum wages.[23]

Although there is more disagreement among economists about the employment and hours effects of U.S. minimum wage increases, the strongest evidence still points to adverse employment effects for low-skilled workers, whom the minimum wage affects most directly.[24]

Until very recently, a strong consensus existed in the labor economics literature that minimum wage increases were ineffective at reducing poverty.[25] These results were primarily driven by two factors: (a) the low rate of steady employment and low share of minimum wage earners among those living in poor and near-poor families and (b) the adverse employment and hours effects of minimum wage increases among individuals living in poor and near-poor families.[26]

In the main, the findings in this literature suggested that minimum wage increases had no *statistically significant* impact on poverty. Most studies found that a 10 percent increase in the minimum wage was associated with somewhere between a statistically insignificant 2 to 3 percent *increase* and a 1 to 3 percent *decrease* in poverty, with overall effects centering on zero.

Yet a recent study by University of Massachusetts Amherst economist Arindrajit Dube—cited by the Congressional Budget Office and in congressional testimony—directly challenges this consensus, suggesting a large poverty-reducing effect of minimum wage increases.[27]

Dube uses historical data from 1983 to 2012 and estimates that a 10 percent increase in the minimum wage reduces longer-run poverty by up to 5 percent among nonelderly individuals, 5 percent among those without a high school degree, and 9 percent among blacks and Hispanics. These effect sizes are very large. Taken at face value, these findings would reverse a long-standing policy conclusion.

However, an April 2023 National Bureau of Economic Research study by Richard Burkhauser, Drew McNichols, and me examines Dube's conclusions on three fronts: (a) the appropriateness of his empirical research design, (b) the robustness of his findings to the post–Great Recession era, and (c) the evidence on the mechanisms through which minimum wage increases could generate such large reductions in poverty.[28]

First, Dube's research design compares "treatment states," which raised their minimum wages, with geographically close "control states," which did not raise their minimum wages or raised them by less than treatment states. However, our review of the data suggests that states farther away were often better controls because they had more similar poverty rates and macroeconomic conditions to treatment states in the years leading up to the minimum wage increase (the "pretreatment" period).[29] When we allow the data to construct a counterfactual via a "synthetic control" design that pulls from both geographically close states and states located farther away, we find no evidence that minimum wage increases reduced poverty, either during the period Dube studied or over a longer period—from 1983 through 2019.

We also show that one of Dube's approaches of disentangling the poverty effects of the business cycle from the poverty effects of the minimum wage—controlling for the unemployment rate in his regression model—may overstate the benefits of raising the wage floor. That is because this control may "net out" the negative effects of the minimum wage on employment, thereby estimating poverty effects only for the "winners" who did not lose their jobs. Using alternative macroeconomic controls, such as the House Price Index and the higher-skilled unemployment rate, we find that Dube's central finding again disappears.

Second, when evaluating state minimum wage hikes enacted in the wake of the Great Recession—which were more frequent and larger in magnitude than in prior decades—we again find no evidence of minimum wage hikes reducing poverty, even using Dube's flawed research design. This is still true even if we measure poverty using the SPM rather than the OPM and is consistent with findings from my previous research, which showed that minimum wage hikes fail to reduce food insecurity, financial hardship, and health-related hardship.[30]

Third, when examining mechanisms that could explain the most likely ways in which minimum wage hikes could reduce poverty, our research showed that (a) less than 10 percent of individuals living in poor families were minimum wage workers, and (b) minimum wage increases reduced employment and hours worked for less experienced, less educated, low-skilled workers. Each fact substantially limits the scope for minimum wage increases to reduce poverty.

Thus, despite modern policymakers' hopes, our research suggests that minimum wage increases continue to be an ineffective policy for delivering income to the working poor.

Better Ways to Reduce Poverty

The small share of poor families that include a minimum wage worker and the minimum wage's adverse employment effects are two important reasons why the minimum wage is an ineffective anti-poverty tool. But even if raising the wage floor did not generate adverse employment effects, recent proposals to substantially raise minimum wages would be a highly inefficient means of delivering income to the working poor.

The reason is that the relationship between earning a low wage and living in poverty has become substantially weaker over time. In 1939, following the introduction of the first national minimum wage, nearly 90 percent of low-wage workers (defined as workers earning less than half the average private-sector wage) lived in poor households.[31] By 2000, this number had fallen to under 20 percent. This result can be explained by the dramatic increase in second and third earners in households over that period—particularly the rise of female labor force participation—that broke the "single breadwinner" model, as second and third earners began to supplement the primary earner's contribution to the family's income. This change weakened the relationship between a single worker's wage rate and total family or household resources.

Using census data, our study projects that fewer than 10 percent of workers who would be affected by a $15 (or $17, for that matter) federal minimum wage live in poor families and about 18 percent live in families with incomes less than 150 percent of the poverty threshold. A far larger percentage (68 percent) live in families with incomes twice or more than the federal poverty line, and about half live in families with incomes three or more times the federal poverty line. Even under the rosy scenario of no adverse employment or hours effects from minimum wage increases, raising the federal wage floor is likely to be a blunt policy tool to combat poverty.

Rather than tighten wage controls, policymakers should explore more effective and efficient strategies to reduce poverty. The strongest strategies for achieving this objective on the income side are pro-work policies targeted at individuals living in poor and near-poor families. For example, the Earned Income Tax Credit provides wage subsidies to employed individuals who earn low incomes, which encourages recipients to work and is well targeted to the working poor.[32] Investments in human capital acquisition, such as schooling and job training, have also been shown to be highly effective at substantially increasing worker productivity and longer-run earnings.[33] Finally, regulatory reform to unlock cheaper food, housing, and energy—such as liberalizing trade, reforming land use and zoning, and streamlining permitting—could also enhance the poor's real living standards for any given money income by reducing prices of essential items.[34]

Advocates who claim minimum wage increases will alleviate poverty are largely delivering only symbolic hope to the working poor. The most credible empirical evidence suggests that government-mandated wage floors are an antiquated, ineffective, and inefficient means of reducing poverty. The unintended consequences of minimum wage hikes risk leaving many of the nation's most vulnerable worse off.

CHAPTER 17

Price Ceilings of Zero Can Cause Deadly Shortages

Peter Jaworski

More than 4,000 Americans will die this year for want of a kidney. More than 4,000 died last year, and more than 4,000 will die next year. They will die because we have shortages of willing kidney donors, and we have shortages of willing kidney donors because we control the price of donations of kidneys at zero dollars. No one needs to die for want of a kidney, but we would have to allow payment for kidney donations to stop the deaths.

Kidneys are just one example of an unusual category of items that are perfectly legal for us to have and share with others, as long as we give them away for free. The government won't stop you if you want to donate your kidney, but in every country except Iran, you will end up in significant legal trouble if you get money for your donation.

In essence, we applaud the selfless act of giving away one's kidney without financial compensation, but we frown on and penalize attempts to sell it. The same is true of blood plasma, sperm, and ova in most countries outside the United States. It is legal and considered noble to gift them, but illegal and considered ignoble to sell. It's as if many of us believe that monetary transactions can corrupt the nobility of these otherwise altruistic acts, in a similar way that kryptonite weakens Superman.

The philosopher Margaret Jane Radin called this distinct category of items "market-inalienable" goods and services.[1] They are things we can alienate in many ways, just not through conventional markets. Something about mixing markets with kidneys, plasma, sperm, ova, and so on tends to turn many stomachs. That is why Nobel Prize–winning economist Alvin Roth calls this category of exchanges "repugnant" markets,[2] and why the philosopher Debra Satz calls them "noxious" markets.[3] This disgust is a powerful force. Even when all the parties to an exchange are competent adults who would emerge from the transfer better off by their own lights, many still find such exchanges for money distasteful enough to want to prevent them from happening at all.

Compare that with a different group of things—like murder or slavery. We ban the sale of assassination services and people not because we object to those markets, but because we object to the acts themselves. Or consider countries that ban drugs like heroin—they ban not just the drug's exchange within markets, but its use altogether. In such cases, it is the acts or substances themselves that are seen as the problem. Yet when it comes to things like a human kidney or liver, you are not only free to donate them, but can expect to be applauded for your generosity. A kidney donor is seen as a life-saving hero; a kidney seller is seen as a money-grubbing criminal.

We can think of our policy responses to these two categories (outright illegal activities and activities for which only their sale is criminalized) in terms of prices. When we try to eliminate something, bans that result in jail time or fines are like a price for producing, possessing, exchanging, doing, or consuming it. We are trying to make the thing more expensive by raising the costs of engaging in the activity, and our hope is that this will mean much less of it will be produced, much less will be demanded, and so we'll have much less of it overall. Sometimes this works out as we hope (as with slavery), but other times, as with prohibited drugs such as heroin, we still see markets develop, albeit illicitly.

When we are seeking to ban just the sale of something, but not its possession or exchange in some nonmarket way, as with kidneys, our approach is instead akin to imposing a specific price control: a price ceiling of zero dollars. We hope that despite only allowing zero-dollar offers to providers, people will still provide the items in sufficient quantities to help those in need. But in case after case, our hopes usually prove futile, and too few people volunteer. The price of zero dollars nearly guarantees that the quantity demanded will exceed the quantity supplied. The result is a shortage, and all the downstream consequences that come with it.

Shortages in Organ, Blood, and Other Markets

Consider the case of kidneys in a bit more depth. In the United States alone, about 100,000 people are on the kidney waiting list. Most of us have an extra kidney that we could spare, but hardly any of us make any effort to give one to those 100,000 people. We may be very kind, but we are not kind enough to give away an organ, even a superfluous one. Of those waiting, many will suffer through dialysis before they meet with an early grave. Each year, thousands of people around the world tragically and needlessly die for lack of an appropriate kidney donor. In 2014, over 4,000 people died in the United States because they didn't get a kidney in time, and more than 3,000 people were removed from the waiting list because they were too sick for a transplant.[4]

The same is true for other people with rare diseases. In the European Union, about 300,000 patients rely on medicines made from the proteins found in our blood plasma (the yellow part of our blood). They rely on medicines like immunoglobulin, albumin, and clotting factors made from other people's proteins because their own bodies don't make them, don't make enough of them, or sometimes make proteins that don't work as they should.

Immunoglobulin, classified as an essential medicine by the World Health Organization, is vital for individuals suffering with immune deficiencies; their survival is often contingent on access to the therapy. But access is precarious. For instance, during the COVID-19 pandemic, even high-income countries like France and Spain found themselves rationing immunoglobulin therapy.

The cause of this predicament lies in the fact that 23 of the 27 member countries of the European Union operate with plasma collection deficits. These are the same countries where donors are prohibited from receiving any financial compensation for their plasma donations. The other four—Austria, the Czech Republic, Germany, and Hungary—have plasma collection surpluses.[5] The amount that donors can legally receive is set by the government and capped and controlled, but in Austria you can get about €30 (just over $32) for a donation, which is enough to get a lot of people to roll up their sleeves.[6] However, the surplus plasma in these four countries isn't sufficient to make up for the shortfalls in the other 23. So the European Union does what the rest of the world does: turns to the United States, where there are no price controls on plasma donation. American donors now supply around 40 percent of the plasma needed in the European Union, and a remarkable 70 percent for the entire world. That includes more than 80 percent in my home country of Canada, nearly 50 percent of Australia's, about 15 percent of New Zealand's, and basically all of the United Kingdom's therapy needs.

Speaking of Canada, American men also provide the majority of sperm donations used by Canadian women, and for similar reasons. Canadians used to donate sperm at rates that met domestic demand for it, but then the Assisted Human Reproduction Act was amended to set a price of zero dollars for sperm in 2004.[7] What happened? Canada went from 40 sperm donation centers to just 1 in Toronto, and the number of sperm donors was estimated to have collapsed to between

30 and 70 in 2010. In 2010, 80 percent of the sperm used in Canadian fertility clinics was sourced from American men.[8]

The Morality of Prices

Why do countries' governments control the prices of things like kidneys, plasma, and sperm at zero dollars, even when this leads to shortages? One reason has to do with the belief that a market price will corrupt altruism. Take an example from Canada, where paying plasma donors is illegal in the provinces of British Columbia, Ontario, and Quebec. In 2018, Sen. Pamela Wallin tried to pass a nationwide ban on paying plasma donors. Although the bill didn't make it out of committee, Wallin argued that "Canada's blood collection system must remain one that is driven by the human instinct to help one another, not by personal gain or the profit of a company. We must encourage giving."[9] In Senator Wallin's mind, there is a conflict between paying people more than zero dollars and the "human instinct to help one another."

The social theorist Richard Titmuss offered similar arguments back in the 1970s.[10] Titmuss tried to show that the UK system of mandatory zero-dollar donations of blood and plasma was much better than the mixed U.S. system, where some companies offered no compensation but others were permitted to offer more. He contended that any price above zero suppressed altruistic behavior and weakened the sense of community solidarity.

But altruism and community solidarity are among the least persuasive reasons for zero-dollar price controls. That's because they are beside the point for the primary objective. We collect plasma not to encourage giving, foster altruism, or promote community solidarity, but to gather enough plasma to meet patients' needs. Suppose we discovered or invented some kind of effective plasma substitute, eliminating the need for donations. We wouldn't continue asking for plasma donations purely for the sake of altruism, solidarity, or to encourage giving. We would just stop collecting plasma from people. Saving lives should supersede these other considerations, especially when there are countless other ways to manifest altruism and generosity or to promote solidarity.[11]

It is also a bit strange how selective we are when it comes to the purported incompatibility between payment for money and altruism. Jurisdictions that ban donor compensation don't ban compensation for nurses or phlebotomists. The doctor who extracts a donor's kidney isn't a volunteer. Yet we don't view the compensation of nurses or doctors as conflicting with the human instinct to help others, or as suppressing altruism, or as undermining community solidarity. If we paid nurses and doctors zero dollars, we would reasonably anticipate hugely damaging shortages in these critical health care roles.

Some are concerned that payments using money will change our attitudes—that we will begin thinking of our bodies or the bodies of others as mere commodities. When the law that set a price of zero dollars for organs was being discussed in the United States before its enactment in 1984, for example, a statement from the Senate Labor and Human Resources Committee said: "It is the sense of the Committee that individuals or organizations should not profit by the sale of human organs for transplantation . . . . The Committee believes that human body parts should not be viewed as commodities."[12]

If you were to ask your friends, they would likely say that we ought to view our body parts with reverence and respect, and they would likely say that money and markets, as a domain of instrumental self-regard, are likely to get us to treat and regard kidneys and other body parts much like we do mufflers—replaceable spare parts.[13] But aren't our lives more sacred than our ostensible spare parts? Even if a price greater than zero dollars for a kidney were to make us think of our kidneys like we do mufflers, our motivation for lifting the price control would be in response to the reverence and respect that we have for life. And this would reinforce, rather than diminish, the thought that it's our lives that are sacred and special.

We might also wonder why our attitudes should be expected to change at all. Plenty of things having a price tag greater than zero dollars still manage to retain their noncommodity status. We respect professors and admire athletes, for example, even though they both work for money—and in the case of the latter, are "traded" between teams and have their every move tracked, evaluated, and calculated. Many of us bought the cats and dogs we love just like members of our family. Why would kidneys or other organs be any different?

A final concern is distributional—the idea that poorer people will sell their kidneys or plasma out of financial desperation, that donors will be coerced by their circumstances or exploited by rapacious companies. In 1983, for example, former senator and then a future presidential candidate Al Gore expressed a common concern when he worried that payment for kidneys "would make the poor a source of spare parts for the rich."[14] And this lifting of price caps, it was feared, would not only mistreat the vulnerable, but risk the health of people who may give plasma or go under the knife despite it being medically unwise.

The latter concern seems to overlook that we have doctors and nurses whose job it is to ensure that no one goes under the knife if doing so presents an unwarranted medical risk. The proposal to repeal a price ceiling of zero dollars is neither a proposal to repeal professional medical ethics nor a liability for negligently allowing someone to be operated on when they shouldn't. Hospitals don't want to be sued, and doctors don't want to lose their licenses. Although this might be something of a concern when it comes to kidneys, it's difficult to see why it would be so concerning when it comes to plasma. In the United States, donating plasma is no big deal, and you can typically get between $50 and $65 for an hour and a half of your time.

It's also not clear why anyone who believes that plasma donation is exploitative thinks the status quo leads to less exploitation. Countries that impose a price ceiling of zero dollars on plasma donations simply import therapies made from the plasma of paid donors in other countries. That doesn't fix the perceived problem of "exploitation"; it just makes these recipient countries' policies hypocritical.

When it comes to kidneys, it is also often family members who are a match and so expected to offer one of theirs to desperately ill relations who are stuck on a waiting list. This expectation will often produce an intense social pressure to help that raises more significant coercion concerns than cases where potential donors seek money.

The arguments for these bans for payments are speculative; however, here's what we do know: price controls that institute a price ceiling of zero dollars predictably result in shortages. They contribute to needless suffering and unnecessary deaths when it comes to kidneys and plasma. They result in frustrated would-be parents when it comes to sperm or eggs. Often, bans on nonzero prices just result in people paying a nonzero price elsewhere, as the world does legally by buying plasma from the United States and as many do illegally by buying kidneys on the black market. The net result is more often much worse than it would be if we were to lift these price controls and allow prices above zero dollars.

PART 3

Value

Value: An Introduction

Ryan Bourne

Much of the impetus for *The War on Prices* stems not from well-thought-out economic reasoning against market prices, but from moral intuitions. Certain prices are simply viewed as wrong, unfair, or not reflective of how much "we" as a society should value a good or service.

Rents, for example, are often said to be "too high," whereas prices for unhealthy foods are considered too low.[1] CEOs are paid too much, whereas essential workers are paid too little.[2] Gender pay gaps or differential pricing of goods marketed to men and women are slammed as inherently unfair, as is the practice known as "dynamic pricing," whereby companies charge consumers different prices at different times for what customers judge the same product.[3] Sometimes, even the absence of a market price is held up as evidence of how little we as a society value something like, say, the Amazon rainforest.[4]

Some of these complaints stem from interesting philosophical discussions about what should be traded in markets. But most of them amount to shooting the price messenger, or at least rejecting its message. Price changes are regularly seen not as an outcome of a market process by movements in supply and demand, but as if they've been decreed or determined by some malevolent actor. That view leads to their disdain. People see large discrepancies between the market price and what they think the good should be valued at, or what they are willing to pay for it, and conclude that market prices must be wrong.

That conclusion then encourages the use of price controls and other business regulations. But it's important to realize that the popular rejection of market prices does not stem just from the distributional consequences of market outcomes, but also from a misunderstanding of how to think about *prices*, compared with the very different concept of *value*.

How Do Economists Think about Value?

Before the 1870s, classical economists believed that a good's price largely reflected the value of the inputs that had gone into it. Since the price of inputs reflected the value of the labor that went into producing them, a good's value was therefore thought to reflect the amount and intensity of labor required to produce it. This value was seen as "objective." It could be calculated by the labor time necessary to produce the good. And this would ultimately be reflected in prices: if a wooden chair took 10 hours to produce and a handwoven basket 5 hours to produce, then the chair should be double the exchange price of the basket.

This "labor theory of value" was near useless, without severe qualifications, in explaining many phenomena we see in markets. It's clear, for example, that demand from consumers matters greatly in determining prices in many markets. Prices are context dependent; after a day in the desert, for example, the price I'd be willing to pay for water would be much higher than after a day at work when I'd had plenty of water available to drink. Yet the labor that went into collecting that water from a given source might be the same. Quality matters too. The quality of two, say, bedside tables could be very different after the same amount of labor and time were put into them, resulting in very different prices.

To keep the labor theory compatible with real-world evidence, one needs to weasel out of the stronger claim about some inherent labor value to talk about what labor would be "strictly necessary" to produce a good of a given quality, given the available technologies and other factors of production. To escape the realities of fluctuating demand affecting prices, one likewise must also restrict the analysis to considering some long-term typical situation.

The marginal revolution in the late 19th century helped resolve these problems. Led by economists such as Carl Menger, William Stanley Jevons, and Léon Walras, it marked a pivotal shift in economic thought, transitioning from classical theories about objective values and aggregate quantities to a new framework that emphasized the subjective value of goods and the incremental impact (or "marginal" effect) of individual decisions on economic outcomes.

Those 19th-century economists' subjective theory of value posited instead that the value of a good is not inherent or fixed, but grounded in how much individuals desire or need it. This desire is influenced by a variety of factors, including an individual's personal preferences, the scarcity of the good, and the presence of alternative goods. How valuable a good or service is to any of us is thus a judgment in our own minds, in that place and in that context. Value is in the eye of the beholder—hence, it is subjective.

An umbrella will be more valuable to someone getting off a train to find a rain-soaked city than to someone on a 10-hour flight. The value of products therefore derives from our individual assessment of their usefulness to us in today's conditions, not the good's inherent physical properties or how much labor went into it.

That flipped the labor theory of value on its head: goods aren't valuable because labor has gone in to producing them; inputs like labor and land are valuable because they can produce goods that we as individuals deem valuable enough to purchase.

The Link between Subjective Value and Price?

If price isn't linked to some "objective" value like the labor inputs that produce a good, then how is a market price determined?

As noted, consumers each have their own subjective valuation of a good or service based on their preferences, needs, and the other choices available to them. On the basis of this valuation, buyers decide how much they are willing to pay for specific goods or services. Those decisions mark the highest price they would consider reasonable, given the marginal satisfaction they expect to gain from buying the next unit of a product—their marginal utility. A rational consumer will continue to consume a good up to the point where the price—that is, its cost—equals the marginal utility obtained from it.

This behavior forms the basis of an individual's demand curve, which slopes downward because the additional utility from each additional unit tends to fall as the consumption of a good increases. The overall demand curve for the market is just the addition of the quantities demanded by all individuals at each price level.

A similar story plays out from sellers' point of view, but in regard to revenues and costs. Sellers think about the additional marginal cost of producing one more unit of the good or service, and what they would need to charge to cover their costs and make a profit. A rational producer will continue to produce if the price, or marginal revenue, is higher than or equal to the marginal cost. This behavior forms the basis of the business's supply curve for a good. The market supply curve sums across all businesses, sloping upward—with suppliers willing to produce more when the price is higher.

Let's presume there's a competitive market. The intersection of the demand and supply curves represents the equilibrium price that markets will tend toward. At that point, the price is such that the quantity of goods consumers want to buy equals the quantity producers want to sell. In other words, the marginal utility to consumers equals the marginal cost to producers, ensuring that resources are allocated efficiently.

Changes in consumer tastes and preferences can affect buyers' marginal utility and so shift the demand curve. Alterations in the marginal cost of production driven by, say, new technologies can shift the supply curve. Both create a movement toward the new price under the new conditions. These effects help explain why goods with the same inherent properties can differ in price in different contexts.

In reality, markets aren't perfectly competitive. Yet supply and demand are still crucial to setting prices even in markets where firms can differentiate their products in some way. In fact, even monopolist firms are disciplined by a downward-sloping demand curve. What's more, experiments from Nobel Prize–winning economist Vernon Smith suggest that markets tend to converge toward the equilibrium prices and quantities predicted by marginalist economics, even when participants do not have perfect information or do not act fully rationally.

Do Prices Show Us What "Society" Values?

Former Bank of England governor Mark Carney is one prominent figure who has bemoaned what market-generated prices say about what society values.[5] In a speech in late 2020, he said, "Increasingly, the value of something, some act or someone is equated with its monetary value, a monetary value that is determined by the market."[6] Market prices, in other words, are widely considered synonymous with how socially valuable different activities are, even when those market prices do not reflect what we might—collectively—know to be important.

How often have you heard people denouncing how absurd it is that sports stars earn so much more than doctors and nurses? Does this notion not also reflect something being fundamentally wrong with how markets value different activities?

Or consider an example Carney puts forth: Amazon, the company, at the time of his writing, had a \$1.5 trillion equity valuation, whereas the biodiversity of the Amazon rainforest appears on no ledger, at least not until it is converted to farmland.[7] Doesn't this disparity in pricing high-light the warped priorities that come about in a free-market exchange system? You hear different versions of these same arguments all the time: the existence of a gender pay gap shows societal discrimination against women, for example, or that high CEO pay shows how markets misvalue lower-ranked employees relative to their true social worth.

Yet this critique of market prices misunderstands how to interpret the information prices convey. Market prices cannot, do not, and should not be thought to reflect the collective valuation society places on a good, service, or job. Market prices arise because of the combination of subjective valuations at the margin interacting with supply decisions at the margin. This is not a deliberative process of society coming to a collective decision about something's inherent worth or value to society as a whole.

Food is clearly valuable to sustaining human life; the next apple for someone in Richmond, Virginia, to consume might not be. Individuals' decisions to buy a good or service at a certain price tell us that they, personally, value the good at least as much as the total cost they bear in exchange. Yet that same transaction doesn't tell us anything about the inherent "worth" of the activity or social value—not least because, as we've seen, value is not objective.

No economist or thinker well versed in the workings of a market economy would therefore claim that market prices reflect inherent social worth, nor even what people "deserve." What prices really reflect is the interaction of the supply and demand for a particular good or worker—influenced, certainly, by the individual valuations of consumers purchasing or businesses hiring, but not reflective of some valuation by "society" writ large.

As the Austrian economist F. A. Hayek—widely regarded as one of the most prominent free-market thinkers—wrote in *Law, Legislation and Liberty*:

> The manner in which the benefits and burdens are apportioned by the market mechanism would in many instances have to be regarded as very unjust if it were the result of deliberate allocation to particular people. But this is not the case.[8]

In a free market, the wage that people earn in performing an occupation is not determined by how meritorious people think the profession is, but by how much people are willing to pay for the service provided. If that were not the case, and we rewarded professions financially according to some societal notion of merit or worth, it would be difficult to avoid a situation in which people were not free to choose their own occupation.

As Hayek, again, explained:

> In a free society, we are remunerated not for our skill but for using it rightly; and this must be so as long as we are free to choose our particular occupation and are not directed to it. . . . In a free system it is neither desirable nor practicable that material rewards should be made generally to correspond to what men recognize as merit.[9]

Why, then, rely on market prices or market wages to allocate goods, services, and set remuneration? Couldn't we aspire to something better, where people get what "we"—through government—decide they deserve?

As we read in Part 2, market-generated prices are important because they provide information to producers and consumers about which products, services, skills, and attributes are wanted or needed by people at that time, how much people are willing to pay for them, and suppliers' capacity to provide them. The function of prices in enhancing our well-being is not to reward people for past acts or achievements, but to provide signals and incentives in regard to what they ought to do in the future.

In a market economy, the earnings of people in a profession are largely driven by the demand for and supply of labor in that field. Athletes earn high salaries because they have rare skills that attract large audiences, leading to substantial revenue through ticket sales, broadcast rights, and merchandise. The supply of individuals with the talent and ability to perform at such a high level is also limited, which further drives up those individuals' wages.

On the other hand, although we all certainly value the work of nurses, their pay is influenced by different market dynamics. The skills required for nursing, while critically important, can be acquired by a larger proportion of the population, which increases the supply of potential nurses. Demand is also a factor; although society certainly needs nurses, the financial revenues that nurses generate through their work are typically less than those generated by top-tier football players.

Trying to ignore or override these price signals—which provide incentives to both producers and consumers to change their behavior—would have very bad consequences overall. If it were decreed, after the COVID-19 pandemic, that nurses had some kind of intrinsic value greater than their market wage, justifying their wages being fixed much higher to reflect "society's" values, what might we expect to happen?

Despite hospitals wishing to employ more nurses at a wage at which they were willing and able to work, hospitals would cut back on employment, as workers would now be much more expensive. As a result, care standards would suffer. In time, we'd likely see hospitals try to replace more expensive workers with labor-saving technologies, especially for the more physical tasks that require significant human input.

What's more, the higher wage would attract more people to the nursing profession. Better-qualified people who could do jobs that require higher levels of education and prolonged training might choose to become nurses instead, whereas people who have the appropriate level of skills for nursing would be unable to find work because the demand for labor in nursing would be insufficient to take up the supply of people willing to work in the field. Vacancies for teachers and other occupations would remain unfilled while would-be nurses would be unemployed, leading to vast damage to many people's career prospects.

If we were to try to replace market-generated prices with some politically determined price setting based on a consensus of "social value," we'd create large surpluses and shortages, depending on whether the price was set too high or too low. We'd encourage resources to be deployed in the wrong industries such that economy-wide production fell, making us poorer.

Do Market Prices Indicate Extensive Discrimination?

Market prices can result in large disparities: between genders (on pay and prices of gendered goods), types of workers (on pay), and different consumers of the same product (on prices). Many see these disparities as inherently unfair, and they get discussed as if their occurrence reflects a nefarious plot by some segments of society to entrench bias, discrimination, or unfairness. This perspective often drives calls for government intervention through price controls, minimum wages, or regulations on business.

It's true that overt discrimination exists; however, competitive markets provide powerful incentives against its persistence. Businesses that discriminate in their hiring practices, for example, limit their pool of potential employees. They risk overlooking talented individuals who could enhance productivity and profitability. More-over, if a business pays certain employees less than their productivity justifies, competitors can lure those employees away with better wages. The same is true with firms that charge different types of customers different prices, since consumers can often find ways to acquire those goods more cheaply elsewhere or have others purchase for them.

True, not all markets are competitive, and there is no doubt that some overt discrimination or unsavory behavior exists. The point is, given the role that supply and demand play in setting prices, we can't just presume that price or wage disparities across genders, workers, or customer groups reflect *harmful* discrimination or inherent bias against certain groups. Instead, we should ask what factors—relating to costs, technologies, or tastes and preferences—might help explain these differential market prices, beyond group bias. In doing so, we usually find that these supply-and-demand factors can help solve much of the puzzle.

In trying to weed out how much explicit bias is in individual markets where price disparities exist, we must be careful not to explain away too much in answering the question above. For example, if women tend to work in lower-paying industries but earn the same as men for the same work within those industries, it would be rash to conclude that discrimination against women simply doesn't exist. The distribution of men and women across industries might itself be a result of systemic biases in our education system or discriminatory societal expectations, which influence career choices.

The point is, observing market price differentials alone simply cannot tell us what is causing the disparity. Price or wage differences might reflect a variety of factors, some benign and others not. They could result from people's free choices, determined by personal preferences, or they could reflect deeply rooted societal biases. A simple gap alone gives us no useful causal information.

Whatever their driver, controlling or rejecting market prices can lead to harmful outcomes. If forced to pay employees the same amount or charge different consumers the same amount, a discriminating business may just cease to hire or cater to the individuals they are strongly biased against or raise prices for everybody. A gap or disparity in prices or wages may be an interesting topic to explore, but the statistic alone tells us little about whether we should be worried about it, let alone the potentially perverse consequences of trying to eliminate it.

CHAPTER 18

The Labor Theory of Value Is Mistaken

Deirdre Nansen McCloskey

The topic warrants a two-step dance. Step 1: The labor theory of value appears to be simple, intuitive, and ethical. Step 2: No, it's not. It's wrong as economics and ultimately confused and unethical too. When used as a basis for state intervention, all sorts of harmful effects ensue.

Step 1. The Labor Theory of Value

The value of a diamond or of a drink of water sounds plain enough. For the first century of the political economy born in the 1700s, economists such as Adam Smith and Smith's follower Karl Marx thought they had "value" figured out. Simple. Surely value is the "labor content," or, in Marxist terminology, the "socially necessary labor time" to get a diamond wrested from the earth or a drink piped from the well.[1] Tough, realistic, and dead easy to calculate.

The labor theory seems intuitive. Remove the hours of human labor and you're left with nothing relevant to human life. The drill press sits idle, which anyway has not been manufactured in the first place. The very word "manufactured" comes from Latin meaning "made by a human hand." Labor is certainly needful. That an item gets value from the toil to produce it seems the merest common sense.

And it seems just. People's toil should be rewarded. When nurses strike for higher pay, we're naturally on their side, saying, "After all, they work harder than most." To quote a famous first-century rabbi, "The laborer is worthy of his wages." His disciple Paul of Tarsus said, "He who does not work, should not eat." With exceptions for children and the handicapped, we say, "Damned right." Put your hand to work making goods and services. That's value, even in God's eyes.

The labor theory of value therefore sounds tough yet ethical. Most people care, or should care, about ordinary people, not things or kings. An acre of land in Iowa or a drill press in a factory in Manchester is a dead thing, not a person you can love. And the things were made or tended to earlier by painful labor. Labor is put "inside" the thing. The king didn't do it.

Such thought extends to the value of other inputs, like land. The massively influential pioneer of the liberal idea that only workers and their works matter, John Locke, declared in 1689: "The Labour of [a person's] Body, and the Work of his Hands, . . . are properly his. Whatsoever . . . he hath mixed his Labour with . . . makes it his Property. This Labour . . . excludes the common right of other Men."[2]

Obtaining things to consume is effort-full, in other words, so it must be the human effort to produce that gives things value, right? When the C+ student complains to her teacher, "But I worked *so hard* on it," she's invoking the labor theory of value. Surely what should figure in the end is the suffering of people, the toil or the damage to you and me and the student in making things, yes? That's how the prices of things should in justice be determined, *sí*?

What is ethically attractive about Locke's, and the student's, labor theory is the liberal conviction that *people* are the bottom line. And so they surely are. What we value, and should value, is not the glory of the king, the holiness of the Church, or the profit of the corporation. No, it's the person, the worker, and *therefore* the result of her toil.

The labor theory embodies the noblest of modern ethics, the liberal conviction that people matter first and last. It was understandable that the early economists believed it, even if some ran with it further than others. Marx, for example, like Rep. Alexandria Ocasio-Cortez (D-NY) today, who concludes that workers were being paid "less than the value they create," believed that the very existence of that wretched extraction, profit, was evidence of capitalist exploitation.[3] Some ethical people and modern Marxist economists—such as the Frenchman Thomas Piketty and the Italian American Mariana Mazzucato—adhere to a variant of the labor theory still.

Step 2. Subjective Value Theory

But, shockingly, against all this apparent common sense and ethical appeal, the labor theory is wholly mistaken as a matter of economics. It's deeply screwy, scientifically, and evil in its ethics.

The Argentine economist Martin Krause imagines an earnest Lockean deciding to build an auto solely with his own labor, making the required steel and rubber and so forth. It's "manufactured," made by his hands, and so valued. But it takes years of exhausting labor to produce a very bad little auto, because his labor lacks the thousands of varied skills that go into making a good one. Self-sufficiency denies him the great productivity of others specializing in glassmaking or door design, and then trading in markets. That's the meaning of the Marxist ploy of adding "socially necessary" to the labor theory. Our Lockean/Marxist toiler then goes to market to sell his very bad auto at the "just price" of his labor content. He offers it for $500,000, to reflect his efforts. But in a market of specialists trading with each other, whatever the labor content, a comparably bad auto only sells for $500. Uh-oh.

About the year 1867, the year in which Marx in *Das Kapital* attributed all output to labor in a Lockean and Adam Smithian way, three young economists from different countries concluded that attributing all value to the "frozen labor" in the item cannot explain market prices. William Stanley Jevons in Britain in 1862, Carl Menger in Austria in 1871, and Léon Walras in French Switzerland in 1874 independently realized why the labor theory was screwy.[4] The troika invented what came to be called "the marginal utility theory of consumer goods and the marginal productivity theory of distribution." It is the correct and modern theory of what prices are, and should be, to get the most out of what we have.

In other words, the new theory is about efficiency, not justice. In God's eyes the price of bread should be zero for a virtuous pauper and the wage zero for a sinful brain surgeon. But here below, "marginalism" in economics says that the subjectivity of demanders and suppliers will and should rule in pricing the last hour of the worker and the last drink of water. The price of water is not about the virtue of its total labor cost but about a subjective valuation of a little bit more to drink, however it was acquired, whether or not with toil. Value is not "objective" and ethical. It depends on how far water and diamonds and labor itself go toward fulfilling human wants. And it comes from humans' subjective valuations.

In musing on "value," Smith had remarked in 1776, "Nothing is more useful than water; but it will purchase scarce anything; scarce anything can be had in exchange for it. A diamond, on the contrary, has scarce any value in use; but a very great quantity of other goods may frequently be had in exchange for it."[5] Smith was puzzled, because value in use did not correspond with his labor-input theory.

Smith was, uncharacteristically, making a big scientific mistake. He confused the *total* value of a thing in use with its actual market price "at the margin," as the economists a century after him put it. An extra ounce of water is not worth much in most circumstances, even though the total of the water consumed in a year is extremely valuable, a necessity of life—in a way that diamonds in any amount are decidedly not.

Wanting an "objective" answer to why anything has value, Smith and Marx looked to *history* to determine value, in the way a lawyer does in deciding who is guilty of a murder. Justice is served. Damned right. The economists of 1862–1874 and beyond replied, "No, not for the best present decision about the *future*."

The bottle of water's use in the future, not justice in the past, determines one's willingness to pay. A consumer does not consult what he's already spent, and a businessperson does not consult past profits when making present decisions. The proverbial wisdom is, "Bygones are bygones." To do best, look forward, not back.

That the Lockean automaker spent $500,000 of his labor is beside the point. His Lockean/Marxist labor was wasted, in the precise sense that it would have been better employed in some other opportunity, for which people would be willing to pay. By the same logic, the modern economist says: "The businessperson, in making the marginal decision to hire another worker, or spend a little more in advertising, should forget about the fixed costs of running a business, such as the cost of paying off the loan. Look now at what will change in the future if you do this or that." That's the "margin."

The 1870s' Theory Solves Pricing Puzzles

On the eve of a predicted hurricane, a four- by eight-foot sheet of plywood is very valuable. Never mind how much it cost to produce, in labor, or in any other input for that matter. People will complain about "price gouging," as they did when ventilators for breathless patients became temporarily expensive during the COVID-19 outbreak of 2020. But the complaint is childish. Do you want the plywood sheet or the ventilator more than someone else, who *is* willing to pay the "gouged" price, right now, history aside? If not, fine. Go spend your money on something you do want more than the other people in society. That's better for you and for society. Fixing prices at their historical labor content instead ensures that items will go to the wrong people, not to those who value them most.

The racehorse Secretariat (1970–1989), under a labor value theory, would have sold for his cost of production at the stables in Doswell, Virginia—perhaps a few tens of thousands of dollars. But his proper value when he was retired was his prospective value as a stud, $6 million at the time (equivalent to $40 million in 2022 dollars), paid voluntarily by the syndicators in expectation of watchers of races featuring his numerous offspring. Look forward to find value.

And so economics shifted in the 1870s from a historical, total-value, labor-theory, and mistaken science to a forward-looking, marginal-value, subjective, and correct science. When you buy a bottle of water, you do not pay the "total" value—its life-sustaining value over a week or a life of drinking. You pay what you value it at for your next drink and in your present condition. "Value," in other words, depends on circumstances. The third ice-cream scoop in 15 minutes is not as delight producing as the first. Sunscreen is more valuable in Cancún at noon in summer than at midnight in Oslo at Christmas.

Subjective value theory thus turns the labor theory on its head. The value of outputs isn't determined by the value of labor inputs (from which, if you're a Marxist or Alexandria Ocasio-Cortez (AOC), capitalists then "steal" profits). No. The value of inputs like labor, or land, or capital is determined by the value that their outputs could have in terms of usefulness in the future to others, at the margin. Not in total, and not in the past.

Such prices arise naturally from human interaction. People facing them will make the correct decisions about what to do next. The Marx-AOC prices would need to be coerced by the state and lead to the incorrect decisions about what to do next. Inefficient. And they would be unjust, too, because every input could claim the whole product. The Marx-AOC economy becomes a class struggle, in which poor or virtuous people do not always win. Human life becomes poor, nasty, brutish, and short.

In our market economy, for labor, the "marginal productivity" theory applies, and should. The nurses on strike are life-giving, like bottles of water. But their value in use for patients and the hospitals representing the patients is determined at the margin, by how much the next hour of one more nurse would contribute, and what people are willing to pay. That's why nurses typically earn much less than, say, sports stars. And it's why when COVID-19 ravaged New York City in the spring of 2020, increasing their marginal value, traveling nurses could command $10,000 per week.[6]

So too with land. It has value not, as according to Locke, because labor went into tilling it in the past. No, its value stems from its potential offerings tomorrow, like growing crops or situating a home. Value resides, and prices should reside, in how much the most eager people on the scene value, subjectively, what they think they can get in the future in use or pleasure or capital gain from a little more of it, considering what else they could direct their bank account toward.

The New Humanist Value Theory and Policy

In the end, the marginalist and subjective theory comes back to the same liberal impulse of the labor theory—only human valuation matters. Yet it's now valuation *by* humans thinking ahead right now, rather than the valuation of human labor in the past.

Justice is backward looking and should be. Did he do the deed, the rat? But getting the most out of what we have now requires looking forward. What more could that potential worker add—his "marginal product"? If the star Red Sox baseball player was paid the total product of "his" labor, there would be nothing left for other players, or the stadium, or the bats and balls. By contrast, paying all inputs exactly their marginal value uses up all the revenue from the product, exactly, instead of attempting to overpay everyone—which is impossible.

The scientific logic of subjective value matters for policy. In 1862, the Homestead Act let pioneers have 160 acres of land in the West, but only if they went out to cultivate it. The policy was Lockean, justice oriented, backward looking. Mix your labor with the land, and it's yours. Though usually viewed as lovely, the act led to gross inefficiencies. People were tempted to the frontier prematurely, because they got the whole land value as a prize. If the land had been sold instead to speculators who then sold it to farmers after holding it for a while, the new farmer-workers would have gone to Nebraska only when the marginal product of their labor justified the move—that is, when what they earned from working the land, not the total value of the land plus their labor, was more than what they could earn back in St. Louis. Labor would then be properly allocated for the benefit of everyone. Under the Homestead Act, it was not.

Under Soviet central planning, only historical labor counted, not, say, evil capital embedded in machinery at its present opportunity cost. A hideous green raincoat used 20 hours of labor to produce, and so it sold at the same price as a beautifully designed scarf produced by machines valued at their historical labor cost, also from 20 hours of labor. At those prices, the raincoats sat in stores unpurchased, and the scarves were snapped up instantly. Stupid policy, bad for poor people.

Today, the old labor theory has legs in public narratives indirectly affecting government policy. Half-Marxists, like AOC, see profits as exploitative, demanding "pro-worker" offsets. The clerisy of journalists and professionals complain that CEOs don't work so much harder than employees to justify earning 324 times median workers' pay.[7] And "equal pay for equal work" is the call when movie costars are paid less than A-listers, ignoring the supply and demand for the marginal actor.

The labor theory underpins much of the war on prices by sustaining the drumbeat for correcting perceived injustices. But it's faulty. In justice, the war-of-all-against-all struggle of trying to pay every input the total product hurts everyone. And those "unfair" market prices yield efficiency in use, allowing society to enrich the poor, which is the greater fairness.

CHAPTER 19

Market Prices and Wages Do Not Reflect Ethical Value

Deirdre Nansen McCloskey

You're worth more than you're paid.

No doubt about it. Your husband values you more than the pathetic salary you earn as a nurse, surely. A registered nurse in the United States earns about $80,000 a year, a nurse in the United Kingdom about £33,000 ($42,000). In both cases, they earn only a little above each nation's median income—this despite the years of education, the high skill, the large effort, and the great responsibility.

Your mother, to keep you alive, would willingly hand over everything she owns. Your friends would likewise contribute significant amounts for the same project, which added together would surely exceed the lifetime income that society would pay you. They love you that much.

Even the hospital where you work as a nurse could pay you more. The management hired you voluntarily. No one put a gun to the head of the supervisor who decided the intensive care unit urgently needed another 40 hours a week of nursing. Therefore, the hospital expected to obtain a net gain, small or big, from hiring you. Any deal that occurs freely in markets makes both sides better off, a little or a lot, at least in the participants' opinions at the time of the transaction. Economists call such feelings "consumer and producer surplus." Both sides end up satisfied, if not ecstatic. That they agree voluntarily, without coercion, implies that the trade improves their lives in some way.

Yet each side can also feel, if it indulges such an emotion, resentment at not getting *more* from the deal. Why not seize more of the hospital's net gain and give it to the nurse doing the work? An idiot footballer gets paid more in a week than a nurse in a year. Jeff Bezos earns billions for the mildly clever idea of reinventing, a century on, the mail-order company, similar to the once-mighty U.S. retailer Sears, Roebuck or its even older Austrian counterpart Kastner & Öhler.

And God, after all, values you at the infinite value of your soul. You reply that God doesn't deal in profane money. Yes, it's true, ultimately and in a sound theology. Yet the Hebrew Bible is filled with stories about Yahweh making secular deals, such as with Abraham to spare the righteous of Sodom, or giving back riches to Job. And the New Testament, after all, centers precisely on a deal of virtue supported by unwarranted grace for the gain of salvation, often expressed metaphorically in monetary terms, "a pearl of great value."

All this is true. It's why in cases of legal liability for the death of a breadwinner, it's inadequate for the court to calculate her worth as just her future money income. Income is not synonymous with worth to family, friends, and God. Yet in courts of law, that calculation is used daily. It's popular because it's easy to compute the physical livelihood lost compared with actual, ethical worth.

Such is another example, you will say, of the corruption of values from letting money talk. Yes. A line of argument in economic policy speaks of "comparable worth" and wants to close by state coercion the gap between what, say, a comparably skilled woman and man earn. The median U.S. salary in 2021 for men was $50,391, which was 27 percent higher than the median salary for women of $36,726.[1] Mind the gap, you say, following "social justice." Let's close it. Let's pay people what they are worth.

The former governor of the Bank of England, the Canadian economist Mark Carney, complains that Jeff Bezos's Amazon is worth billions whereas the Amazon rainforest, a major sink for excess carbon dioxide in the atmosphere, has no money ledger and so gets chopped down.[2] Let's value it correctly.

Market Prices Aren't Social Judgments

But here's the thing: prices in a market do not reflect ethical or personal or environmental worth. Nor do we liberals, supporters of price mechanisms, pretend otherwise.

Jeff Bezos made a good bet, and the permission to make the bet turned out well for us all. To induce his competitors, and new Jeff Bezoses and new Amazons, to have a go at innovation, we need to have prices and profit reflect what you and I value in cash about his online mail-order service. By willingly paying for shipment by Amazon we send the message, "Suppliers, please do more of that stuff, quick as you can." Do Bezos's startling billions, though, signal that he's a good guy? No. He may or may not be. Even if he acquired his monetary wealth, as Elon Musk or Liliane Bettencourt or Bill Gates did, perfectly legally and even ethically, he may, as an individual man, be an evil jerk or a wonderful saint. Can't tell. Earnings are about what other people are *willing to pay for the next little bit of your services.*

Nor do market prices or wages necessarily reflect who is "deserving" according to our stated preferences or priors. In a 2017 poll, Americans deemed high-skilled scientists, manufacturing company founders, inventors of new products or services, and technology entrepreneurs as deserving of wealth, on net.[3] Top sports stars, pharmaceutical companies, and senior bankers—not so much. But prices and wages are prices and wages—what we value their services at through our decisions.

Robert Nozick, the liberal philosopher, suggested that "capitalism" was unpopular with intellectuals precisely because its rewards

were not apportioned to what those intellectuals deemed just—
namely, what they were good at.[4] They were whip-smart at school,
earning high grades and the approval of teachers. They then went
out into the labor market and, though still pretty well rewarded,
looked around to see car dealers and TV celebrities and sports stars
and financiers with better houses and higher pay. They resent it. A
market system is not, they come to think, really "meritocratic"—that
is, if merit is defined by grades at school, not the ability to sell cars
or score goals.

True, the price mechanism doesn't or cannot distribute riches or
costs based on this or that ethical judgment or objective criterion like
intellect or hard work. The economist and philosopher F. A. Hayek
understood the gap between subjective conceptions of worth and market prices very well. "The manner in which the benefits and burdens
are apportioned by the market mechanism," he wrote in 1976, "would
in many instances have to be regarded as very unjust if it were the
result of deliberate allocation to particular people. But this is not the
case."[5] Yes, but as he also said, it's irrelevant to how they help deliver
the efficient working of an economy.

Justice is a matter of individual ethical valuation. You can be *blamed*
for injustice if you steal holy water from the font in a church. But the
going price of water, or the wage of an academic, is not a decision like
whether or not to steal. It's the result of thousands and thousands
of voluntary and anonymous and innocent interactions in a market.
Prices and wages thus depend not on what you "deserve," but on what
people are willing to pay.

It is a huge intellectual error, in fact, to view the rewards of a market as if they are a societal judgment on what "we," collectively, value.
The outcomes are neither individual, to which we can sensibly assign
blame, nor a national decision by a tyrant, such as deciding to kill
6 million Jews or starve 2 million Ukrainians. It's an example, like

language or social custom or the history of music or science, of what Hayek called a "spontaneous order" and Adam Smith called (though only twice in his writings) "the invisible hand."

The price of water, or the wage of the academic, is not intended by a person or a group, neither by you nor by a tyrant nor by a lovely committee of wise economists. So it can no more be praised or blamed ethically than the weather or the varied gifts people have from birth or the course of the Big Bang. The phrase on many lips of "social justice," Hayek argued, is nonsense. Society does not, in a collective, deliberative, planned human act, settle the price of water or pearls or nurses.

In 1866, as belief in a benevolent God was fading among British intellectuals, the novelist and poet Thomas Hardy wrote:

> How arrives it joy lies slain,
>
> And why unblooms the best hope ever sown?
>
> —Crass Casualty obstructs the sun and rain,
>
> And dicing Time for gladness casts a moan.[6]

All right, Tom, life is tough and then you die. Then, unreasonably, he issues an *ethical* complaint against casualty, the dicing, the outcome of merely natural and unblameable forces:

> These purblind Doomsters had as readily strown
>
> Blisses about my pilgrimage as pain.

Well, dear, dear Tom, grow up. Stop attributing ethical weight to cloudy days and hopes dashed by no individual or state-level human decision to behave badly. You too, Mark Carney, on the matter of the Amazon rainforest versus Amazon, the company. Quit implying that market values show the warped nature of "our values," as if prices are determined by a hive mind.

That Doesn't Mean We Should
Tamper with Market Prices

Now, some might reply, "Why not give up the price system, as a merely arbitrary tax imposed on us by the greed of sellers or a crazy undervaluation to society of the worth of a nurse or a friend or the Amazon rainforest?" Ask, should we replace the price system with a state-enforced just price, a living wage, a controlled price, a family income, or some other scheme suggested by good people such as Pope Francis or Sen. Elizabeth Warren (D-MA)? The economist answers, "No, not if we want to have the wherewithal to have good lives and to permit good lives for poor people and to offer good help to the halt and the lame."

To charge money prices for deals or graceful gifts unrequited among family and friends would be crazy and offensive. You don't send your six-year-old into the market to earn enough to buy lunch. But for deals among strangers, to follow Pope Francis and Senator Warren in abandoning money prices and the property rights to buy and sell voluntarily leads straight to poor lives.

Prices and wages are important not because they reflect what an individual *deserves*, but because they provide information to producers about which products, services, skills, and attributes *people are willing to give up some of their hard-earned labor to purchase*. Prices aggregate information from myriad individual transactions, providing a signal and an incentive that shifts resources toward people's needs and desires. Houses in San Francisco. Steaks in Omaha. Dentists in Oregon.

Water is essential for life, yet a pearl of great value is only a trinket. But water sells for much less per ounce than pearls. To explain such an apparent "paradox of value," the economist replies, "An ounce of water is cheap *at the margin*, for the last sip, considering the easy availability of supply in normal circumstances." Supply and demand in a market determine the going, and usually low, price of an ounce of water compared with the high price of an ounce of pearls.

The merit of markets is that the price that has been accepted on both sides leaves what an economist calls a "surplus" to both suppliers and demanders, what normal people call a profit or a gain. Trades, in economic jargon, are positive sum. Violent coercion, by contrast—such as private hired thugs or public tax gatherers extracting goods from one person to give to another—yields one person a gain and the other a loss. It's zero or even negative sum.

In the market in New York City, you gladly pay one cent for one sip of excellent water. But you value it, psychologically, in your heart, at up to three cents. You would be willing to pay that if somehow required to do so by an evil genius exercising monopoly power, who could engage in what economists call "perfect price discrimination." But when you close a deal with the ordinary, nonevil monopoly and drink the sip, you get a consumer's surplus, a two-cent gain, a profit. It's wholly analogous to the profit a seller of water can get, called *producer* surplus. But of course, in *total*, to get water at least every three days is worth the whole value of your life, like oxygen is every three minutes and food every 30 days. Outside such emergencies, though, a drink, a breath, or a bite sells for little or nothing. Thus is resolved the so-called paradox.

Letting prices work in the way they do, the economist argues, leads to a pretty good outcome, socially speaking. Why? Because if resources are not put to their most valued use, entrepreneurs like Bezos can reallocate them a little to get the unclaimed profit. In a poker metaphor, if money is left on the table, someone has an incentive to scoop it up. The outcome, by and large, is that no money is left on the table. We want to do things well for all of us. Market prices for scarce things lead us to do so.

Sure, there are thornier problems—certain "externalities" and "unpriced" things we (collectively) might value. The Amazon rainforest's biodiversity is scarce and lacks a money price. What's the best way of keeping the carbon-storing gain from the rainforest in good order? Plan the use of each hectare of it by a civil servant in Brasília? Or perhaps a committee of brilliant economists in Brussels? Usually, no. Better to put a price on it. Nonscarce goods—whose present use doesn't reduce the future amount available—don't need pricing. Sunlight, for example, or any fixed cost, such as the history of our culture up to the present, should not be priced, because they have no opportunity cost—that is, you don't have to give up something else to enjoy their benefits. For the rest, including the Amazon, the better plan is to move *away* from intentional, blamable human acts of planning, by devising a price system for the rainforest, enforced by law, leaving the preservation of environmental value to supply and demand at its efficient price.

In other words, if a hectare of the Amazon rainforest is owned by someone who can benefit from selling its market value in carbon capture on a market, the rainforest gets used well. The socially sensible move then is to create markets where there are none, not abolish them by collectivization or price controls. Some of the worst environmental disasters, in fact, such as the 40 percent draining of the Aral Sea in the Soviet Union between 1960 and 1987, happened under state planning.

The price system doesn't guarantee nirvana, heaven, perfection. But beware of making the imagined perfect the enemy of the actual pretty good. Money prices don't value us ethically. But they have yielded a 3,000 percent increase in human material welfare since 1800.

Not too shabby. Let's keep it going.

CHAPTER 20

Market Prices Are Not Inherently Corrupting

Deirdre Nansen McCloskey

Two characters debate "cynicism" in Oscar Wilde's play of 1882, *Lady Windermere's Fan*:

> GRAHAM. What *is* a cynic?
>
> DARLINGTON. A man who knows the price of everything, and the value of nothing.
>
> GRAHAM. And a sentimentalist, my dear Darlington, is a man who sees an absurd value in everything and doesn't know the market price of any single thing.[1]

That first, much-quoted, definition applies certainly to an economist, or any other professional cynic, like a lawyer or journalist. But Graham's retort, too, a cynic would reply, has its own truth. It's a mixed bag.

Some years ago, a daycare center in Israel had a problem with parents arriving late to pick up their kids. A cynic, or an economist, would suggest: "Impose a fine on the late parents. That gives them a price incentive to show up on time." The daycare center tried it for an economic field study.[2] The result? *More parents were late.* Huh? What was going on? This: before the regime of a money fine, parents who came late felt guilty, ethically, because they were violating a sacred social norm to not take advantage of others. They responded to a moral incentive to be on time—their actions were part of a social, rather than a market, exchange. So they didn't arrive late often. But when the fine was introduced, it changed the nature of the transaction. They said to themselves: "Oh, it's not any more in the realm of the sacred. It's just a money price, the realm of the profane. Good deal. At that low price, I'll buy extra time taking care of my kid."

Weeks later, the daycare removed the fine again. What happened? Newly tardy parents did not go back to being punctual—even more were now late at the new price of zero.[3] The temporary infusion of a market price, in other words, shifted the exchange from a social to a market one, semipermanently.

Prices Are a Necessity for Strangers

For some, the Israeli daycare is a cautionary tale: markets with prices corrupt social norms, and so, ultimately, corrupt us. We become driven by greed and selfishness rather than, say, altruism, generosity, and solidarity. And yet market exchange, coordinated by prices, clearly allows us to harness "self-interest" to socially productive ends. What gives?

We get an advantage from people when we pay them, in money or favors, to do things for us they otherwise would not do. Give a hot dog for cash; give a nice dinner party to "pay" for one you attended; give extra childcare for money. A mother, in contrast, doesn't charge her kid for cooking lunch, nor does a friend for giving advice.

In contrast to the personal and sacred realm, when dealing in a big, specialized modern economy, we are implicitly giving and getting goods and services directly or indirectly to and from millions upon millions of strangers. The local ice-cream shop, dealing routinely with strangers, does not hand out ice cream gratis. With broader networks, depending on exchanging monetized favors is only sensible.

Why "sensible"? A price system for ice cream or nursing or housing and so forth induces and allows strangers to give advantages to others. The price system induces and allows a form of altruism. Deep personal love, alas, is limited. Thankfully, though, by the system of priced supply and demand, a similar result is achieved, with people we do not especially love. As Adam Smith put it, noting that a man's coat is made by thousands directly and indirectly, "In civilized society [a man] stands at all times in need of the cooperation and assistance of great multitudes, while his whole life is scarce sufficient to gain the friendship of a few persons."[4]

A hospital could ask you as a nurse to volunteer gratis. But outside the happy obligations of love or faith or charity, such as a Catholic nun trained also as a nurse, you won't do it. The hospital you work for bids your services away from their other uses, perhaps in other hospitals, by paying you money. If it doesn't, you will go elsewhere, presumably to a less urgent job. Your skills are misallocated. A sensibly organized society wants you to work in the exact place that values the contribution of your last hour the most. The test of such a material "contribution" to patients in a commercial society is paying in money prices. Wages.

Any other arrangement—such as one ordered by the Gosplan out of Moscow, or from Whitehall, or Washington, by planners who do not know the usefulness of an hour of your work at 4:00 p.m. this Thursday in the intensive care unit at Hampstead Royal Free Hospital—is, to use the economist's beloved word, "inefficient." With an efficient system of prices, society gets the most out of what it produces. This charging of prices that cause goods and services to be allocated "best," materially speaking, gives us prosperity.

Prices are suitable, then, for dealing with 330 million strangers. Not with lovers. If your husband leaves a $100 bill on the bed after having sex, it sends a most unwelcome message. The Dutch economist Arjo Klamer imagines that you go to George, a dear friend, spilling out your troubles over coffee for an hour. At the end, George says, "That'll be $100, for psychological counseling." Setting a direct money price is friendship destroying because it shifts what you thought was a sacred gift of love, or grace, into a profane transaction at a market price. It's the cynic's "price of everything."

"Between friends all is common," the 16th-century liberal Erasmus of Rotterdam wrote in his editions of Greek and Latin proverbs.[5] Yes, certainly. If you bring a large pizza to a lovely little party of friends, but then announce "pay up or I'm eating all of it"—end of sacred friendship. Yet no one objects to your selling a pizza slice to a stranger, to the benefit of you both.

Different societies, and even different people, demarcate the two spheres differently. In Japan, people keep account of nonmonetized advantages given and received, such as gifts, with a precision for balance that Europeans would deem churlish.[6] Yet Japan is also famous for its devotion to sacred things and ceremonies that others overlook, or that Westerners pay money for, as merely profane things.

In the grand sweep of things, however, there's little indication that more marketized societies have more corrupted values. The economist Herbert Gintis examined 15 tribal societies worldwide, including "hunter-gatherers, horticulturalists, nomadic herders, and small-scale sedentary farmers—in Africa, Latin America, and Asia." He found that all "exhibited a considerable degree of moral motivation and a willingness to sacrifice monetary gain" for fairness and reciprocity. Great. But his experiments found that those societies more exposed to markets and exchange were *more* motivated by nonfinancial fairness considerations than those that were not. "The notion that the market economy makes people greedy, selfish, and amoral is simply fallacious," he concluded.[7]

Too right. As Gintis notes, "Movements for religious and lifestyle tolerance, gender equality, and democracy have flourished and triumphed in societies governed by market exchange, and nowhere else."[8] The tension between the market domain and the social domain is real and ever present. But market norms do not make us inherently greedier or less altruistic, en masse.

Prices Conserve Resources

Market money prices are regularly criticized by what Graham in Wilde's play would call the sentimentalists. The Harvard political philosopher Michael Sandel in his book *What Money Can't Buy* criticizes using a price for entry to watch Shakespeare in New York's Central Park.[9] Sandel wants to show that money prices can be unjust. And the supporting axiom he advances is that someone having more money than another to pay the price is also unjust.

That would be fine if seats in the audience were not scarce, such that every person in New York with a taste for *Hamlet* could attend. But it's not so. If the seats are allocated by, say, standing in line for three hours to get a ticket, then hours, which are better used elsewhere, are being thrown away for the purpose of deciding who gets what. It's better socially to charge dollar bills, which are merely paper tokens for value, not the valuable thing itself, such as hours spent working or jogging or eating.

"Resources," in the sense of "all inputs"—how economists use the word—are conserved when we don't throw them away to compete for scarce things. We could compete for seats by, say, entering a crazy contest to burn the most books, or by making weapons to be able to extort tickets from others by violence. Book burning and weapon making waste resources that are better used to satisfy human wants directly. Money prices, however, don't incur such waste. They just shuffle the bills around, directing the ticket and the nurses and the daycare and the psychological counseling to this person or that person who values each item the most.

Once we agree on the line between sacred and profane, price is therefore not corrupting. The very definition of such corruption is "crossing the line, substituting money for, say, duty." In 1905, the politician George Washington Plunkitt, looking back on his corrupt career in New York City, declared that he only took "honest graft." What's that? Well, it's "honest" not to go directly to the city's treasury and grab money from it. Instead, he used his inside knowledge as a city councilor to secretly buy up land at bargain prices, knowing the city was planning to lay roads, and so pocketing a healthy capital gain. "I seen my opportunities, and I took 'em," he said.[10] We regard it as corrupt because he crossed over to the profane, leaving behind his sacred duty to New York's citizens.

By bringing demands into line with supplies, markets can often help *prevent* corruption. The suppressed market caused by U.S. prohibition of alcohol from 1920 to 1933 notoriously made specialists in violence rich, Al Capone among them. Similarly, today's war on drugs has corrupted every police force from Kabul to Kansas City. It makes ordinary supply and demand, without interference in other people's habits of consumption, look pretty good.

Prices Elevate Prospects for All

But wait a minute. Suppose a poor person loves *Hamlet* very, very much. Isn't it unfair to price the ticket? Sandel thinks so. Handing over money prices, after all, mixes the value of love for the Bard with one's spending capacity, money income. As Sandel notes indignantly, the rich have more money, whereas the poor have a better shot if goods are allocated through standing in line. So why allocate by money prices?

The economists' reply to this sentimentalism is fourfold. First, as we've just seen, allocating by price avoids the wasteful use of time in queues or other resource-wasting ploys. Second—a leading theme of this book—a free price mechanism encourages theater companies to find ways to serve the pent-up demand for affordable Shakespeare. Put on performances elsewhere. Extend the show for another few weeks. Televise it and offer it free on PBS, or for that matter NBC.

But there are more profound stakes. Third, deciding to allocate Hamlet outside of a market raises a question: What else should we allocate by nonprice means? Clothing and cable TV or Fritos? A 100-foot yacht? Where exactly should we draw the line? An unwillingness to draw any line between sacred and profane descends quickly to the economic logic of North Korea. Allocate everything by Communist Party membership, say. Prices are in this sense egalitarian. A millionaire's dollar has the same purchasing power as a pauper's, even if the millionaire belongs to a favored race or religion or gender or whatever. Yes, the millionaire has more dollars. But the price system has a form of fairness in not depending on who you personally are. It's in that sense anonymous, colorblind.

And that sets up the fourth point. Poverty and inequality of incomes exist, of course. But differences in brains and energy to earn the money incomes, or luck, or inequality of beauty, or differential parenting, or any other advantages massively affect the possibilities for achieving high income. Some have more such qualities, some less. It is impossible to actually achieve the goal of equal opportunity, lovely as it sounds. Equal permission to run the race *can* be achieved by eliminating legal obstacles to permissions, such as state segregation of people by skin color, or laws against women piloting airplanes, or whatever. Exactly equal permission to run the race we can achieve, as it were, this afternoon, but not ever exactly equal starting points, or equal outcomes.

The ethical case is to face the reality. St. Paul noted in his first Epistle to the Corinthians that "there are differences in the graces bestowed" by God or nature or chance of family or past effort or present effort. To make the best of human diversity is to let people with various graces exchange with each other, by offers and acceptances of prices. The result? Massive improvements in the condition of the poor, without the corruptions of Communist Party membership or the gross inefficiencies of Sandelian schemes of "social justice."

Trying by coercive measures instead to get to an imagined but impossible world of equality of opportunity or outcome is, notice, materialistic, necessarily violent, and in a literal sense counter-productive. It makes people nastier and poorer. If a brain surgeon and a street sweeper were paid the same in the money price of labor, we would have too few brain surgeons and too many sweepers. For the same reason that without prices the Shakespeare ticket is allocated to the wrong hands, without unequal wages the labor is misallocated.

In short, there's nothing inherently corrupting about market forces determining prices. In fact, paying your way is dignifying. Think back to the pride you had earning your first paycheck. That the police in his Tunisian city routinely stole from street vendor Mohamed Bouazizi, reducing him to the indignity of a slave to state power, unable to support his family, drove him in 2010 to douse himself with gasoline and light the match.[11] It initiated the Arab Spring, the unsuccessful revolt against the indignity of societies and economies run by the masters, not by markets. Egypt's economy is still owned by the army and works about as well.

Yes, attaching a price to sacred goods can violate social norms. We must choose properly what is for sale and what is not. Voluntary slavery and serfdom, for example, are rightly outlawed. You might think they're impossible anyway. But in 16th-century Russia, desperately hungry people did sell themselves and their descendants into serfdom. Let's not.

Some economists and their disciples still recommend markets in everything. But, of course, if, say, grades at university were for sale, standards of excellence become meaningless. Yet even here, we must examine the counterfactual. The same degradation occurs with the move to meaningless high grades for all, and easy courses, or when ideologically pure professors are demanded by students.

Most often, and especially when dealing with strangers, money prices take an item out of the political or ethical realm in a way that paradoxically purifies it. Allocating goods by social class or race or violence or political pressures or party membership is disgraceful. A price for most goods is merely a price. No shame attached. As the U.S. proverb has it, "You pays your money, and you takes your choice."

The sentimentalist would interfere and use police and prisons to alter prices. The underlying motive is often pure. We wish to help the poor. Controlling the rents paid, as in Paris from World War I onward, or the minimum wage one can legally earn, as in South Africa nowadays, is seen as a direct route to helping.

Yet the motive, the cynic reminds us, is often swiftly corrupted into cruel protection for one group of Paris voters or South African trade unionists over others. It's usually better to let prices work, so that the Parisian apartments are allocated efficiently, and the half of South African youth now unemployed can get jobs.

Having permitted prices to yield efficiency, we'll have the prosperity to give a hand up to the poor, at prices that make economic and ethical sense. The right signals for overall prosperity will be sent. Running the race will be permitted, to the benefit of all. Even the poor benefit from brain surgeons. We all benefit from inventions. Without prices, neither efficiency nor innovation happens.

Market prices are the only noncorrupting system for allocating nonsacred goods. Their appropriate extension leads to enrichment, and justice.

CHAPTER 21

The Gender Pay Gap Isn't about Workplace Discrimination

Vanessa Brown Calder

Recent U.S. data indicate that median weekly earnings for women working full-time are just 83 percent of men's.[1] This statistic is widely known as the "gender pay gap." Despite the growth in women's freedoms and wages in recent decades, as well as the pay gap's continued decline across countries and time, this gap continues to receive substantial attention both in the United States and around the world.

Researchers and commentators regularly attribute this unequal outcome, explicitly or implicitly, to unfair treatment, discriminatory practices, or prejudices that hold women back in the workforce or in society at large. A 2022 Economic Policy Institute report on the gender pay gap states, for example, that "even though women disproportionately enter lower-paid, female-dominated occupations, this decision is shaped by discrimination, societal norms, and other forces beyond women's control."[2] A U.S. Department of Labor publication has said, "Women-dominated jobs, including care work, have been devalued."[3]

Politicians often misrepresent what the gender pay gap statistic shows, conflating this difference in pay between the median male and female worker across the whole population with the very different concept of "equal pay for equal work"—the idea that women should be paid the same as men for doing the exact same job. President Joe Biden, for example, has stated that "in nearly every job—more than 90 percent of the occupations—women still earn less than men: 82 cents on the dollar on average." The confusion is not helped by the fact that a campaign day to bring awareness to the crude gender pay gap is called Equal Pay Day, echoing the name of the 1963 legislation that outlaws gender discrimination on pay for the same job within a company.[4]

This misperception feeds into proposed legislation designed to counter the gender pay gap. Vice President Kamala Harris, for example, has previously invoked the overall gender pay gap as justification for her proposal to require individual businesses to report their own company gender pay gaps, controlling for "differences in job titles, experience, and performance," under the threat of higher taxes for firms with unequal outcomes.[5]

More generally, those concerned about the gender pay gap often seem unable to comprehend the decentralized nature of wage setting. They talk in reified abstractions as if market wages reflect a deliberate, collective societal judgment that women's work is just inherently less valuable than men's, rather than the reality of pay being set on an individual basis, according to supply and demand in different markets.

In competitive markets, genuine discrimination and prejudice are punished. If women are paid less despite being as productive as men, then other firms have a profit incentive to hire women at higher wages until the pay gap for a given level of performance is eliminated. However, real-world markets are imperfect, and some discrimination surely exists despite countervailing market forces. A closer look at the factors behind the economy-wide gender pay gap helps us better understand how much.

What's Behind the Gender Pay Gap

Are American employers biased against women? Many factors influence differences in pay beyond gender, and the cited gender pay gap is a superficial measure that ignores many such factors. Substantial evidence indicates that the gap is largely a result of differences in the average man's and average woman's backgrounds and roles and the way they combine family obligations and work.

For instance, one key contributor is that men and women tend to work in different industries. Women constitute only 38 percent of professionals involved in securities, commodities, funds, and trusts, and only 26 percent of professionals engaged in architecture, engineering, and related services. In contrast, women dominate the fields of social assistance, holding 84 percent of all jobs, and education, where they hold 75 percent of jobs in elementary and secondary schools.[6]

Occupation matters for the gender pay gap, in part because, as one study describes it, "Individuals working in more time intensive occupations have a substantially higher hourly wage."[7] The study finds that the occupation-level difference in hours worked is large and explains approximately half the gender pay gap. Other key factors include differences in years of experience, education level, age, employer, and location. Accounting for these factors allows for a more apples-to-apples comparison between men and women with similar backgrounds and roles. After controlling for them, as well as occupation and industry, a 2019 Glassdoor study based on 425,000 full-time U.S. workers' salaries found that the measured gender pay gap fell from almost 21 percent to less than 5 percent.[8]

Although the Glassdoor study considers a variety of factors, researchers typically do not have access to data reflecting every job characteristic that may affect wages beyond discrimination. For instance, risk tolerance or average hours worked by full-time employees—both outside the scope of Glassdoor's data—may also vary between the average man and woman. Men often engage in more unpleasant work or jobs that are more physically demanding or unsafe, for which we'd expect "compensating differentials" or higher pay in lieu of such risks. Indeed, other research finds that the number of hours worked and workers' risk tolerance provide important explanations for pay gaps. One Stanford study found that male Uber drivers made 32 percent more than female Uber drivers per week.[9] Even when adjusting for overall hours worked, male Uber drivers still made 7 percent more per hour than female drivers.

This result is interesting because, on the platform, riders were unable to discriminate by gender on which driver they were assigned. Nevertheless, a 7 percent pay gap per hour remained. Researchers found that driver risk preferences and experience levels explained it: specifically, a higher average male driving speed accounted for half the remaining gap, location choices of where and when to operate explained one-fifth of the gap, and average experience with using the platform (i.e., higher productivity) explained one-third of the gap, owing to male drivers being less likely to quit driving and typically driving more hours per week.

National data suggest that adjusting for hours worked is critical in fairly comparing men's and women's pay. The American Time Use Survey data show that the average full-time woman works a little over four hours fewer per week than the average full-time man.[10] When controlling for hours worked, as well as job title, education, experience, industry, and job level, a 2023 Payscale report estimates that a 17 percent crude pay gap falls to just 1 percent.[11]

This difference in hours worked is not because women are less industrious: the average woman absorbs more childcare and housework at home, or "domestic labor." This makes some sense given that biology necessitates that women absorb the early physical and emotional labor associated with pregnancy, childbirth, and breastfeeding. In line with that fact, a Danish study found that, following the arrival of the first child, women's earnings fall by about 30 percent relative to their previous earnings.[12]

This fall in earnings is explained by a decline in hours worked, falling labor force participation, and reduced wage rates following birth, with each factor about equally important. The authors found that women's wage rates fell because they frequently change to more family-friendly roles after birth and are less likely to be promoted or become managers. Although this differential declines to about 20 percent over the subsequent 20 years, it does not recover completely. Meanwhile, fathers' earnings following childbirth are unaffected.[13]

Danish women's experiences are consistent with women's experiences in other Western countries. In a follow-up study, the authors found that this impact on mothers' earnings also exists in the United States, where the long-run earnings decline for mothers is approximately 31 percent.[14] The decline in mothers' earnings is even larger in other European countries, like Germany and the United Kingdom, despite those countries having extensive social programs, which, it's frequently argued, would help close the gender pay gap here.

Nobel Prize–winning economist Claudia Goldin's work on the gender pay gap provides additional insights. In one study, Goldin and coauthors compare elite Master of Business Administration (MBA) graduates and find that male and female MBAs earn almost identical amounts following graduation.[15] However, motherhood precipitates career interruptions, reductions in hours, and increasing preferences for job flexibility that help explain the widening gender gap for female MBA graduates compared to male MBAs.

Goldin likewise finds that the gender pay gap varies considerably by occupation and, even more so by the nonlinear returns to hours worked in certain professions.[16] Many jobs in client-facing roles and high-pressure office environments pay a premium wage rate for longer and more continuous hours worked, with greater round-the-clock availability. This helps explain why the pay gap grows following motherhood: mothers often find it more challenging to be available in roles with these demands, take time out of the labor force, or choose less time-intensive work opportunities after childbirth.

A Societal Problem?

Some commentators acknowledge the aforementioned evidence but argue that societal bias and prejudice are reflected in the education and career choices that women make along the way, and that gender expectations unfairly shape women's professional, educational, and childcare decisionmaking. That is a contentious claim: It could be that outcomes reflect women's true revealed preferences given their opportunities, tradeoffs, and tastes. It could be that society is fundamentally prejudiced toward women. Or it could be anything else. The mere existence of a gender pay gap provides no insight on its cause.

As an example of cultural pressures potentially affecting career decisions, one study found that highly qualified single women reported lower levels of career ambition and leadership ability when they knew that their classmates could access the information about their preferences, relative to that information being collected privately.[17]

The effects were large: those who thought the information was disclosed said they desired $18,000 less in annual compensation, were willing to travel seven fewer days per month, and were willing to work four fewer hours per week than those who thought the survey responses were private. Notably, married women and men did not adjust their answers when they knew their answers would be public. This behavioral difference may reflect disparities in what men and women value in the dating market and suggests that cultural expectations affect single women's career decisions.

Then again, if women are pressured to select lower-paying, less traditionally "male" areas of study or careers against their will, we would expect to see women opt into these traditionally male areas of study with greater frequency in countries where women have educational, economic, and political opportunities that are close to, or on par with, men. In fact, research finds the opposite pattern, with *fewer* women selecting into science, technology, engineering, and mathematics (STEM) in *more* gender-egalitarian countries, including the Nordic countries, and *more* women selecting STEM fields in *less* gender-egalitarian countries, like Algeria or Turkey.[18] Women apparently exhibit significantly different average career preferences than men under conditions of greater freedom and opportunity.

Similarly, if inherent discrimination or bias against women causes the pay gap, we would expect it to show up in comparatively lower pay throughout women's working lives. However, as Goldin's work highlights, the gender gap tends to widen as individuals age.[19] Reporting indicates that in the Los Angeles, New York, and Washington, DC, metropolitan areas, women under 30 years old earn as much as or more than men.[20] Women likely outperform men's pay in these areas at least in part because these women have high levels of education and delay childbearing later than female peers in other locations.[21] Across the country overall, however, the pay gap is also smaller for younger women.[22] This evidence suggests that both previous generations' educational opportunities and family obligations related to motherhood are important sources of the gap.

It's crucial to remember that there's no amorphous planner called "society" that determines wages in particular sectors. Pay levels in markets are determined by worker productivity in the service of profit, which is driven by consumers' tastes and preferences and the relative availability of substitutable labor. Pay gap activists often compare two different jobs—say, stockers in warehouses and stockers in stores—that seem similar on the surface, and then assume gender discrimination if there's a pay premium for the male-heavy job type—in this case, warehouse stockers. On closer inspection, we often find that the male industry is less pleasant, is riskier, and in many cases requires working less sociable hours. If "society"—in reality, politicians—were to enforce equalized pay between such roles, we'd see shortages of workers for warehouses and an oversupply for stores.

What Are the Policy Implications?

Given that most of the pay gap is attributable to characteristics outside of workplace discrimination, it is difficult to imagine what policy would successfully close the gap without significant economic damage and curbs on free choice. It is not even clear whether policymakers should aim to remedy it, if the gap reflects decisions grounded in women's preferences. Certainly, most major policies proposed to date do not address drivers of the gap, including average differences in occupation or the way that women combine work and family obligations.

The most popular proposals might even harm some women by reducing their employment and income opportunities. The Paycheck Fairness Act, for example—reintroduced in Congress in 2023—would put the onus on employers to prove that gender pay differences are the result of "a bona fide factor . . . such as education, training, or experience . . . [that] accounts for the entire differential in compensation."[23] Yet pay differences are typically the result of many factors beyond education, training, and experience, so most employers could easily fail this test.

Moreover, sometimes pay differentials between employees don't result from "bona fide" differences between workers at all, but from a combination of the timing of hiring and budget realities. Ignoring these realities would have adverse consequences: if a private school sees an additional math teacher as adding significant value, limiting what it can offer based on the pay of other existing staffers of a different gender could negatively affect the children served.

The Paycheck Fairness Act would increase litigation in several ways, including by increasing the associated benefits for plaintiffs and by automatically enrolling class members in class-action lawsuits.[24] As a result, employers will be eager to reduce their legal liability. That might mean adopting rigid pay structures less reflective of an employee's prior experience or performance. Importantly for women, that could make employers less willing to grant alternative pay-benefit bundles, including flexible work hours, which could be detrimental to women's continued labor force participation.[25]

Greater social spending also doesn't seem likely to close the gap. One implication of Goldin's work is that policies like paid leave have ambiguous effects on the pay gap: on the one hand, they may keep women better connected to jobs; on the other, paying women to spend longer periods outside the labor force may exacerbate the pay gap for jobs where presence, long hours, and continuous active employment lead to higher wage rates.

Indeed, research finds that government-funded paid leave and child-care programs have little or no effect on mothers' earnings. Economists Henrik Kleven, Camille Landais, and Jakob Egholt Søgaard find that the gender pay gap is converging across all countries, and "though [the United States and Sweden or Denmark] feature different public policies and labor markets, they are no longer very different in terms of overall gender equality."[26]

Although proposed public policies are unlikely to meaningfully close the gap, policymakers should seek to remove government-imposed barriers to employment and workplace flexibility, thereby providing women with more options and opportunities generally. For instance, polling suggests that women value work flexibility highly and are more likely than men to work irregular hours for personal reasons like caregiving for a family member.

Eliminating burdensome occupational licensing laws, home-based business zoning, and local labor regulations could make employment less rigid and more flexible.[27] Current labor rules, intended to "protect" workers, could also be reformed. The Fair Labor Standards Act—a federal regulation that requires workers to be compensated for overtime with payment, rather than future time off—currently makes balancing work and family life more difficult. Then there are state staffing regulations on childcare that drive up prices, making it more difficult for mothers to find affordable and flexible care around their work schedules.

In summary, although substantial evidence supports the idea that the gender pay gap does not result significantly from workplace bias, that's not to say that women are never passed over professionally because of discrimination. Fortunately, the broader evidence suggests that workplace discrimination is not the typical cause of gender pay differences and women can make various academic, career, and personal decisions to improve their pay. This empowering message should be readily welcomed by working women of all backgrounds.

CHAPTER 22

The Pink Tax Is a Myth

Ryan Bourne

Do businesses engage in "sexist" pricing? That has been a long-standing accusation. "The Pink Tax Costs Women Thousands of Dollars over Their Lifetimes," boomed *U.S. News & World Report* in April 2023.[1] It wasn't referring to a tax in the usual sense, of course, but to the idea that manufacturers and retailers routinely charge more for ostensibly similar products marketed to women rather than men.

In 2015, the New York City Department of Consumer Affairs compared 397 pairs of "gendered" products across 24 New York City retailers.[2] It found that products aimed at women—grouped into categories of toys, kids' clothes, adults' clothes, personal-care items, and senior health care products—were, on average, 7 percent more expensive than for men. The premiums ranged from an average of 13 percent more for personal-care products to 4 percent more for children's clothing and weren't driven by extreme outlier price differences. Women's versions were the more expensive of product pairs 42 percent of the time, against 18 percent for men's items.

A Radio Flyer Red "My 1st Scooter" for children, sold at Target, was advertised at $24.99, for example, whereas a Radio Flyer Sparkle Pink "Girls My 1st Scooter" was $49.99. Adult dress shirts were found to be 26 percent more expensive for women, on average, while a packet of five Schick Hydro Silk women's razor cartridges was $18.49, against $14.99 for an equivalent blue packet.

The New York City Department of Consumer Affairs acknowledged that men's and women's products were not exactly the same. Different ingredients, materials, packaging, branding, advertising, and market research costs may all contribute to these observed price differences. Yet that was not the narrative the report emphasized. The message instead was that companies charged women more than men for nearly identical products, squeezing higher markups from women. The reason was not because of higher production costs or differentiating products in ways women preferred. No, the report implied this was overt *price discrimination*, undergirded by sexism. Given that products were commonly "gendered" by virtue of their packaging and coloring, often pink for women, the term the "pink tax" took off.

Since then, studies from a member of Congress, the Government Accountability Office, and academics have reported similar results.[3] Newspapers regularly repeat the narrative, running their own crude analyses on samples of goods, typically comparing gendered personal-care products like razors, hair-care products, deodorants, and body washes, but also clothes, footwear, and more.[4] "Are Shoe Brands Charging You More Based on Your Gender?" is a typical headline.[5]

This common belief that women are being fleeced by manufacturers and retailers through higher markups even produced a legislative backlash. New York City (from 2020) and California (from 2023) passed laws prohibiting charging different amounts for "substantially similar" goods marketed to different genders.[6] That is, if manufacturers and retailers charge different prices for gendered products that have the same materials, uses, features, and branding, despite no major difference in production techniques, time, or cost, they are liable for civil penalties. For the first violation, the fine can be up to $10,000 in California and $250 in New York City, and $1,000 and $500, respectively, for subsequent violations. Varying the color of the product or packaging would not be enough to escape these penalties under either bill.

Although no general federal law yet exists prohibiting charging men and women different prices for goods or services (except in credit and real estate), former representative Jackie Speier (D-CA) tried to introduce a Pink Tax Repeal Act four times. This act would have instituted a law like California's nationwide.

Is This Gender Bias from Businesses?

Basic economics should make us skeptical about gender bias explaining these price differences. Why? If consumers regarded a pair of gendered products as nearly perfectly substitutable, then women would have a huge incentive when facing higher prices to buy the male or gender-neutral variants. That would make the differential pricing strategy unprofitable for companies and lead to eventual price equalization.

In the case of clothing and footwear, of course, such substitution is less practical. But when it comes to personal goods used privately at home, such as razors, shaving cream, and hair-care products, the barriers to shifting are low. Markets therefore provide incentives to arbitrage away pricing based on pure gender bias.

We might therefore hypothesize that the existence of an apparent "pink tax" reflects a failure to account for genuine, though perhaps small, differences in products that are being marketed to men and women. Perhaps the goods have different attributes, ingredients, or scents. Or indeed, maybe the size of products, production scale, advertising costs, and packaging are different—meaning that, combined with the average woman preferring the female version, its price is higher.

As almost all research on this topic acknowledges, it is hard to account for all these factors to make like-for-like comparisons.

Still, recent research commissioned by the Federal Trade Commission and conducted by economists Sarah Moshary, Anna Tuchman, and Natasha Bhatia Vajravelu looked comprehensively at the highly gendered market for personal-care products. Their findings across thousands of stores suggest the pink tax is more a story of product differentiation than gender bias.[7]

They looked at the price per unit for "gendered" items across nine categories (bar soap, body wash, deodorant, hair coloring, razor blades, disposable and nondisposable razors, shampoo, and shaving cream). On a crude basis, they confirmed an average 10.6 percent "pink price gap." Women's items were significantly pricier in four categories, with no statistically significant difference in the other five.

However, to compare products that were "substantially similar," the researchers then controlled for active and key inactive product ingredients, manufacturer, and retailer. Doing so showed that most products targeted at one gender were differentiated—with very limited overlap in any ingredients for bar soap, body wash, deodorant, hair coloring, shampoo, or shaving cream. Of products that were directly comparable, the women's versions were only 0.1 percent more expensive. On this like-for-like basis, body wash, shampoo, and shaving cream marketed to women were cheaper than those marketed to men, deodorant was roughly the same, whereas women's bar soap was still pricier.

In short, the "pink tax" narrative implies that women are charged more for the same products because of gender bias. For goods in the personal-care market, at least, women really pay more for products they prefer that are differentiated by ingredients. Far from costing them thousands of dollars through their lifetimes, these results suggest that the average household would save less than 1 percent of spending on these items by opting for the cheaper gendered version of genuinely similar products, by ingredients. Both theory and this evidence caution against assuming "sexist" pricing.

Cost Differences or Higher Markups?

Prices per unit are often higher for women, as they don't view men's versions as equivalent products, given these goods' different formulations. However, this still leaves several possible economic explanations for the crude price differentials we see.

They might arise because women choose products that are costlier to produce, which means firms aren't really profiting more from them. The gap might arise because women select items from less competitive product markets, where firms have more market power to raise prices. Or it could be that women show more loyalty to certain branded goods (in economics-speak, that they have less elastic demand, which means they are less likely to reduce the amount they buy when prices rise, allowing companies to charge more).

University of California, Berkeley, economists Kayleigh Barnes and Jakob Brounstein have sought to disentangle these mechanisms. Their work looks at overall purchase histories of men and women from single-member households using the Nielsen Consumer Panel Survey, combined with store-level data on prices and quantities sold in big-box and grocery stores. Any product bought over 90 percent of the time by one gender is deemed a "gendered product."[8]

Again, they find a crude, unsophisticated gender price gap exists: women pay an average of 15 percent higher prices on "gendered" products relative to men (and 3.9 percent higher prices on ungendered products). Women also tend to purchase a wider variety of goods, with larger consumption baskets that are 27 percent more diverse than men's in general and 54 percent more diverse for health and beauty products.[9]

However, Barnes and Brounstein conclude that this is not indicative of companies obtaining higher markups, and so profiting more, from women. Women actually shop in less concentrated product markets, where one could imagine that greater competition might help keep prices down. They also find women have more elastic demand than men—meaning women are more sensitive to price changes, consistent with the stereotype of their being careful shoppers, rather than blindly loyal to certain brands.[10]

No, looking at five "gendered" product markets in detail—yogurt, protein bars, deodorant, disposable razors, and shampoo—instead suggests that, except for protein bars, women are voluntarily buying products with higher marginal costs of production and distribution. They tend to pay higher prices because they opt for goods that are more expensive to supply.

There are numerous reasons why marginal costs might be higher for products marketed and bought by women. For health and beauty lines, the ingredients and formulations could simply be more expensive. Men's products tend to be larger in size, potentially leading to some volume cost savings in production. Research in other areas has found that advertisers have greater demand for women's impressions, leading to higher prices for female eyeballs and so, potentially, a higher marginal cost of obtaining a new customer.[11]

In other markets beyond these studies, men's clothes and shoes tend to be more standardized than women's.[12] This is one reason why dry cleaners often have higher standard charges for women's clothing, since it often cannot be handled in the same way because of style variations. Many children's toys for which people complain of a "pink tax" are those traditionally targeted at boys, such as scooters, helmets, and arm pads and kneepads. Given that demand levels are much higher for the boy versions, perhaps economies of scale in production or marketing are passed through into lower prices.

Each market will be different. Yet the evidence we do have for retail and personal-care products suggests that women often voluntarily opt for products with higher marginal costs of production. This is not a story about companies exploiting women.

Market Innovation versus Legislation

As we've seen, gendered goods that are cherry-picked and deemed directly comparable by commentators and activists in crude analyses are often not considered substitutable by female consumers. Yet the enduring price differences between men's and women's products nevertheless annoy many people, who demand "solutions" to this "problem."

Markets themselves provide one source of remedy. The New York City Department of Consumer Affairs claims that paying higher prices is "mostly unavoidable for women" given that "consumers do not have control over the textiles or ingredients used in the products marketed to them."[13] This is nonsense: there is nothing to stop a woman buying a product marketed to men, or vice versa.

Indeed, the Federal Trade Commission research shows that households could save themselves up to 9 percent on personal-care products if they were willing to opt for differentiated formulations marketed toward the other gender. The fact that most do not suggests that enough women highly value features targeted at them, despite being aware of men's products. After all, data show that married women, at least, often buy male toiletries for their husbands when shopping.[14] They aren't ignorant of the options.

Some argue that there's an expectation for how women should look and smell, or what they should buy, leaving them, in effect, limited by societal norms to purchase higher marginal-cost products marketed for them, despite their true preferences. Disentangling what people really want from what they buy is difficult, but some women say they'd prefer more genderless products. Former UK Women and Equalities Committee chair Maria Miller has said on gender pricing, "At a time when we should be moving towards a more de-gendered society, retailers are out of step with public opinion."[15]

As it happens, the Government Accountability Office reports that federal agencies received very few complaints from the public about gendered pricing, as of 2018.[16] But even if Miller's dissatisfaction were widely shared, markets would provide a huge entrepreneurial incentive for companies to produce unisex or gender-neutral products.

Some already do. Bic, for example, launched gender-neutral facial moisturizer, body lotion, and shaving cream in 2020.[17] Younger customers say they are willing to try gender-neutral toiletries. Existing lines of gender-neutral skin-care and other products are often more expensive than gendered goods, as they market themselves as premium performance products. There's no reason why this market wouldn't expand and diversify if that's what customers truly want.

It's true that some areas of gendered pricing are less explainable. Hairdressers often charge more for women's haircuts, even when a woman seeks the same style as a man. In setting gendered prices, hairdressers gauge, on average, that women have longer hair, have more varied styles, or are fussier customers and so price by stereotypes. One can see why affected women with short hair find this unjust, and online reviews provide a vehicle for complaint.

Likewise, some government tariffs represent a literal "pink tax"— charging higher tax rates on imports of, say, women's underwear (15.5 percent) compared with men's (11.5 percent), as well as more for women's golf shoes, suit jackets, insoles, and more.[18] Perhaps politicians should examine what they can control before reaching for new laws on gendered pricing.

California and New York City, of course, now have legislation to prohibit gendered pricing. Yet there's a paradox at the heart of these laws. As currently constructed, they would barely dent the supposed "pink tax" that a rough analysis identifies, but if they were broadened to deal with the examples generating outrage, they would have harmful effects.

The reason is, as we've seen with personal-care products, many goods are differentiated enough on materials, uses, features, and branding not to fall afoul of the laws' "substantially similar" criterion. It's thus difficult to argue that there's unjustified and substantial injury to consumers from the more significant gendered product differentiation we do see, because it diversifies product availability and women could still opt for men's or gender-neutral marketed goods if they prefer a different, cheaper option.

Even in cases where today there are clear product analogs by gender, such legislation, by creating legal uncertainty, may lead manufacturers to simply discontinue the less profitable variants. That would reduce options available to all consumers, harming their welfare.

The most likely long-term outcome of this legislation is that its narrow application will disappoint consumer activists. In time, demands for tighter rules to police supposedly spurious product differentiation will arise. The idea of "equal prices for equal products," with broader definitions of what constitutes "equal" products, would risk creating great uncertainty and a legal minefield. Companies would likely avoid producing gendered products entirely, which could again harm consumers by reducing the variety of goods available.

In short, the pink tax as conceived is largely a myth. Product preferences vary, on average, across genders, with markets providing subtly differentiated products for which women often willingly pay more.

CHAPTER 23

High CEO Pay Is Not a Simple Story of Rent Seeking

Alex Edmans and J. R. Shackleton

High CEO pay is under attack on both sides of the Atlantic. For example, American journalist Timothy Noah writes: "Shareholders couldn't be clearer: they think CEO pay is out of control. This isn't an offense just to lefty egalitarians. It's an offense to old-school market capitalists too."[1] Meanwhile, one British critic says, "Excessive pay packages awarded by remuneration committees represent a significant failure in corporate governance and perpetuate the idea of a 'superstar' business leader when business is a collective endeavor and reward should be shared more fairly."[2]

Measures of pay differentials vary, but the Economic Policy Institute estimates that CEOs at the largest 350 publicly owned U.S. firms were paid 399 times as much as typical workers in 2021 (compared with 36 times in 1980).[3] London's High Pay Centre reports median pay for CEOs on the FTSE100 Index at 109 times the median UK full-time worker.[4] These figures aren't directly comparable as the metrics differ between the studies, and U.S. corporations anyway tend to be larger than their UK equivalents. Nonetheless, both organizations conclude that the gap between CEO pay and that of ordinary employees has grown, is far too large, and is a cause for concern.

Politicians and regulators share that concern. Corporate governance rules have been tightened to put executive pay under the spotlight and to invite shareholders to query how it is determined. Both countries now have regulations guaranteeing shareholders the right to a nonbinding vote on specific executive compensation—a "say on pay."[5] Although some evidence indicates that say on pay has had an impact, it has not satisfied those who want further clampdowns on high CEO pay, which they see as a market failure.[6]

Is High CEO Pay Driven by Market Forces?

Critics of high CEO remuneration claim that shareholders want to see lower pay, and large numbers of "say on pay" votes have indeed gone against the pay levels or pay structures proposed by remuneration committees and endorsed by boards. However, such gestures may reflect disgruntlement over company performance and attempts to punish executives rather than anything more fully reasoned. It is instructive to note that when large shareholders have a real say in companies, as they do when private equity firms and hedge funds take charge, they rarely choose to cut CEO pay. They may make major changes to the business, including firing the CEO, but not to CEO pay.[7]

Defenders of high CEO pay often claim that an increasingly competitive labor market is driving rising executive pay, and they can point to several plausible arguments. Most obviously, globalization produces larger companies, greater competition for top executives, and movement of talent between countries. In this sense, top executives are increasingly like movie actors, musicians, and professional sports stars—except that executives probably earn less relative to their responsibilities. "Celebrity bosses" with strong reputations for turning companies around are in high demand, with financial analysts often claiming to buy shares because of the CEO's reputation. When a star CEO moves from one company to another, the share price in the company the CEO has left falls, while the share price of the new company rises. When Pat Gelsinger left VMware in 2021 to head Intel, the former's share price fell by 7 percent and the latter's rose by 8 percent.[8] Unexpected departures of talented CEOs can likewise cause large share price declines.[9] For example, Namal Nawana's 2019 resignation as CEO of UK medical device firm Smith & Nephew was associated with a 9 percent share price fall.[10]

The increasing scale and scope of modern companies (given how many corporations now operate in many different products markets) may require a wider range of knowledge and skills for CEOs than in the past. The obstacles to successful management today include ever more intrusive regulation across numerous countries; rapid technological change; international competition; and the demands of environmental, social, and governance (ESG) lobbyists and the diversity, equity, and inclusion movement. Arguably, these pressures make it more likely that CEOs will fail and be dismissed.[11] This heightened risk of job loss in turn increases the remuneration executives expect.

At a personal level, constant travel, the need to be on call 24-7, and the incessant scrutiny associated with mainstream and social media can play havoc with family life. It requires a particular type of personality to stand up to these pressures—but also a substantial compensating differential in pay to offset the demands of the top job.

A failure to recognize that there is a need to compete for scarce talent in an international market for CEOs is potentially damaging to a country's economy. Julia Hoggett, head of the London Stock Exchange, has said that UK executives should be paid more if the country wants to retain talent and deter companies from locating overseas.[12] Against a background of shareholder revolts against pay recommendations at Unilever and Pearson, two of the largest London Stock Exchange firms, she said: "We should be encouraging and supporting UK companies to compete for talent on a global basis, so we remain an attractive place for companies to base themselves, stay and grow. The alternative is we continue standing idly by as our biggest exports become skills, talent, tax revenue and the companies that generate it."[13]

CEO Pay and Company Performance

These factors notwithstanding, much of the debate has turned on how CEO pay is linked to company performance. In August 2022, the U.S. Securities and Exchange Commission began forcing disclosure of the relationship between companies' executive compensation and financial performance over the previous five years.[14] In the United Kingdom, regulations came into force in 2019 that require quoted companies on the London Stock Exchange with over 250 employees in the country to "disclose and explain their top bosses' pay and the gap between that and their average worker."[15]

Economists have had much to say on this since Michael C. Jensen and Kevin J. Murphy wrote their seminal article about it over 30 years ago.[16] Their work was based on principal-agent theory. Risk-neutral "principals" (the shareholders) hire risk-averse "agents" (CEOs) to manage firms. However, there is an informational asymmetry in this relationship; shareholders cannot costlessly observe either the top managers' efforts or the quality of their decisionmaking. The efficient form of contract is said to be one that minimizes monitoring costs by linking CEO pay to company performance, ideally to shareholder returns as reflected by a company's performance on the stock market.

Jensen and Murphy found that a CEO gains only $3.25 when firm value rises by $1,000—an effective equity stake of 0.325 percent.[17] They concluded that CEOs were "paid like bureaucrats." However, economists Brian Hall and Jeffrey Liebman argued that the relevant measure of incentives is how much the CEO gains from a percentage, not dollar, increase in firm value.[18]

The reason is that CEO actions can have multiplicative, rather than additive, effects on firm value. For example, if the CEO introduces a program that increases efficiency, it can improve firm-wide performance. For firms that are highly valuable to begin with, even small percentage improvements can generate a lot of value. In fact, Hall and Liebman found that the CEO gains significantly from a one percentage point increase in firm value, and this sensitivity has risen over time. More recent data gathered by economists Alex Edmans, Xavier Gabaix, and Dirk Jenter find that the average CEO in the S&P 500 gains $670,000 from such an increase.[19] Thus, CEOs are highly incentivized to work to increase their firms' value.

Despite this rigorous academic research, many practitioner studies claim that CEO remuneration is barely affected by poor performance. An often-cited 2016 study by the data provision company MSCI is titled "Are CEOs Paid for Performance?," to which the authors' succinct answer is "In a word, no."[20]

These findings are widely shared through traditional and social media, potentially given confirmation bias, but the authors make a fundamental error: they only study how salaries and bonuses change with firm performance, even though those are a small part of a CEO's overall incentive package. The biggest component is the CEO's stock and option holdings. Some studies take account of stock and options granted in the relevant reporting year, but we really need to understand *all* stock and options granted across previous years. What matters is *wealth-performance sensitivity*—the sensitivity of the CEO's entire wealth to how well the company is run (as studied by the earlier-cited papers)—not *pay*-performance sensitivity.

Activists and politicians who insist that very high pay cannot be justified by CEOs' performance—in some cases even deeming it a reward for failure—reject the idea that contracts have been designed by boards, albeit imperfectly, to motivate executives to maximize shareholder value. Rather, they see the process of setting executive compensation as captured by CEOs and their cronies as a form of rent extraction.

This view was articulated at length by Harvard Law School's Lucian Bebchuk and Jesse Fried in their widely cited 2004 book *Pay without Performance: The Unfulfilled Promise of Executive Compensation*. The U.S.-focused book claimed to provide "a detailed account of how structural flaws in corporate governance have enabled managers to influence their own pay and produced widespread distortions in pay arrangements."[21] They argue that boards have not been operating at arm's length from the executives whose pay they set. Again, by calculating pay-performance sensitivity, rather than wealth-performance sensitivity, they erroneously conclude that executives' incentives are not aligned with shareholders' interests.

The debate on executive pay is often polarized between the "efficient contracting" view (that boards are perfectly aligned with shareholders and observed contracts are optimal) and the "rent extraction" perspective (that boards are in CEOs' pockets); however, a May 2023 academic survey of directors and investors—conducted in part by one of us (Edmans)—suggests that reality lies between the two extremes. Boards and investors often disagree, but not because boards are trying to enrich CEOs and investors are trying to rein them in.[22] Instead, both parties want to maximize shareholder value, but they have different conceptions of how to do so.

In the survey, investors emphasize the need to design forward-looking pay structures to motivate the CEO, whereas directors prioritize attracting the right individual in the first place. Indeed, evidence suggests that board members may feel hampered by shareholders in the search for CEO talent in highly competitive executive labor markets. As many as 77 percent of directors in the survey report shareholder constraints forcing them to offer lower pay levels than they deem appropriate for their CEO, while 72 percent report shareholders forcing them to offer an inferior pay structure. If directors are correct about how to set pay to attract talent, shareholder power may reduce shareholder value.

The same survey also suggests that incentives may play a different role than that assumed by agency theory. Rather than pay motivating future behavior, top executives see their pay as a reward for past achievement, a retrospective validation of their performance. Thus, the high incentives found by academic research need not be caused by CEOs being lazy and only exerting effort if given a substantial bonus. Instead, even an intrinsically motivated CEO may believe that it is fair to be rewarded for a job well done.

Should CEO Pay Be a Matter of Public Policy?

The belief that high CEO pay stems from rent extraction rather than from market forces is said to justify regulatory interventions. But it's shareholders who bear the cost of executive pay (both directly and indirectly, if pay leads to poor incentives or demotivates other workers), so it's unclear why corporate regulation is warranted. To the extent that there are wider societal impacts of pay not borne by shareholders (e.g., increased inequality), governments already tax all highly paid professions through income taxes. There's no need to regulate CEO pay separately.

Nevertheless, many critics of high pay argue that government intervention is required. Too often their proposals are based on gut feeling rather than evidence. For example, in the United States, the Economic Policy Institute has argued for higher corporate taxes for firms with higher ratios of CEO to worker pay, which has been tried on a limited scale in Portland, Oregon.[23]

Such a rule would impose a higher tax burden on corporations in sectors with large numbers of low-paid part-time workers, such as retail, or else force those firms to reduce their CEOs' pay. In industries with few low-paid workers but extremely highly paid executives, such as finance, the tax disincentive could handicap firms in the competition for top CEO talent. It would also encourage companies to outsource low-paid work to lower the ratio. In Britain, the former general secretary of the Trades Union Congress Frances O'Grady has said, "It's time to set a maximum ratio between the top earner in each firm and other workers,"[24] which is probably even worse than the Economic Policy Institute's proposal in that it substitutes a graduated penalty with an absolute limit.

Sen. Bernie Sanders (I-VT) has suggested CEO pay could be checked by having worker representatives on company boards, whereas the UK's High Pay Centre wants workers represented on remuneration committees. If implemented, these types of policies would likely lead to compressed pay structures within firms, and worker representatives could influence companies against certain types of investment or layoff decisions. One famous study of Germany (where employee representatives have been on supervisory boards for years) found that labor union opposition to restructuring cost West German firms about a quarter of shareholder value.[25] Faced with this outcome, we might find many companies delisting and talented executives migrating to private equity businesses. Whether it would affect CEO pay levels much is difficult to say: German CEOs, though paid less than those in the United States, are still paid quite highly.

Another popular proposal is to tie executive pay to ESG goals. Most companies already do this. Advocates claim that adherence to ESG investing criteria will ultimately boost shareholder value, a win-win for both shareholders and stakeholders. However, if this is true, it is unclear why investors—or worse, government—need to set the targets. Whether it be tractors in the Soviet Union or today's reductions in energy use or more ethnically diverse recruitment, attention to specific metrics can cause businesses to miss the bigger picture.

If the "rent extraction" thesis is correct and the aim is to restore shareholder value, the only logical type of regulation is one that increases shareholder power. This is the Bebchuk-Fried view: shareholders are too weak and have been captured by management, and this justifies a range of corporate governance initiatives. However, the rise in CEO pay has coincided with greater shareholder power and shareholder activism, which is surely inconsistent with pay rising because of rent extraction rubber-stamped by inattentive shareholders. Moreover, if shareholders are uninformed about the specifics of a particular company situation and impose one-size-fits-all guidelines, more shareholder power may constrain boards from offering optimal contracts and so erode shareholder value.

We prefer simple, transparent, and sustainable incentives for CEOs. We need to replicate the incentives faced by owner-entrepreneurs. Pay them like owners, with long-term shares they cannot sell for 5 to 10 years and must retain after departure. We shouldn't overthink payment schemes but should be prepared to pay top dollar to acquire top talent. Successful corporations can work this out for themselves without further government intervention.

CHAPTER 24

Dynamic Pricing Can Benefit Consumers

Liya Palagashvili

In early 2023, the *Wall Street Journal* reported on a customer's anger at a small-town bowling alley. The bowling alley had introduced a pricing system that charged three times more than the normal rate for a family game during winter break. As access to algorithmic technologies have widened, more and more companies, including restaurants, gyms, and golf courses, are experimenting with this so-called dynamic pricing.[1] Consumers aren't always enamored with it.

Sometimes referred to as "algorithmic," "demand-based," or "surge" pricing, dynamic pricing is a practice in which the price of a good or service fluctuates in real time based on market supply and, especially, demand conditions. That makes it different from fixed or static pricing, where the price remains relatively constant over some period. For example, the apple at your local grocery store will likely stay at about the same price over a week, irrespective of how busy the supermarket is.

In economic parlance, dynamic pricing is a form of "price discrimination," whereby firms can segment customers within a market by time, charging different prices based on when the consumer purchases or wants to access a good or service. Dynamic pricing is why you can get a cheap flight to Italy if you book in advance for the "low demand" colder months but will pay a high price for a last-minute trip in July during the "high demand" school holidays. It's a deeper application of the principle that underpins why theaters charge less for low-demand matinees and also why winter clothes are sold at a discount in the spring.

Yet there have been controversies surrounding dynamic pricing as greater computing power and algorithmic technologies have seen it rolled out into new sectors, allowing price changes to occur more frequently and quickly, sometimes instantaneously.

Ridesharing services such as Uber and Lyft have taken flak for their real-time "surge pricing," with news articles bemoaning extortionate prices after major events and emergencies.[2] Concertgoers have been angered by Ticketmaster using dynamic pricing too.[3] Bruce Springsteen tickets were at one point selling for as much as $5,000 each under dynamic pricing.[4] When fans refused to pay that much, prices fell. In the end, more than half of all fans paid less than $200 per ticket for the concert, but the anger at the higher prices remained.[5]

Now, more transportation, hospitality, and e-commerce platforms use dynamic pricing in industries where customers have traditionally seen more price stability. Some consumers consider it "unfair" to charge customers different amounts at different times for the "same product." Others dislike the apparent lack of transparency and the uncertainty associated with rapidly changing prices. Then there are the usual complaints about "price gouging" when the explosion of demand is driven by emergencies or natural disasters.

As algorithmic technologies and internet search engines make dynamic pricing more appealing, it's therefore necessary to remember the economic benefits of letting prices float, more regularly, according to market conditions.

The Economics of Dynamic Pricing

Most business don't price dynamically. At your grocery store, you will often see consistent, static pricing of goods throughout the day, without shelves ever becoming barren. Supermarkets instead manage demand fluctuations by forecasting demand, maintaining a backup stock of certain products, automatically reordering when a stock level dwindles, and leveraging real-time inventory tracking to ensure that they can fulfill customers' demand. Consumers pay slightly higher prices for each item—a convenience premium—to have the goods available to them at a consistent price throughout the day or week.

For example, when you walk into a McDonald's, you don't pay different prices depending on how long the line is. Prices don't even rise at lunch- and dinnertimes, even though the company knows the restaurants will be busier. McDonald's has calculated that keeping prices constant—and maintaining some spare capacity to ensure that wait times don't get too long—better protects their brand and the certainty that consumers crave.

These examples highlight how firms usually consider it more profitable, on balance, to avoid surprising consumers, or to invest in systems that keep supply more elastic in response to predictable demand shifts. Yet there are costs to this uniform pricing, relative to pricing dynamically. In supermarkets, there's extensive food waste because of consumers' reluctance to buy expiring produce, empty shelves during very high demand times like just before hurricanes, and long checkout lines during rush-hour shopping. At McDonald's, long lines at lunchtime raise the effective price of a McDonald's meal to customers, potentially deterring consumers who place a high value on their time.

Dynamic pricing occurs when businesses consider that varying prices by time will instead increase the profitability of the company. It's an attempt to discriminate by different customers' time- and context-specific willingness to pay for the good or service. In general, it tends to be used in two types of markets: (a) where there is a short-term flexible supply that can move to meet demand, like in ride-sharing; or (b) where there is fixed or limited capacity that needs to be efficiently allocated in a market with uncertain demand, as with hotels and airlines.

Ridesharing is perhaps the quintessential example of dynamic pricing. Surge pricing for rideshare companies like Uber helps ensure that no large mismatches of supply and demand result in cars sitting around idle or customers waiting for ages for pickups.

If a subway malfunction increases the demand for ridesharing services, like Uber, prices surge. This result has two important effects. First, customers who wanted an Uber at the old price must reconsider and decide whether to walk, stay longer in the office until the price falls, cancel their plans, or pay up at the higher rate. This rationing by price ensures a reduction in the quantity demanded and that those who value the rideshare highly are more likely to get a ride. Second, drivers see that they are being offered a higher price for servicing that particular area at that time. This encourages more of them to get out or remain on the road, supplying more rides to the area to meet demand. It also encourages them to hit the road the next time a similar event occurs.

Services like Uber judge that consumers value a consistent service more than consistent pricing. They seem to be right. Gett—"the Uber without surge pricing"—failed to create a sustainable business model after launching in the United States. Faced with instances of surging demand, the company had to either allow long wait times or eat the cost of paying more drivers to get on the road, despite the lack of price incentives for them to do so.[6] Most analyses have found that surge pricing in this sector therefore significantly increases the welfare of consumers.[7] Those who value rides highly get a timely pickup; those who prefer lower prices can opt to wait. In instances where Uber has seen outages in its surge system, wait times have soared.[8] Surge pricing helps calibrate supply with demand.

The economics of short-term fixed-supply markets, like those for concert seats or airline tickets, are slightly different. Here, dynamic pricing helps allocate goods in high demand to those who value them most, which also allows companies to maximize revenues. This approach can help ensure that those who really want seats during high-demand periods can go or fly, while broadening access for off-peak performances or flights to more marginal customers. The higher profits can also encourage more capacity expansion or entry into the sector, widening access further in time. But there's no sugarcoating that some consumers will pay more and be worse off than when prices are uniform.

Dynamic pricing at the point of sale helps allocate seats to the fans who value them most in the same way that secondary markets or touts used to operate. If Taylor Swift concert tickets online were fixed at a "cheap" price of $100 per seat, an influx of marginal fans could mop up the tickets on a first-come, first-served basis. Many "true" Taylor Swift fans who would be willing to pay much more would be left ticketless. If the price was a fixed $500, those who do not value the Taylor Swift concert for at least $500 would drop out, leaving more available seats for those "true" Taylor Swift fans. If priced at $5,000, however, there'd probably be empty seats in the stadium.

Airlines also price-discriminate on numerous margins when selling scarce seats, including the flight's time of departure. A marginal tourist can get a cheap ticket to Rome during off-peak months, but will be discouraged from flying to Rome during Christmas, when prices are high. This approach frees up seats for Italians living abroad, who may value the ticket more as they seek to fly home to their families for the holidays. Interestingly, airlines also price-discriminate according to when you purchase a ticket. They typically charge less on weekends (when marginal leisure travelers are browsing) than during the week when purchasers are more likely to be price-insensitive business travelers, for whom travel is a necessity.

In operating such dynamic pricing on two dimensions, airlines can exploit variations in consumers' willingness to pay, thus obtaining more revenues and higher profitability, which enables them to run more routes—generating affordable off-peak fares. Several studies analyzing the airline industry have found that overall economic welfare is higher under dynamic pricing, compared with fixed pricing.[9] The major beneficiary is the marginal leisure traveler, who enjoys more flights and cheap fares at low-demand times.

Dynamic pricing can, in the right circumstances, increase economic welfare, expand access to services, and ensure that sales at any given time are devoted to consumers who value the service most. In the absence of dynamic pricing, firms must still find ways to allocate goods, whether it's long lines; first-come, first-served sales; or some other mechanism. Often firms will deem these alternative allocation mechanisms more profitable given the features of their market. But they come with big economic costs, including temporary shortages, the need to maintain spare capacity or inventory to meet high-demand periods, and time spent in lines for consumers—which raises the services' effective price.

A Case Study: Dynamic Pricing for Ridesharing

Uber and other ridesharing services' products are fundamentally different from taxis precisely because of the foundational role of dynamic pricing interacting with a flexible fleet of drivers. The sector provides a case study of dynamic pricing that highlights its benefits: (a) calibrating supply to demand, (b) reducing wait times, (c) reducing wasteful down periods for drivers, and (d) making consumers better off overall.

In one study on surge pricing, for example, economists M. Keith Chen and Michael Sheldon confirmed that drivers extended their sessions and provided significantly more rides when "surge pricing" occurred in a particular geographic area. Indeed, the median driver on the Uber platform works less than 3.5 hours per session and varies the length of that session significantly to take advantage of surge pricing.[10] This supply response can be large. In New York City, taxicabs have no dynamic pricing beyond peak-hour fare increases twice a day. A 2018 study found the number of Uber and Lyft rides rose by 22 percent during rainstorms, compared with just 5 percent for ordinary taxis.[11]

When dynamic pricing encourages more drivers to get out on the road, that translates to shorter wait times. When calling a taxi to their home, just 35 percent of San Francisco residents said they usually waited less than 10 minutes on a weekday. In comparison, 90 percent of residents said they waited less than 10 minutes for an Uber or Lyft. Another recent study confirms that dynamic pricing strategies reduced wait times for riders.[12]

Drivers are less likely to drive around idly without passengers under dynamic pricing. Economists Judd Cramer and Alan Krueger found that the capacity utilization rate—measured by "the fraction of time a driver has a fare-paying passenger in the car while he or she is working, and by the share of total miles that drivers log in which a passenger is in their car"—is significantly higher for UberX drivers than for taxi drivers, who often drive around without a passenger during off-peak periods.[13]

Finally, consumers benefit most from dynamic pricing in ride-sharing services. Economist Juan Camilo Castillo, analyzing data from Uber in Houston during the spring of 2017, found that consumers are significantly better off under dynamic pricing relative to static pricing in ridesharing because surge pricing allows riders who highly value their time (e.g., they need to be punctual for an appointment or to catch their flight) to be picked up more quickly.[14] Customers who don't put as high a premium on their time can always wait until surge diminishes or take another form of transport. Under static pricing, only riders who are lucky to be near a driver get a ride, irrespective of how much they value it.

Concerns about Dynamic Pricing

Three major concerns are voiced about dynamic pricing. The first is that charging different customers different prices for what is, ostensibly, the same product or service, is inherently unfair. Imagine if dynamic pricing hit your local grocery store: there would be outrage if the same apple jumped from $1 to $20 later that evening during rush-hour shopping. Aside from consumers valuing certainty, the underlying fear is that more goods will become unaffordable at certain popular times for low-income and financially strained individuals.

This is closely related to a second concern that dynamic pricing "exploits" customers during emergency situations as a form of price gouging. When Uber or Lyft prices surge by 10 times the normal fare in response to a shooting or natural disaster, customers view this as Uber and Lyft taking advantage of vulnerable individuals who may have difficulty affording these essential services during a desperate situation.[15] Indeed, there have been several instances where Uber had agreed to limit dynamic pricing in an emergency because of public backlash.[16]

These two complaints largely reflect that many customers consider it illegitimate for companies to raise prices when demand surges, as opposed to in response to rising costs. The problem is that many customers do not naturally connect the "dynamic pricing" mechanism with the supply response. To them, the perceived alternative is that they can get both low prices *and* access to the good or service, when in fact the real alternative in many cases is low prices *and* no access for large numbers of customers.

Yes, some individuals will get lucky under uniform pricing, obtaining both low prices and access to the services in a period of high demand. But that leaves many customers without access, even though their willingness to pay might be much higher. Imagine a working-class Italian who desperately needs to fly home at late notice to take care of his elderly parents over the holidays. A uniform price of $200 per flight from New York to Rome would see American tourists with more free time on their hands snatching all the seats earlier, preventing the Italian from flying.

People also forget that fluctuating prices mean that prices move both *up* and *down*. Dynamic pricing allows consumers to access a good or service that is below a normal fare when demand is low or when they book far in advance—for example, airline tickets have been affordable for many millions of Americans for advance flights and off-peak hours. In this sense, dynamic pricing allows customers with a high willingness to pay to subsidize the product or service at low-demand times.

A counterintuitive point here is that sharp price increases associated with high-demand periods provide a signal to improve long-term supply too. Just as surge pricing for rideshares at the end of a baseball game encourages more drivers both now and after future sporting events, the price signal from a bowling alley being full on weekends despite prices being higher may encourage new entrants to the industry or capacity expansions from the provider. This is a crucial point with regard to the "fairness" of high prices, which are often judged on a very static basis.

A third concern is that dynamic pricing can lack transparency. In the early days of rideshare apps, customers would see a message that said something like "Demand is high so we're increasing prices sixfold," but they couldn't see the final price before booking a trip.[17] This made consumers inherently suspicious. Venues such as restaurants, museums, and state parks are also realizing that customers dislike prices that are unclear.[18]

Yet this problem can be overcome with better information provision. The rideshare example is instructive. When customers demand transparency, markets are incentivized to provide it. Uber and others have since shifted to highlight the full price, including the high-demand surcharge, up front. Likewise, third-party institutions, such as travel sites like Expedia and Google Travel, today provide calendars of airline fares and price comparisons across providers. Airlines and rideshare companies also showcase ranges of prices and travel options during times of high and low demand. If consumers want transparency, there's nothing inherent about dynamic pricing that means companies can't provide it.

At least some of the backlash to dynamic pricing appears to arise from bad marketing. Few bargoers complain that bars charge excessive prices for drinks outside of happy hour. That's because the latter is marketed as a discount. Rather than surges at high-demand times, if off-peak times were labeled as discounted, maybe there'd be fewer concerns.

Most economists, regardless of political affiliation, agreed in a 2014 survey that dynamic pricing tends to raise consumer welfare by increasing the supply of services, allocating them to people who desire them most, and reducing search and queuing costs.[19] Although every business must decide for itself whether to prioritize consistency of supply or consistency in prices, according to its own assessment of profitability, we'd be worse off if public or political pressure were to lead to anti-dynamic-pricing legislation, as it has with price gouging.

NOTES

Introduction

[1] Bureau of Labor Statistics, "Consumer Price Index for All Urban Consumers: Food at Home in U.S. City Average [CUSR0000SAF11]," Federal Reserve Bank of St. Louis, May 2023.

[2] Bureau of Labor Statistics, "Consumer Price Index for All Urban Consumers: Used Cars and Trucks in U.S. City Average [CUSR0000SETA02]," Federal Reserve Bank of St. Louis, May 2023.

[3] Bureau of Labor Statistics, "Consumer Price Index for All Urban Consumers: Electricity in U.S. City Average [CUUS0000SEHF01]," Federal Reserve Bank of St. Louis, January 12, 2023.

[4] Bureau of Labor Statistics, "Consumer Price Index for All Urban Consumers: Coffee in U.S. City Average [CUUR0000SEFP01]," Federal Reserve Bank of St. Louis, June 13, 2023.

[5] Bureau of Labor Statistics, "Nonfarm Business Sector: Real Hourly Compensation for All Workers," Productivity and Costs, accessed at FRED, Federal Reserve Bank of St. Louis, on September 1, 2023.

[6] Ryan Bourne, Testimony on "(Im)Balance of Power: How Market Concentration Affects Worker Compensation and Consumer Prices" before the House Select Committee on Economic Disparity and Fairness in Growth, 117th Cong., 2nd sess., April 6, 2022.

[7] Taylor Orth and Carl Bialik, "More Americans Now Blame Inflation on Large Corporations Than Did So Last October," YouGov, July 7, 2023.

[8] Ryan Bourne, "A New, Depressing Survey on Inflation," *Cato at Liberty* (blog), Cato Institute, July 21, 2023.

[9] Meg Jacobs and Isabella M. Weber, "The Way to Fight Inflation without Rising Interest Rates and a Recession," *Washington Post*, August 9, 2022.

[10] Joe Biden (@JoeBiden), "Let me be clear to any corporation that hasn't brought their prices back down even as inflation has come down: It's time to stop the price gouging. Give American consumers a break," X post, November 30, 2023, 10:29 a.m.

[11] Paul Krugman, "I Was Wrong about Inflation," *New York Times*, July 21, 2022.

[12] Paul Krugman (@paulkrugman), "So, we're right back on the prepandemic Phillips curve. It takes real intellectual gymnastics *not* to see this as a transitory adverse supply shock," X post, January 25, 2024, 9:43 a.m.

[13] Ryan Bourne, "Yes, Demand Can Explain (Most of) the American Disinflation," The War on Prices (blog), January 3, 2024.

Part 1: Inflation

[1] Frank Newport, "How Do Americans View Higher Inflation?," Gallup, June 10, 2022.

[2] "Most Important Problem," Gallup, 2023.

[3] "Inflation, Health Costs, Partisan Cooperation among the Nation's Top Problems," Pew Research Center, June 21, 2023.

[4] "Consumer Price Index," U.S. Bureau of Labor Statistics, last updated June 2023; "Personal Consumption Expenditures Price Index," U.S. Bureau of Economic Analysis, May 26, 2023.

[5] U.S. Bureau of Economic Analysis, "Personal Consumption Expenditures: Chain-Type Price Index [PCEPI]," Federal Reserve Bank of St. Louis, last updated May 26, 2023.

[6] Milton Friedman, "Counter-Revolution in Monetary Theory," Wincott Memorial Lecture, Institute of Economic Affairs Occasional Paper no. 33, 1970.

[7] Robert E. Lucas Jr. Prize Lecture: "Monetary Neutrality," NobelPrize.org, December 7, 1995.

[8] DataBank World Development Indicators, "Broad Money (Current LCU)," World Bank, accessed September 2023; and DataBank World Development Indicators, "Inflation, Consumer Prices (Annual %)," World Bank, accessed September 2023.

[9] Milton Freidman, "The Fed's Thermostat," *Wall Street Journal*, August 19, 2003.

[10] M2, FRED Economic Data, accessed on August 25, 2023.

[11] Axel Leijonhufvud, "Costs and Consequences of Inflation," UCLA Discussion Paper no. 58, May 1975.

Chapter 1: Rising Product Prices and Inflation

[1] Alyssa Fowers, "What Is Causing Inflation: The Factors Driving Prices High Each Month," *Washington Post*, July 26, 2022.

[2] Martin Arnold, "Rising Inflation in France and Spain Fuels Fears of More ECB Rate Increases," *Financial Times*, February 28, 2023.

[3] In economic parlance, goods or products typically include services, except when the context clearly indicates otherwise.

[4] It is important to understand that all the curves on the graph are indexes set to 100 in June 2014. Their heights above the horizontal axis do not indicate in any way that one good costs more or less than another, only that the highest one has increased more rapidly since June 2014.

[5] "Uncooked Beef Roasts in U.S. City Average, All Urban Consumers, Not Seasonally Adjusted," BLS, accessed March 2023; "Rent of Primary Residence in U.S. City Average, All Urban Consumers, Not Seasonally Adjusted," BLS, accessed March 2023; and "Gasoline (All Types) in U.S. City Average, All Urban Consumers, Not Seasonally Adjusted," BLS, accessed March 2023.

[6] Hie Jo Ahn and Matteo Luciani, "Relative Prices and Pure Inflation since the Mid-1990s," Finance and Economics Discussion Series no. 2021-069, Board of Governors, Federal Reserve System, 2021, pp. 3–15 passim.

[7] Bureau of Labor Statistics, *Handbook of Methods*, Chap. 17, "The Consumer Price Index" (Washington: BLS, 2018).

[8] Evaluating human welfare, that is, the welfare of several individuals, cannot anyway be done with only information on prices and quantities. See Paul A.

Samuelson, "Evaluation of Real National Income," *Oxford Economic Papers* 2, no.1 (1950): 1–29.

[9] Michael Parkin, "Inflation," *New Palgrave Dictionary of Economics* (London: Palgrave Macmillan, 2017), pp. 6433–81. For an interesting educational resource, see Scott Wolla, "Money and Inflation," Federal Reserve Bank of St. Louis, n.d.

[10] John C. Frain, "Inflation and Money Growth: Evidence from a Multi-Country Data-Set," *Economic and Social Review* 35, no. 3 (2004): 251–66. See also the charts in my post "How Could Inflation Ever Be Stopped?," EconLog (blog), May 11, 2022.

[11] Jerome H. Powell, Chair, Board of Governors of the Federal Reserve System, Testimony on "Oversight on the Monetary Policy Report to Congress Pursuant to the Full Employment and Balanced Growth Act of 1978," hearing before the Senate Committee on Banking, Housing, and Urban Affairs, 117th Cong., 1st sess., February 23, 2021.

[12] Hugh Rockoff, *Drastic Measures: A History of Wage and Price Controls in the United States* (Cambridge: Cambridge University Press, 1984).

[13] Max Colchester and Paul Hannon, "U.K. Government to Cap Household Energy Prices for Two Years," *Wall Street Journal*, September 8, 2022.

[14] Jerome H. Powell, "Monetary Policy in the Time of COVID," speech at the "Macroeconomic Policy in an Uneven Economy" economic policy symposium, Jackson Hole, WY, August 27, 2021.

Chapter 2: The Wage-Price Spiral

[1] Jenni Reid, "Bank of England Governor Says the UK Is Facing a Wage-Price Spiral," CNBC, May 18, 2023.

[2] Michael Race and Vishala Sri-Pathma, "Bank of England Economist Says People Need to Accept They Are Poorer," BBC, April 26, 2023.

[3] Talmon Joseph Smith, "Wages May Not Be Inflation's Cause, but They're the Focus of the Cure," *New York Times*, April 7, 2023; and Jerome H. Powell, chair, Board of Governors of the Federal Reserve System, Testimony on "The Federal Reserve's Semi-Annual Monetary Policy Report" before the House Financial Service Committee, 118th Cong., 1st sess., March 8, 2023.

[4] See "Inflation" in the *Concise Encyclopedia of Economics*. For additional details on inflation: Lawrence H. White, "Inflation," Econlib, 2023.

[5] This example assumes the economy is in a steady-state equilibrium. However, the economy does not instantaneously move from one steady-state equilibrium to another because of a variety of factors that create what economists call "nominal rigidities." For example, although the arithmetic relationship between the variables described in this example must always hold at any point in time, a change in the growth rates of the money supply will affect money velocity and real income differently in the short run than in the long run.

[6] "Union Members Summary," Bureau of Labor Statistics news release no. USDL-23-0071, January 19, 2023.

[7] The Federal Reserve does not create a projection for nominal income growth, but one can be inferred from the "Summary of Economic Projections" by combining

the median projection of real income growth and inflation. For the final 2019 projections, see "FOMC Projections, Materials, Accessible Version," Board of Governors of the Federal Reserve System, December 11, 2019. For the data on nominal income, see Bureau of Economic Analysis, "Gross Domestic Product [GDP]," FRED, Federal Reserve Bank of St. Louis.

[8] Inflation in this chart is based on the Personal Consumption Expenditures price index, which is the Federal Reserve's preferred price index. For data on the inflation rate and the level of employment, see Bureau of Economic Analysis, "Personal Consumption Expenditures: Chain-Type Price Index," FRED, Federal Reserve Bank of St. Louis.

[9] Bureau of Economic Analysis, "Personal Consumption Expenditures: Chain-type Price Index [PCEPI]," Federal Reserve Bank of St. Louis; and Bureau of Labor Statistics, "All Employees, Total Nonfarm [PAYEMS]," Federal Reserve Bank of St. Louis.

[10] The pre-pandemic trend reflects the average monthly inflation-adjusted wage growth between January 2015 and December 2019. See Bureau of Labor Statistics, "Average Hourly Earnings of All Employees, Total Private [CES0500000003]," FRED, Federal Reserve Bank of St. Louis. Wages have been deflated using the personal consumption expenditures: Chain-Type Price Index from the St. Louis FRED website, using January 2020 as the base year. The chart is denominated in January 2020 dollars.

[11] Bureau of Labor Statistics, "Average Hourly Earnings of All Employees, Total Private [CES0500000003]," Federal Reserve Bank of St. Louis.

[12] Since this adjustment process takes time to complete, the wage-price pass-through may continue even after the growth of nominal income has started to slow. Note, however, that this differs from higher wages *causing* higher prices. The ultimate cause was the excessive nominal income growth. See Olivier J. Blanchard, "The Wage Price Spiral," *Quarterly Journal of Economics* 101, no. 3 (1986): 543–66.

[13] See, for example, Romain A. Duval et al., "Labor Market Tightness in Advanced Economies," International Monetary Fund Staff Discussion Notes no. 2002/001, March 31, 2022.

[14] Measuring inflation using price indexes is far from perfect. For example, changes in the prices of some goods relative to others may not be adequately reflected in these indexes. As a result, the sort of shift described in this example may have a measurable effect on the price indexes used to calculate inflation. However, the measurement issue does not invalidate the theoretical point about the two price effects offsetting each other.

Chapter 3: Greed and Corporate Concentration

[1] Tom Polanseck, "U.S. Senator Warren Calls for Probe of Soaring Poultry Prices," Reuters, November 22, 2021.

[2] Catherine Rampell, "An Inflation Conspiracy Theory Is Infecting the Democratic Party," *Washington Post*, May 12, 2022.

[3] Jon Sindreu, "'Greedflation' Is Real—and Probably Good for the Economy," *Wall Street Journal*, May 25, 2023; Jana Randow and Aaron Eglitis, "ECB Wakes Up to

Greedflation as Key Culprit in Price Struggle," Bloomberg, April 27, 2023; Emily Peck, "Once a Fringe Theory, 'Greedflation' Gets Its Due," Axios, May 18, 2023; Juliana Kaplan, "The Real Monster behind Soaring Prices," Insider, May 2, 2023; and Talmon Joseph Smith and Joe Rennison, "Companies Push Price Higher, Protecting Profits but Adding to Inflation," *New York Times*, May 30, 2023.

4 Hal Singer, managing director, Econ One Research, Testimony before the House Committee on Economic Disparity and Fairness in Growth, 117th Cong., 2nd sess., April 6, 2022.

5 "Inflation, Market Power, and Price Controls," Clark Center Forum, January 11, 2022.

6 Emily Peck, "Once a Fringe Theory, 'Greedflation' Gets Its Due," Axios, May 18, 2023.

7 Brian Albrecht and Alexander Salter, "Lina Khan Won't Solve Inflation," *The Hill*, February 14, 2022.

8 Ryan A. Decker and John Haltiwanger, "Surging Business Formation in the Pandemic: Causes and Consequences," working paper, rdecker.net, 2022.

9 Falk Bräuning, José L. Fillat, and Gustavo Joaquim, "Cost-Price Relationships in a Concentrated Economy," Federal Reserve Bank of Boston, May 23, 2022; and Bräuning, Fillat, and Joaquim, "Cost-Price Relationships in a Concentrated Economy," Elsevier, June 28, 2022.

10 Ryan Decker and Jacob Williams, "A Note on Industry Concentration Measurement," Board of Governors of the Federal Reserve System, February 3, 2023.

11 Nathan Miller et al., "On the Misuse of Regressions of Price on the HHI in Merger Review," *Journal of Antitrust Enforcement* 10, no. 2 (July 2022): 248–59.

12 Oscar Arce, Elke Hahn, and Gerrit Koester, "How Tit-for-Tat Inflation Can Make Everyone Poorer," *ECB Blog*, March 30, 2023.

13 Isabella M. Weber and Evan Wasner, "Sellers' Inflation, Profits and Conflict: Why Can Large Firms Hike Prices in an Emergency?," *Review of Keynesian Economics* 2, no. 2 (April 2023): 183–213.

14 Tracy Alloway and Joe Weisenthal, "How 'Excuseflation' Is Keeping Prices— and Corporate Profits—High," Bloomberg, March 9, 2023.

15 Josh Hendrickson, "Price Theory as an Antidote," *Economic Forces* (blog), February 9, 2023.

16 Andrew Glover, José Mustre-del-Río, and Jalen Nichols, "Corporate Profits Contributed a Lot to Inflation in 2021 but Little in 2022—A Pattern Seen in Past Economic Recoveries," Federal Reserve Bank of Kansas City, May 12, 2023.

17 Weber and Wasner, "Sellers' Inflation, Profits and Conflict."

18 Brian Albrecht, "Is Inflation Demand or Supply Driven?," *Economic Forces* (blog), June 16, 2022.

19 Adam Hale Shapiro, "How Much Do Supply and Demand Drive Inflation?," Federal Reserve Bank of San Francisco, June 21, 2022.

20 "Supply- and Demand-Driven PCE Inflation," Federal Reserve Bank of San Francisco, 2023.

21 Isabella Weber, "Could Strategic Price Controls Help Fight Inflation?," *The Guardian*, December 29, 2021.

22 "Inflation, Market Power, and Price Controls," Clark Center Forum, January 11, 2022; and Edward Malnick, "Rishi Sunak Will Ask Stores to Cap Basic Food Prices," *The Telegraph*, May 27, 2023.

Chapter 4: Supply Shocks and the Ukraine War

[1] For more on the importance inflation was playing in the 2022 elections, see Frank Newport, "How Do Americans View Higher Inflation?," Gallup, June 10, 2022.

[2] Another important reason is that most observers, including Fed officials and professional economic forecasters, simply assumed that the low inflation of the past few decades would soon return. It was tough for many to imagine a sustained inflation surge after such a long run with low inflation.

[3] Ben Bernanke and Olivier Blanchard, "What Caused the U.S. Pandemic-Era Inflation?," Hutchins Center Working Paper no. 86, Brookings Institution, Washington, June 2023. This paper found that most of the commodity price surge in 2021 was due to strong aggregate demand growth.

[4] Aggregate supply, in other words, becomes inelastic with significant acceleration of total dollar spending.

[5] a. "The Budget and Economic Outlook: 2020 to 2030," CBO, January 28, 2020; and "Nominal Gross Domestic Product for United States [NGDPSAXDCUSQ]," Federal Reserve Bank of St. Louis. b. "The Budget and Economic Outlook: 2020 to 2030," CBO, January 28, 2020; and BEA, "Real Gross Domestic Product [GDPC1]," Federal Reserve Bank of St. Louis. c. "The Budget and Economic Outlook: 2020 to 2030," CBO, January 28, 2020; and BEA, "Gross Domestic Product: Implicit Price Deflator [GDPDEF]," Federal Reserve Bank of St. Louis; International Monetary Fund, "Nominal Gross Domestic Product for United States [NGDPSAXDCUSQ]," Federal Reserve Bank of St. Louis.

[6] a. David Beckworth, "Measuring Monetary Policy: the NGDP Gap," Mercatus Center at George Mason University, December 1, 2023. b. "Cyclical and Acyclical Core PCE Inflation," Federal Reserve Bank of San Francisco. c. Author's modeling.

[7] "Budget and Economic Data: Historical Data and Economic Projections," Congressional Budget Office, Washington, February 2023; and Jason Furman, comments on Ben Bernanke and Olivier Blanchard's "What Caused the U.S. Pandemic-Era Inflation?," Brookings conference on "The Fed: Lessons Learned from the Past Three Years," Brookings Institution, Washington, May 23, 2023.

[8] David Beckworth, "Measuring Monetary Policy: The NGDP Gap," Monetary Policy Data Visualizations, Mercatus Center at George Mason University, Arlington, VA, August 15, 2023.

[9] The model is a vector autoregression, where the NGDP gap, the NGDP gap squared, cyclical core PCE inflation, and acyclical core PCE inflation are included as endogenous variables. The model is estimated with quarterly data, uses five lags, and runs the sample period of second quarter 1996 to first quarter 2023. A dynamic counterfactual forecast is created by setting the NGDP gap and the NGDP gap squared to zero starting in second quarter 2021 and staying at that value through first quarter 2023.

Chapter 5: World War II Price Controls

[1] Meg Jacobs and Isabella M. Weber, "The Way to Fight Inflation without Rising Interest Rates and a Recession," *Washington Post*, August 9, 2022.

[2] Stephen D. King, *We Need to Talk about Inflation: 14 Urgent Lessons from the Last 2,000 Years* (New Haven, CT: Yale University Press, 2023), p. 115.

[3] Hugh Rockoff, "Price and Wage Controls in Four Wartime Periods," *Journal of Economic History* 41, no. 2 (1981): 381–401.

[4] Stephen B. Reed, "One Hundred Years of Price Change: The Consumer Price Index and the American Inflation Experience," *Monthly Labor Review*, Bureau of Labor Statistics, April 2014.

[5] Milton Friedman and Anna J. Schwartz, *Monetary Trends in the United States and United Kingdom: Their Relation to Income, Prices, and Interest Rates, 1867–1975* (Chicago: University of Chicago Press, 1982), p. 101.

[6] Friedman and Schwartz, *Monetary Trends in the United States and United Kingdom.*

[7] Bureau of Labor Statistics, *The General Maximum Price Regulation* (Washington: Department of Labor, 1946).

[8] Greg Rosalsky, "Price Controls, Black Markets, and Skimpflation: The WWII Battle against Inflation," National Public Radio, February 8, 2022.

[9] "Consumers' Prices in the United States, 1942–48: Analysis of Changes in Cost of Living," *Bulletin of the United States Bureau of Labor Statistics*, no. 966," December 15, 1949.

[10] Steven Horwitz and Michael J. McPhillips, "The Reality of the Wartime Economy: More Historical Evidence on Whether World War II Ended the Great Depression," *Independent Review* 17, no. 3 (2013): 325–47.

[11] Reed, "One Hundred Years of Price Change."

[12] Bureau of Labor Statistics, " *General Maximum Price Regulation.*

[13] Geofrey Mills and Hugh Rockoff, "Compliance with Price Controls in the United States and the United Kingdom during World War II," *Journal of Economic History* 47, no. 1 (1987): 197–213.

[14] Hugh Rockoff, "Price and Wage Controls in Four Wartime Periods," *Journal of Economic History* 41, no. 2 (1981): 381–401.

[15] Meg Jacobs, "How About Some Meat?: The Office of Price Administration, Consumption Politics, and State Building from the Bottom Up, 1941–1946," *Journal of American History* 84, no. 3 (1997): 910–41.

[16] Grover J. Sims, *Meat and Meat Animals in World War Two* (Washington: Bureau of Agricultural Economics, U.S. Department of Agriculture, 1951).

[17] Robert Higgs, "Wartime Prosperity? A Reassessment of the U.S. Economy in the 1940s," Independent Institute, Washington, March 1, 1992.

[18] "Inflation, Market Power, and Price Controls," Clark Center Forum, January 11, 2022.

Chapter 6: Modern Monetary Theory

[1] Eliza Relman, "Alexandria Ocasio-Cortez Says the Theory That Deficit Spending Is Good for the Economy Should 'Absolutely' Be Part of the Conversation," Insider, January 7, 2019.

[2] Stephanie Kelton, *The Deficit Myth: Modern Monetary Theory and the Birth of the People's Economy* (New York: PublicAffairs, 2020).

[3] Stephanie Kelton, "Learn to Love Trillion-Dollar Deficits," *New York Times,* June 9, 2020.

[4] "COVID-19 Relief: Funding and Spending as of Jan. 31, 2023," Government Accountability Office, February 28, 2023.

[5] "Modern Monetary Theory," Clark Center Forum, March 13, 2019.

[6] Neil Irwin, "The Clash of Liberal Wonks That Could Shape the Economy, Explained," *New York Times*, February 8, 2021.

[7] J. W. Mason, "The American Rescue Plan as Economic Theory," *Slackwire* (blog), March 15, 2021.

[8] David Beckworth, "Nathan Tankus on the Future of MMT and How to Avoid U.S. Debt Default," interview with Nathan Tankus, Macro Musings podcast, May 8, 2023.

[9] Scott Fullwiler, Rohan Grey, and Nathan Tankus, "An MMT Response on What Causes Inflation," *Financial Times*, March 1, 2019.

[10] Mason, "American Rescue Plan as Economic Theory."

[11] Matthew C. Klein, "Understanding COVID-Flation," *The Overshoot* (blog), January 19, 2022.

[12] BLS, "Consumer Price Index for All Urban Consumers: All Items Less Food and Energy in U.S. City Average [CPILFESL]," Federal Reserve Bank of St. Louis.

Part 2: Prices and Price Controls

[1] Ben Casselman and Jeanna Smialek, "Price Controls Set Off Heated Debate as History Gets a Second Look," *New York Times*, January 13, 2022.

[2] Robert L. Schuettinger and Eamonn F. Butler, *Forty Centuries of Wage and Price Controls: How Not to Fight Inflation* (Washington: Heritage Foundation, 1979).

[3] Sascha Becker, Lukas Mergele, and Ludger Woessmann, "The Separation and Reunification of Germany: Rethinking a Natural Experiment Interpretation of the Enduring Effects of Communism," *Journal of Economic Perspectives* 34, no. 2 (2020): 143–71.

[4] Alex Tabarrok, "A Price Is a Signal Wrapped Up in an Incentive," *Marginal Revolution* (blog), February 10, 2015.

[5] Hugh Rockoff, "Price Controls," *Concise Encyclopedia of Economics* (Carmel, IN: Econlib, 2002).

[6] "Inflation, Market Power, and Price Controls," Clark Center Forum, January 11, 2022.

[7] "Inflation, Market Power, and Price Controls."

[8] "Rent Control," Clark Center Forum, February 7, 2012; "Price Gouging," Clark Center Forum, May 2, 2012; "Price Gouging," Clark Center Forum, June 7, 2022.

Chapter 7: Price Controls throughout History

[1] Robert L. Schuettinger and Eamonn F. Butler, *Forty Centuries of Wage and Price Controls* (Washington: Heritage Foundation, 1979).

[2] Meg Jacobs and Isabella M. Weber, "The Way to Fight Inflation without Rising Interest Rates and a Recession," *Washington Post*, August 9, 2022.

[3] Todd N. Tucker, "Price Controls: How the US Has Used Them and How They Can Help Shape Industries," Roosevelt Institute, New York, November 16, 2021.

[4] Mary G. Lacy, "Food Control during Forty-Six Centuries," *Scientific Monthly* 16, no. 6 (1923), reprinted by the Foundation for Economic Education, Irvington-on-Hudson, NY, pp. 3–4; and Jean-Philippe Levy, *The Economic Life of the Ancient World* (Chicago: University of Chicago, 1967), pp. 40–42.

[5] Antony Fisher, *Must History Repeat Itself?* (New York: Transatlantic Arts, 1974).

[6] Samuel Noah Kramer, *The Sumerians: Their History, Culture, and Character* (Chicago: University of Chicago, 1963), p. 79.

[7] Chilperic Edwards, *The Hammurabi Code and the Sinaitic Legislation* (Port Washington, NY: Kennikat Press, 1904), pp. 69–72.

[8] W. F. Leemans, *The Old Babylonian Merchant: His Business and His Social Position* (Leiden, Neth.: E. F. Brill, 1950), p. 122.

[9] Huan-Chang Chen, *The Economic Principles of Confucius and His School* (New York: Longmans, 1968), pp. 168, 174.

[10] *Kautilya's* Arthaśāstra (Mysore, India: Wesleyan Mission Press, 1923), pp. 148, 249, 252.

[11] Aristotle, *The Constitution of Athens,* 51.3; M. I. Finley, *The Ancient Economy* (London: Chatto & Windus, 1973), p. 170; and Lysias, "Against the Grain Dealers," in *Eight Orations of Lysias,* edited by Morris H. Morgan (Boston: Ginn & Co., 1895), pp. 89–103.

[12] Jean-Philippe Lévy, *The Economic Life of the Ancient World* (Chicago: University of Chicago Press, 1967), p. 55.

[13] Lévy, *Economic Life of the Ancient World,* p. 55.

[14] Lévy, *Economic Life of the Ancient World,* p. 69.

[15] Lévy, *Economic Life of the Ancient World,* p. 55.

[16] H. Michell, "The Edict of Diocletian: A Study of Price-Fixing in the Roman Empire," *Canadian Journal of Economics and Political Science* 13, no. 1 (February 1947): 1–12.

[17] Frank F. Abbott, *The Common People of Ancient Rome:Studies of Roman Life and Literature* (New York: Scribner, 1911), pp. 150–51.

[18] L. C. F. Lactantius, *A Relation of the Death of the Primitive Persecutors,* translated by Gilbert Burnet (Amsterdam, 1697), pp. 67–68.

[19] Samuel Brittan and Peter Lilley, *The Delusion of Incomes Policy* (London: Temple Smith, 1977), p. 74.

[20] W. J. Ashley, *An Introduction to English Economic History and Theory,* vol. 1, part 1 (London: Longmans, 1923–1925), p. 181.

[21] Simon Litman, *Prices and Price Control in Great Britain and the United States during the Word War* (New York: Oxford University Press, 1920), p. 6.

[22] Ashley, *English Economic History and Theory,* p. 191.

[23] Antony Fisher, *Must History Repeat Itself?* (London: Churchill Press, 1974).

[24] Arthur Bryant, *The Fire and the Rose* (New York: Doubleday, 1966), p. 61.

[25] R. H. Inglis Palgrave, ed., *Dictionary of Political Economy* (London: Macmillan & Co.: 1894), p. 431.

[26] Palgrave, *Dictionary of Political Economy,* p. 431.

[27] Ashley, *English Economic History and Theory,* p. 30.

[28] William Holdsworth, *A History of English Law,* vol. 2 (London: Methuen, 1922–1926), p. 377.

[29] John Fiske, *The Unseen World and Other Essays* (Boston and New York: Houghton, Mifflin, 1904).

[30] William Wilson Hunter, *Annals of Rural Bengal* (London: Smith, Elder, 1897), p. 7.

[31] William Weeden, *Economic and Social History of New England, 1620–1789,* vol. 1 (New York, 1890), p. 99; and John Winthrop, *The History of New England from 1630–1649,* vol. 1 (Boston, 1925, and New York: Arno Press, 1972), p. 116.

[32] Weeden, *History of New England, 1620–1789,* p. 99.

[33] Quoted in Alan Reynolds, "A History Lesson on Inflation," *First National Bank of Chicago World Report*, July 1976.

[34] Anne Bezanson, *Prices and Inflation during the American Revolution* (Philadelphia: University of Pennsylvania Press, 1951), p. 35.

[35] Connecticut, *Public Records of the State*, vol. 1 (Hartford, 1894), pp. 62, 366.

[36] Bezanson, *Prices and Inflation*.

[37] Bezanson, *Prices and Inflation*.

[38] *Journal of the Continental Congress*, vol. 21 (New York, 1908).

[39] Charles Francis Adams, *Familiar Letters of John Adams and His Wife Abigail Adams, during the Revolution* (New York: Hurd & Houghton, 1876), p. 307.

[40] "Mémoire sur le Commerce de l'isle Royale Joint à la Lettre de Monsieur Prévost," Canadian Archives, CIIB, XXXIII, p. 124.

[41] Litman, *Prices and Price Control during the World War*, p. 6.

[42] Henry Bourne, "Food Control and Price-Fixing in Revolutionary France," *Journal of Political Economy* 27, no. 3 (February 1919): 188–209.

[43] William Ball Sutch, *Price Fixing in New Zealand* (New York: Columbia University Press, 1932), p. 130; Chapter 6 passim.

[44] *Final Report of the Royal Commission on the Sugar Supply* (London: Her Majesty's Stationery Office, 1921).

[45] Wendy Wilson, "A Short History of Rent Control," House of Commons Briefing Paper no. 6747, March 30, 2017.

[46] James L. Sweeney, *The California Electricity Crisis* (Stanford, CA: Hoover Institution Press, 2002). "The California Crisis Timeline," PBS; Alex Tabarrok, "Price Caps on Electricity Are a Good Idea?," Foundation for Economic Education, New York, October 1, 2001.

[47] Tomas J. Philipson and Troy Durie, "The Evidence Base on the Impact of Price Controls on Medical Innovation," Becker Friedman Institute Working Paper no. 2021-108, September 2021.

Chapter 8: Under Rent Controls, Everyone Pays

[1] Jim Lapides and Lisa Blackwell, "Senator Bernie Sanders Proposes National Rent Control Plan," National Multifamily Housing Council, Washington, September 23, 2019.

[2] Roshnan Abraham, "Economists Support Nationwide Rent Control in Letter to Biden Admin," *Vox*, August 3, 2023.

[3] Elliot Njus, "How Does Oregon's First-in-the-Nation Rent Control Law Work? A Quick Guide," OregonLive, September 25, 2019.

[4] City of San Francisco, "The California Tenant Protection Act of 2019 (AB 1482)," SF.gov, August 25, 2023.

[5] Jeff Shaw, "Rent Control Measures High on Priority List for State Legislatures in 2023," REBusinessOnline, 2023.

[6] One of us (Miron) served as a paid consultant to the campaign that banned rent controls in Massachusetts in 1994.

[7] Kenneth R. Ahern and Marco Giacoletti, "Robbing Peter to Pay Paul? The Redistribution of Wealth Caused by Rent Control," National Bureau of Economic Research Working Paper no. 30083, May 2022.

[8] Anthony Downs, *Residential Rent Control: An Evaluation* (Washington: Urban Land Institute, 1988).

[9] Prasanna Rajasekaran, Mark Treskon, and Solomon Greene, "Rent Control: What Does the Research Tell Us about the Effectiveness of Local Action?," Urban Institute, Washington, January 2019.

[10] "Rent Control," Clark Center Forum, February 7, 2012.

[11] This need not be true in every case since it is possible that regulations are not "binding," in the sense that they allow for prices that are at least as high as the ones that prevail under a free market.

[12] David H. Autor, Christopher J. Palmer, and Parag A. Pathak, "Housing Market Spillovers: Evidence from the End of Rent Control in Cambridge, Massachusetts," *Journal of Political Economy* 122, no. 3 (2014): 661–717.

[13] Joan Monràs and José García Montalvo, "The Effect of Second Generation Rent Controls: New Evidence from Catalonia," Universitat Pompeu Fabra, Department of Economics and Business Working Paper no. 1836, April 2022.

[14] Katie Mather, "TikToker Shares 'Secret' behind How She Got Her Two-Bedroom Apartment in NYC," In the Know, March 2, 2021.

[15] "How Long Does It Take?," Bostadsförmedlingen i Stockholm AB, April 20, 2023.

[16] Rebecca Diamond, Tim McQuade, and Franklin Qian, "The Effects of Rent Control Expansion on Tenants, Landlords, and Inequality: Evidence from San Francisco," *American Economic Review* 109, no. 9 (September 2019): 3365–94.

[17] David P. Sims, "Out of Control: What Can We Learn from the End of Massachusetts Rent Control?," *Journal of Urban Economics* 61, no. 1 (January 2007): 129–51.

[18] Bill Lindeke, "In First Months since Passage of St. Paul's Rent-Control Ordinance, Housing Construction Is Way Down," *MinnPost*, March 10, 2022. Data are from the U.S. Department of Housing and Urban Development (multifamily building permits for Minneapolis and Saint Paul, November–January 2020 versus 2021).

[19] Katie Galioto, "Divided St. Paul City Council Exempts Some Units from Rent Increase Cap," *Star Tribune*, September 22, 2022.

[20] These are often referred to as "second-generation" rent controls.

[21] John F. McDonald and Daniel P. McMillen, *Urban Economics and Real Estate: Theory and Policy* (Hoboken, NJ: Wiley, 2010). An important assumption for this to happen is that access to rent-controlled units does not align perfectly with willingness to pay. At least some of the tenants who get the controlled apartments value them less than individuals who did not get them. In other words, it must be that rent controls introduce misallocation. If access correlated perfectly with willingness to pay, the prices in the unregulated market would not change.

[22] It is important to keep in mind that such new housing is not a benefit, but a cost from the policy.

[23] Andreas Mense, Claus Michelsen, and Konstantin A. Kholodilin, "The Effects of Second-Generation Rent Control on Land Values," *AEA Papers and Proceedings* 109 (May 2019): 385–88.

[24] Pekka Sagner and Michael Voigtländer, "Supply Side Effects of the Berlin Rent Freeze," *International Journal of Housing Policy* 82 (May 2022): 1–20.

[25] David Meyer, "Germany's Top Court Ends Berlin's Rent-Freeze Experiment," *Fortune*, April 15, 2021.

26 Ken Auletta, *The Streets Were Paved with Gold* (New York: Random House, 1979).

27 Lawrence Crook, "An Actress Lived for Decades in This New York City Apartment—for $28 a Month," CNN, May 15, 2018.

28 Edward L. Glaeser and Erzo F. P. Luttmer, "The Misallocation of Housing under Rent Control," *American Economic Review* 93, no. 4 (September 2003): 1027–46.

29 Diamond, McQuade, and Qian, "Effects of Rent Control Expansion."

30 Joseph Gyourko and Peter Linneman, "Rent Controls and Rental Housing Quality: A Note on the Effects of New York City's Old Controls," *Journal of Urban Economics* 27, no. 3 (1990): 398–409; Hans Skifter Andersen, "Motives for Investments in Housing Rehabilitation among Private Landlords under Rent Control," *Housing Studies* 13, no. 2 (1998): 177–94; and Nandinee K. Kutty, "The Impact of Rent Control on Housing Maintenance: A Dynamic Analysis Incorporating European and North American Rent Regulations," *Housing Studies* 11, no. 1 (1996): 69–88.

31 Autor, Palmer, and Pathak, "Housing Market Spillovers," 661–717.

32 Autor, Palmer, and Pathak, "Housing Market Spillovers," 661–717.

33 Ahern and Giacoletti, "Robbing Peter to Pay Paul?"

34 Cities include San Francisco, Los Angeles, and Washington, DC.

35 Alexa Phillips, "SNP closes rent control loophole," *The Telegraph*, October 31, 2023.

36 Ahern and Giacoletti, "Robbing Peter to Pay Paul?"

37 Diamond, McQuade, and Qian, "Effects of Rent Control Expansion."

38 Beacon Economics, *The Economic Impact of Rent Control in Berkeley* (Sacramento: California Apartment Association, 2016).

39 Kate Pennington, "Does Building New Housing Cause Displacement?: The Supply and Demand Effects of Construction in San Francisco," *Urban Economics and Region Studies eJournal* (June 2021); Vicki Been, Ingrid Gould Ellen, and Katherine O'Regan, "Supply Skepticism: Housing Supply and Affordability," *Housing Policy Debate* 29, no. 1 (2019): 25–40; and Evan Mast, "JUE Insight: The Effect of New Market-Rate Housing Construction on the Low-Income Housing Market," *Journal of Urban Economics* 133, no. 8 (2021): 103–383.

Chapter 9: Oil and Natural Gas Price Controls

1 B. Ravikumar and Iris Arbogast, "Long-Term Trends in Gasoline Prices," Federal Reserve Bank of St. Louis *Economic Synopses* no. 14, June 1, 2022.

2 Consumer Fuel Price Gouging Prevention Act, H.R. 7688, 117th Cong., 2nd sess., May 6, 2022.

3 After Hurricane Katrina reduced oil production in the Gulf of Mexico, the Republican-controlled House passed anti-price-gouging legislation in October 2005, the Gasoline for America's Security Act of 2005. The bill gave the Federal Trade Commission the power to define "price gouging" and empowered the agency to impose fines of $11,000 a day on companies found to be gouging the public. The bill got 57 votes in the Senate but failed to get the 60 required to overcome the filibuster. Jerry Taylor and Peter Van Doren, "Economic Amnesia: The Case against Oil Price Controls and Windfall Profit Taxes," Cato Institute Policy Analysis no. 561, January 12, 2006. Although the bill did not pass, the Federal Trade Commission

did issue a report in 2006 that concluded market forces were responsible. See Stephen Labaton, "Gas Prices Legitimate, Study Says," *New York Times*, May 23, 2006.

[4] Joseph P. Kalt, *Economics and Politics of Oil Price Regulation: Federal Policy in the Post-Embargo Era* (Cambridge, MA: MIT Press, 1981).

[5] Kalt, *Economics and Politics of Oil Price Regulation*, pp. 10, 42–44.

[6] Peter M. Van Doren, *Politics, Markets, and Congressional Policy Choices* (Ann Arbor: University of Michigan Press, 1991).

[7] Kalt, *Economics and Politics of Oil Price Regulation*, pp. 9–23, 26–31.

[8] Kalt, *Economics and Politics of Oil Price Regulation*, p. 10.

[9] Arab states have made three attempts to target embargoes against certain Western states: 1956 (targeted at Britain and France, in response to the Suez Canal crisis), 1967 (targeted against Britain, the United States, and West Germany, in response to support for Israel during the Six-Day War), and 1973 (targeted against the Netherlands and the United States, during the Yom Kippur War). All failed to reduce imports into the targeted countries. For a political and economic history of those embargo episodes, see A. F. Alhajji, "Three Decades after the Oil Embargo: Was 1973 Unique?," *Journal of Energy and Development* 30, no. 2 (2005), pp. 1–16.

[10] Thomas Lee, Ben Ball Jr., and Richard Tabors, *Energy Aftermath* (Boston: Harvard Business School Press, 1990), p. 17.

[11] Kalt, *Economics and Politics of Oil Price Regulation*, pp. 12, 18. The definition of "old" oil was quite complicated. Output from a domestic property in each month of 1972 was defined as that property's base period control level (BPCL) for that month. If a property had once produced more than its BPCL, the amount by which production in any subsequent month fell short of the BPCL was added into a property's current cumulative deficiency (CCD). Output in any month less than or equal to the sum of the BPCL and the CCD was defined as "old oil."

[12] Kalt, *Economics and Politics of Oil Price Regulation*, p. 12. Output greater than the sum of a property's BPCL and CCD, or from properties not producing in 1972, was defined as "new oil." Each barrel of new oil brought to market allowed a producer to release a barrel from its old oil classification.

[13] Kalt, *Economics and Politics of Oil Price Regulation*, p. 286.

[14] Kalt, *Economics and Politics of Oil Price Regulation*, p. 14.

[15] Kalt, *Economics and Politics of Oil Price Regulation*, p. 15.

[16] Kalt, *Economics and Politics of Oil Price Regulation*, pp. 15–17.

[17] Under the Energy Policy and Conservation Act, the BPCL for a property in any month was defined as the lesser of average monthly output of "old" oil in 1975 and the average monthly output of all oil in 1972. "Lower-tier oil" was defined as output not in excess of that property's BPCL plus CCD. "Upper-tier oil" was defined as production from pre-1976 properties in excess of the associated lower-tier output and production from properties that began producing after 1975. Lower-tier oil sold at its May 15, 1973, price plus inflation and incentive adjustment factors determined by the U.S. Department of Energy. Upper-tier oil sold at its September 30, 1975, price less $1.32 plus inflation and incentive adjustment factors. Alaskan North Slope crude oil was treated as upper-tier crude for regulatory purposes. Crude from the federal Naval Petroleum Reserves and incremental production from tertiary oil recovery projects were not controlled. The oil release program (established as part

of the EPAA)—under which not only increases in production above base period 1972 levels would be free of price controls, but an equivalent amount of old oil would be released from controls—was repealed.

[18] Kalt, *Economics and Politics of Oil Price Regulation*, p. 17.

[19] Kalt, *Economics and Politics of Oil Price Regulation*, p. 17.

[20] Kalt, *Economics and Politics of Oil Price Regulation*, p. 18; Energy Information Administration, *Annual Energy Review 2004*, (Washington: Department of Energy, 2005), Table 5.21, p. 173.

[21] Kalt, *Economics and Politics of Oil Price Regulation*, p. 233, $14–$50 billion in 1980 dollars; PCE deflator 2023 Q1/1980 = 3.06.

[22] Kalt, *Economics and Politics of Oil Price Regulation*, p. 288.

[23] Kalt, *Economics and Politics of Oil Price Regulation*, p. 287.

[24] Kalt, *Economics and Politics of Oil Price Regulation*, pp. 233–34.

[25] Rodney T. Smith, "In Search of the 'Just' U.S. Oil Policy: A Review of Arrow and Kalt and More," *Journal of Business* 54, no. 1 (1981): 87–116.

[26] Robert Rogers, "The Effect of the Energy Policy and Conservation Act (EPCA) Regulation on Petroleum Product Prices, 1976–1981," *Energy Journal* 24, no. 2 (2003): 63–94.

[27] This section draws on Peter M. Van Doren, *Politics, Markets, and Congressional Policy Choices* (Ann Arbor: University of Michigan Press, 1991), pp. 56–59.

[28] Van Doren, *Politics, Markets, and Congressional Policy Choices*.

[29] Van Doren, *Politics, Markets, and Congressional Policy Choices*.

[30] Van Doren, *Politics, Markets, and Congressional Policy Choices*.

[31] Van Doren, *Politics, Markets, and Congressional Policy Choices*.

Chapter 10: Interest Rate Caps

[1] For example, in 2021, the Veterans and Consumers Fair Credit Act was introduced in the Senate to expand the Military Lending Act to restrict all American consumers (service members, veterans, and citizens alike) from having access to loans with interest rates above 36 percent. Senate Committee on Banking, Housing, and Urban Affairs, "U.S. Senators Seek to Cap Consumer Loans at 36%," Majority news release, July 28, 2021; S. 2508, Veterans and Consumers Fair Credit Act, 117th Congress, 1st sess., July 28, 2021; Diego Zuluaga, "AOC and Sanders' Credit Card Interest Rate Cap Would Be Disastrous," CNN, May 13, 2019; and Thomas W. Miller Jr. and Todd Zywicki, "The Wrong Kicks on Route 36," *RealClearPolicy*, January 8, 2020.

[2] "Durbin, Senators Introduce Bill to Protect Consumers from Shady, High Cost Lending," Dick Durbin news release, July 14, 2021.

[3] 2022 Arizona Revised Statutes, Title 6, Chapter 5, Article 2, Section 6-632(A); 2020 Arkansas Code, Title 4, Subtitle 5, Chapter 57, Section 4-57-104; Arkansas Constitution Amendment 89, Section 7; 2022 Colorado Code, Title 5, Article 2, Part 2, Section 5-2-201; 2022 Connecticut General Statutes, Title 37, Chapter 673, Section 37-4; 2022 Connecticut General Statutes, Title 21, Chapter 409, Section 21-44; 2022 District of Columbia Code, Title 28, Chapter 33, Section 28–3301; 2022 Florida Statutes, Title 33, Chapter 516,

Section 516.031; 2022 Georgia Code, Title 7, Chapter 3, Article 2, Section 7-3-11 and Chapter 4, Section 7-4-2; 2022 Georgia Code, Title 7, Chapter 4, Article 1, Section 7-4-2; 2022 Illinois Compiled Statutes, Chapter 815, Payday Loan Reform Act, Article 2, Section 2-5(2-5); 2022 Indiana Code, Title 24, Article 4.5, Chapter 7, Section 201; 2022 Maryland Statues, Title 12, Subtitle 1, Sections 12-102, 12-103, and 12-104; 2022 Massachusetts General Laws, Part 1, Title 20, Chapter 140, Section 96; 2022 Montana Code, Title 31, Chapter 1, Part 1, Section 31-1-106; 2022 Montana Code, Title 31, Chapter 1, Part 1, Section 31-1-107; 2022 Nebraska Revised Statutes, Chapter 45, Section 45-918; 2022 New Hampshire Revised Statutes, Title 36, Title 399-A, Section 399-A:17; 2022 New Hampshire Revised Statutes, Title 31, Title 336, Section 336:1; 2022 New Hampshire Revised Statutes, Title 36, Title 398, Section 398:11; 2022 New Jersey Revised Statutes, Title 31, Section 31:1-1; Office of the Governor Michelle Lujan Grisham, "Governor Caps Interest Rates on Storefront Loans," Press Releases, March 1, 2023; 2022 New York Laws, PEN, Part 3, Title K, Article 190, Section 190.40; 2022 North Carolina General Statutes, Chapter 53, Article 15, Section 53-176; 2022 Pennsylvania Consolidated Statutes, Title 41, Article 2, Section 201; 2022 South Dakota Codified Laws, Title 54, Chapter 4, Section 54-4-44; 2022 Vermont Statutes, Title 9, Chapter 4, Section 41a; and 2022 West Virginia Code, Chapter 46A, Article 4, Section 46A-4-107.

[4] Senate Committee on Banking, Housing, and Urban Affairs, "U.S. Senators Seek to Cap Consumer Loans at 36%"; "Whitehouse, Warren, Merkley, Reed Introduce Bill to Protect Consumers from Runaway Credit Card Rates," Sheldon Whitehouse news release, April 4, 2019.

[5] "Protecting Americans from Debt Traps by Extending the Military's 36% Interest Rate Cap to Everyone," Hearing before the Senate Committee on Banking, Housing, and Urban Affairs, 117th Cong., 1st sess., July 29, 2021.

[6] 815 ILCS 123, "Predatory Loan Prevention Act"; S. 1230, Protecting Consumers from Unreasonable Credit Rates Act of 2019, 116th Congress, 1st sess., April 29, 2019; H.R. 2930, "Loan Shark Prevention Act," 116th Congress, 1st sess., May 22, 2019.

[7] Bernie Sanders, "Credit Card Interest Rates Are Outrageously High. With @RepAOC, we are introducing legislation to challenge the greed of Wall Street and protect consumers across America," @SenSanders.

[8] Christopher Coyne and Rachel Coyne, *Flaws & Ceilings: Price Controls & the Damage They Cause* (London: Institute of Economic Affairs, 2015).

[9] Diego Zuluaga, "Financial Inclusion without Finance? The Misguided Quest to Limit Choice in Consumer Credit," Cato Institute, October 21, 2019.

[10] Ryan Bourne and Sofia Hamilton, "The Rent Control Bandwagon Rolls On," *Cato at Liberty* (blog), December 9, 2022.

[11] Norbert Michel, "Interest-Rate Caps—Like Other Price Controls—Harm Consumers," Heritage Foundation Issue Brief no. 5205, July 27, 2021.

[12] Paul A. Samuelson, Statement on the "Uniform Consumer Credit Code," *Hearings before the Subcommittee on Consumer Affairs of the Committee on Banking and Currency* (Washington: Government Printing Office, 1969), p. 164.

[13] Claire Kramer Mills et al., "The State of Low-Income America: Credit Access & Debt Payment," Federal Reserve Bank of New York, March 2022; and Rachael Beer, Felicia Ionescu, and Geng Li, "Are Income and Credit Scores Highly Correlated?," FEDS Notes, August 13, 2018.

[14] J. Brandon Bolen, Gregory Elliehausen, and Thomas Miller, "Effects of Illinois' 36% Interest Rate Cap on Small-Dollar Credit Availability and Financial Well-Being," Social Science Research Network, January 2, 2023.

[15] Charla Rios, Diane Standaert, and Yasmin Farahi, *The Sky Doesn't Fall: Life after Payday Lending in South Dakota* (Durham, NC: Center for Responsible Lending, 2020).

[16] Onyumbe Enumbe Ben Lukongo and Thomas W. Miller Jr., "Adverse Consequences of the Binding Constitutional Interest Rate Cap in the State of Arkansas," Mercatus Center at George Mason University, Arlington, VA, October 12, 2017; and Thomas Durkin, Gregory Elliehausen, and Min Hwang, "Rate Ceilings and the Distribution of Small Dollar Loans from Consumer Finance Companies: Results of a New Survey of Small Dollar Cash Lenders," Social Science Research Network, December 2, 2014.

[17] Donald P. Morgan and Michael R. Strain, "Payday Holiday: How Households Fare after Payday Credit Bans," Federal Reserve Bank of New York Staff Report no. 309, February 2008.

[18] Bill Skimmyhorn and Susan Carter, "Much Ado about Nothing? New Evidence on the Effects of Payday Lending on Military Members," *Review of Economics and Statistics* 99, no. 4 (2017): 606–21.

[19] Skimmyhorn and Carter, "Much Ado about Nothing?"

[20] Miller and Zywicki, "Wrong Kicks on Route 36."

[21] Aurora Ferrari, Oliver Masetti, and Jiemin Ren, "Interest Rate Caps: The Theory and the Practice," Word Bank Policy Research Working Paper no. 8398, April 2018.

[22] Dyna Heng, Serey Chea, and Bomakara Heng, "Impacts of Interest Rate Cap on Financial Inclusion in Cambodia," International Monetary Fund Working Paper no. 2021/107, April 29, 2021, p. 1.

[23] Anita Campion, Rashmi Kiran Ekka, and Mark Wenner, "Interest Rates and Implications for Microfinance in Latin America and the Caribbean," Inter-American Development Bank Working Paper no. IDB-WP-177, 2010.

[24] Zuluaga, "Financial Inclusion without Finance?"

[25] F. A. Hayek, "The Use of Knowledge in Society," *American Economic Review*, 1945.

[26] Senate Committee on Banking, Housing, and Urban Affairs, "U.S. Senators Seek to Cap Consumer Loans at 36%."

[27] Department of Defense, "Report on the Military Lending Act and the Effects of High Interest Rates on Readiness," May 2021, p. 3.

[28] Federal Deposit Insurance Corporation, "2021 FDIC National Survey of Unbanked and Underbanked Households," November 14, 2022.

[29] For example, 61 percent of U.S. consumers reported in 2022 that they live paycheck to paycheck, and an estimated 30 percent of Americans had subprime credit in 2021. "Report: 36% of Consumers Earning $250K+ Now Live Paycheck-to-Paycheck," PYMNTS, June 1, 2022; Stefan Lembo Stolba, "Fewer

Subprime Consumers across U.S. in 2021," Experian, June 7, 2021; Kenneth P. Brevoort, Philipp Grimm, and Michelle Kambara, "Data Point: Credit Invisibles," Consumer Finance Protection Bureau, May 2015; and Ivana Pino, "What Is a Payday Loan? What You Might Use One for and When to Avoid Them," *Fortune*, December 7, 2022.

[30] Chris Arnold, "A Ban on High-Cost Loans May Be Coming," National Public Radio, November 7, 2019.

[31] For example, Senator Jack Reed (D-RI) said, "There is no reason consumers should be charged a 300 percent APR to access credit." Senate Committee on Banking, Housing, and Urban Affairs, "U.S. Senators Seek to Cap Consumer Loans at 36%."

[32] In 2021, the average daily rate at U.S. hotels was $125: "Average Daily Rate of Hotels in the United States from 2001 to 2021," Statista, July 26, 2022; Thomas Sowell, "Payday Loans," *National Review*, November 2, 2011; and John Berlau, "The 400 Percent Loan, the $36,000 Hotel Room, and the Unicorn," Competitive Enterprise Institute OnPoint no. 176, February 6, 2011.

[33] Norbert Michel, "Payday Loans Are No Worse Than Avocado Toast," *Forbes*, February 11, 2019.

[34] Zuluaga, "Credit Card Interest Rate Cap Would Be Disastrous."

[35] An estimated 30 percent of Americans had subprime credit in 2021. Stolba, "Fewer Subprime Consumers"; Brevoort, Grimm, and Kambara, "Credit Invisibles."

[36] 12 CFR § 345.12(u)(1); Board of Governors of the Federal Reserve System, "Survey of Consumer Finances, 1989–2019," table: "Transaction Accounts by Percentile of Income," November 2021.

[37] LexisNexis, "True Costs of Financial Crime Compliance Study," 2022; Paul Calem, "Costs and Pricing of Bank-Provided Small Dollar Loans," Bank Policy Institute, Washington, December 15, 2020; Thomas W. Miller Jr., "Interest Rate Caps Harm Consumers," *The Hill*, February 6, 2020; and "The Cost of Providing Payday Loans in a US Multiline Operator Environment," Ernst & Young, September 2009.

[38] LexisNexis, "True Costs of Financial Crime Compliance Study"; and Norbert Michel and Jennifer J. Schulp, "Revising the Bank Secrecy Act to Protect Privacy and Deter Criminals," Cato Institute Policy Analysis no. 932, July 26, 2022.

[39] Norbert Michel, "Price Controls Do Not Work—Even in Credit Markets," *Forbes*, July 27, 2021.

[40] 15 USC § 1693o-2; 12 CFR § 1026.52.

Chapter 11: Abolishing "Junk Fees"

[1] White House, "Remarks by President Biden at the Third Meeting of the White House Competition Council," September 26, 2022.

[2] Brian Deese, Neale Mahoney, and Tim Wu, "The President's Initiative on Junk Fees and Related Pricing Practices," White House, October 26, 2022.

[3] Deese, Mahoney, and Wu, "President's Initiative on Junk Fees."

[4] Junk Fee Prevention Act, S. 916, 118th Cong., 1st sess., March 22, 2023.

[5] Deese, Mahoney, and Wu, "President's Initiative on Junk Fees."

[6] "Service Annual Survey Tables," Census Bureau, last revised November 22, 2022; and Deese, Mahoney, and Wu, "President's Initiative on Junk Fees."

[7] Deese, Mahoney, and Wu, "President's Initiative on Junk Fees."

[8] Bailey Miller, "Some Restaurants Are Adding Surcharge to Bills as a Result of Minimum Wage Increase," Fox10 Phoenix, January 7, 2020.

[9] AT&T, "Understand Early Termination Fees," Support, December 7, 2022; Thurschild74, "Service Commitment," AT&T Community Forums, January 4, 2018.

[10] Penelope Wang, "Protect Yourself from Hidden Fees," *Consumer Reports*, May 29, 2019.

[11] Wang, "Protect Yourself from Hidden Fees."

[12] Joanna Cohen et al., "Credit Card Late Fees," Consumer Financial Protection Bureau, Washington, March 2022.

[13] White House, "Remarks by President Biden."

[14] Ben Baldanza, "Six Useful Insights from the 'Airlines for America' Consumer Survey," *Forbes*, April 25, 2022.

[15] "USDOT Unveils Dashboard, Highlights Progress to Help Parents Avoid Family Seating Junk Fees, Department of Transportation news release, March 6, 2023.

[16] Mary W. Sullivan, "Economic Issues: Economic Analysis of Hotel Resort Fees," Bureau of Economics, Federal Trade Commission, Washington, January 2017.

[17] Junk Fee Prevention Act.

[18] Matthew Yglesias, "A Targeted Crackdown on 'Junk Fees' Makes a Lot of Sense," *Slow Boring* (blog), February 13, 2023; and American Hotel and Lodging Association, "Resort Fees."

[19] American Hotel and Lodging Association, "Resort Fees."

[20] Sullivan, "Economic Issues."

[21] Sullivan, "Economic Issues."

[22] James Mak, "Making Sense of Mandatory Resort Fees," Economic Research Organization at the University of Hawaii, Honolulu, April 10, 2018.

[23] Rule: 12A-1.061: Rentals, Leases, and Licenses to Use Transient Accommodations, Florida Administrative Code and Florida Administrative Register, Florida Department of State, May 9, 2013; "Transient Lodging Establishment Room Tax Instructions & Guidelines," Business License Division, City of Las Vegas, January 2021; "A Guide to Sales Tax for Hotel and Motel Operators," New York State Department of Taxation and Finance Publication no. 848; and "What Is the 'Bed Tax'?," Transient Occupancy Tax, County of Los Angeles Treasurer and Tax Collector.

[24] Xavier Gabaix and David Laibson, "Shrouded Attributes, Consumer Myopia, and Information Suppression in Competitive Markets," *Quarterly Journal of Economics* 121, no. 2 (May 2006): 505–40.

Chapter 12: Price Controls in Health Care

[1] "The Cost of Health Care: How to Make It Affordable," *The Economist* (film), December 1, 2022.

[2] Noam N. Levey, "Why Trump and Sanders Are Praising Healthcare in Other Countries," *Los Angeles Times*, February 29, 2016.

[3] All health insurance reduces consumer price sensitivity and therefore creates at least the potential for higher medical prices. As long as the benefits of risk protection outweigh the moral hazard costs of excessive prices and medical

consumption, health insurance is still economically efficient. Excessive coverage pushes medical prices and consumption beyond that point.

[4] Sherry Glied, "Reinhardt Lecture 2021: Health Care Prices as Signals," *Health Services Research* 56, no. 6 (September 2021): 1087–92.

[5] Anne B. Martin et al., "National Health Care Spending in 2021: Decline in Federal Spending Outweighs Greater Use of Health Care," *Health Affairs* 42, no. 1 (December 2022): 6–17.

[6] National Health Statistics Group, "Table 5: Out-of-Pocket Spending by Sex and Age Group, Calendar Years 2002, 2004, 2006, 2008, 2010, 2012, 2014, 2016, 2018, 2020," Office of the Actuary, U.S. Centers for Medicare and Medicaid Services.

[7] See Laurie McGinley and Sarah Lueck, "As the Medicare Chief Reins in Costs, Opposition Grows," *Wall Street Journal*, July 16, 2003; and Uwe E. Reinhardt, "The Medicare World from Both Sides: A Conversation with Tom Scully," *Health Affairs* 22, no. 6 (November/December 2003): 167–74.

[8] Michael F. Cannon and Jacqueline Pohida, "Would 'Medicare for All' Mean Quality for All? How Public-Option Principles Could Reverse Medicare's Negative Impact on Quality," *Quinnipiac Health Law Journal* 25, no. 2 (2022): 181–258.

[9] Government Accountability Office, "Medicare: Information on Geographic Adjustments to Physician Payments for Physicians' Time, Skills, and Effort," February 2022.

[10] Medicare Payment Advisory Commission, Payment Basics website.

[11] Jeannie Fuglesten Biniek et al., "Half of All Eligible Medicare Beneficiaries Are Now Enrolled in Private Medicare Advantage Plans," Kaiser Family Foundation, May 1, 2023.

[12] Elizabeth Hinton and MaryBeth Musumeci, "Medicaid Managed Care Rates and Flexibilities: State Options to Respond to COVID-19 Pandemic," Kaiser Family Foundation, September 9, 2020.

[13] Charles Silver and David A. Hyman, *Overcharged: Why Americans Pay Too Much for Health Care* (Washington: Cato Institute, 2018), pp. 180–81.

[14] Medicare Payment Advisory Commission, *Report to the Congress: Medicare Payment Policy* (Washington: MedPAC, 2020), p. 152.

[15] Silver and Hyman, *Overcharged*, pp. 180–81.

[16] Liran Einav, Amy Finkelstein, and Neale Mahoney, "Long-Term Care Hospitals: A Case Study in Waste," *Review of Economics and Statistics* 105, no. 4 (July 2023): 745–65.

[17] Medicare Payment Advisory Commission, *Report to the Congress: Medicare Payment Policy* (Washington: MedPAC, 2012), p. 74.

[18] Margot Sanger-Katz, "When Hospitals Buy Doctors' Offices, and Patient Fees Soar," *New York Times*, February 6, 2015; and Ames Alexander, Karen Garloch, and David Raynor, "As Doctors Flock to Hospitals, Bills Spike," *Charlotte Observer*, December 26, 2012.

[19] Federal Trade Commission and Department of Justice, *Improving Health Care: A Dose of Competition* (Washington: FTC and DOJ, 2004), pp. 24–25.

[20] Office of the Assistant Secretary for Planning and Evaluation, *Comparison of U.S. and International Prices for Top Medicare Part B Drugs by Total Expenditures* (Washington: U.S. Department of Health and Human Services, 2018).

[21] Tammy Worth, "Hospital Facility Fees: Why Cost May Give Independent Physicians an Edge," Medical Economics, August 6, 2014.

[22] Melanie Evans, "What Does Knee Surgery Cost? Few Know, and That's a Problem," *Wall Street Journal*, August 21, 2018.

[23] See U.S. Centers for Medicare and Medicaid Services, "Medicare Inpatient Hospitals—by Geography and Service," Average Total Payments for DRG-470 in 2016, accessed June 15, 2023.

[24] Evans, "What Does Knee Surgery Cost?"

[25] See U.S. Centers for Medicare and Medicaid Services, "Medicare Inpatient Hospitals—by Geography and Service," Average Total Payments for DRG-470 in 2018, accessed June 16, 2023.

[26] Evans, "What Does Knee Surgery Cost?; U.S. Centers for Medicare & Medicaid Services, "Medicare Inpatient Hospitals—by Geography and Service," Average Total Payments for DRG-470 in 2016, accessed June 15, 2023; and U.S. Centers for Medicare & Medicaid Services, "Medicare Inpatient Hospitals—by Geography and Service," Average Total Payments for DRG-470 in 2018, accessed June 16, 2023.

[27] Federal Trade Commission and Department of Justice, *Improving Health Care*, p. 26.

[28] Sarah L. Barber, Luca Lorenzoni, and Paul Ong, *Price Setting and Price Regulation in Health Care: Lessons for Advancing Universal Health Coverage* (Geneva: World Health Organization and Organisation for Economic Co-operation and Development, 2019), p. 31. See Ge Bai and Gerard F. Anderson, "A More Detailed Understanding of Factors Associated with Hospital Profitability," *Health Affairs* 35, no. 5 (May 2016): 889–97. "Hospitals . . . in states with price regulation tended to be more profitable than other hospitals."

[29] Medicare Payment Advisory Commission, *Report to the Congress: Medicare Payment Policy* (Washington: MedPAC, March 2023), p. 22.

[30] Federal Trade Commission and Department of Justice, *Improving Health Care*, pp. 24–25.

[31] Medicare Payment Advisory Commission, *Report to the Congress: Medicare Payment Policy* (Washington: MedPAC, March 2018), p. 119.

[32] Office of the Assistant Secretary for Planning and Evaluation, *Comparison of U.S. and International Prices for Top Medicare Part B Drugs by Total Expenditures* (Washington: U.S. Department of Health and Human Services, 2018); and Rachel Dolan and Marina Tian, "Pricing and Payment for Medicaid Prescription Drugs," Kaiser Family Foundation, January 23, 2020.

[33] Mark Duggan and Fiona M. Scott Morton, "The Distortionary Effects of Government Procurement: Evidence from Medicaid Prescription Drug Purchasing," *Quarterly Journal of Economics* 121, no. 1 (February 2006): 1–30.

[34] Loren Adler, "Cost-Shifting in Drug Pricing, or the Lack Thereof," Brookings Institution, Washington, September 24, 2021.

[35] Medicare Payment Advisory Commission, *Report to the Congress: Medicare Payment Policy* (Washington: MedPAC, March 2020), pp. 17, 463; Martin Gaynor, "What to Do about Health-Care Markets? Policies to Make Health-Care Markets Work," Hamilton Project, Brookings Institution Policy Proposal 2020-10, March 2020, p. 11.

[36] Michael A. Morrisey, *Cost Shifting in Health Care: Separating Evidence from Rhetoric* (Washington: AEI Press, 1994).

[37] Jeffrey Clemens and Joshua D. Gottlieb, "In the Shadow of a Giant: Medicare's Influence on Private Physician Payments," *Journal of Political Economy* 125, no. 1 (February 2017): 1–39.

[38] See Chapin White and Christoper M. Whaley, *Prices Paid to Hospitals by Private Health Plans Are High Relative to Medicare and Vary Widely* (Santa Monica, CA: RAND Corporation, 2019); and Charles Blahous, "The Costs of a National Single-Payer Healthcare System," working paper, Mercatus Center at George Mason University, Arlington, VA, July 2018.

[39] See Ryan J. Rosso et al., *Federal Requirements on Private Health Insurance Plans* (Washington: Congressional Research Service, updated 2023) p. 5; and Mark Pauly and Bradley Herring, *Pooling Health Insurance Risks* (Washington: AEI Press, 1999), pp. 69–70.

[40] Tom Murphy, "Exercise Caution with Zero-Premium Medicare Advantage Plans," Associated Press, October 5, 2022; Louise Norris, "Who's Getting Zero-Premium Health Insurance Plans?," healthinsurance.org, January 2024; and Aleka Gürel, "HealthSherpa Enrolls More Than 3 Million People through January 15th, Most Pay Less than $21/Month," *HealthSherpa* (blog).

[41] Norris, "Who's Getting Zero-Premium Health Insurance Plans?"

[42] Cynthia Cox et al., "Explaining Health Care Reform: Risk Adjustment, Reinsurances, and Risk Corridors," Kaiser Family Foundation, August 17, 2016.

[43] David M. Culter and Sarah J. Reber, "Paying for Health Insurance: The Trade-Off between Competition and Adverse Selection," *Quarterly Journal of Economics* 113, no. 2 (May 1998): 433–66.

[44] Joe Davidson, "Caught by a Change in Health Care," *Washington Post*, November 27, 2008; and "Insurer Ends Health Program Rather Than Pay Out Big," *Washington Times*, October 14, 2009.

[45] Medicare Payment Advisory Commission, *Report to the Congress: Medicare Payment Policy* (Washington: MedPAC, March 2023), p. 375.

[46] François Duc de La Rochefoucauld, "Reflections; or Sentences and Moral Maxims," 1678.

[47] Michael Geruso, Timothy Layton, and Daniel Prinz, "Screening in Contract Design: Evidence from the ACA Health Insurance Exchanges," *American Economic Journal: Economic Policy* 11, no. 2 (May 2019): 64–107.

[48] Ron Johnson and Mike Lee, letter to U.S. Senate, July 19, 2017.

[49] Geruso, Layton, and Prinz, "Screening in Contract Design."

[50] Geruso, Layton, and Prinz, "Screening in Contract Design."

[51] Colby Itkowitz, "Parents of a 4-Year-Old with Cancer Can't Buy ACA Plan to Cover Her Hospital Care," *Washington Post*, November 15, 2017.

[52] Mark Shepard, "Hospital Network Competition and Adverse Selection: Evidence from the Massachusetts Health Insurance Exchange," National Bureau of Economic Research Working Paper no. 2600, February 29, 2016.

[53] Michelle Andrews, "For Some Patients in Marketplace Plans, Access to Cancer Centers Is Elusive," KFF Health News, January 3, 2017.

[54] Jay Hancock, "Insurers' Flawed Directories Leave Patients Scrambling for In-Network Doctors," *New York Times*, December 3, 2016.

[55] Geruso, Layton, and Prinz, "Screening in Contract Design."

[56] Beatriz Duque Long, Carl Schmid, and Andrew Sperling, email to Sylvia Mathews Burwell, "Re: 2017 Qualified Health Plan Review and 2018 *Notice of Benefit and Payment Parameters* Rule & Letter to Issuers," August 24, 2016.

[57] David J. Meyers et al., "Comparison of the Quality of Hospitals That Admit Medicare Advantage Patients vs Traditional Medicare Patients," *JAMA Network Open* 3, no. 1 (January 2020): 8–9; Jack S. Resneck Jr. et al., "The Accuracy of Dermatology Network Physician Directories Posted by Medicare Advantage Health Plans in an Era of Narrow Networks," *JAMA Dermatology* 150, no. 12 (December 2014): 1290–97; "Online Provider Directory Review Report," Centers for Medicare and Medicaid Services, January 13, 2017; Government Accountability Office, *Medicare Advantage: Actions Needed to Enhance CMS Oversight of Provider Network Adequacy* (Washington: GAO, 2015), p. 32; and Government Accountability Office, *Medicare Advantage: Beneficiary Disenrollments to Fee-for-Service in Last Year of Life Increasing Medicare Spending* (Washington: GAO, 2021).

[58] Office of the Assistant Secretary for Planning and Evaluation, Department of Health and Human Services, "Individual Market Premium Changes: 2013–2017," May 23, 2017; and Office of the Assistant Secretary for Planning and Evaluation, Department of Health and Human Services, "Health Plan Choice and Premiums in the 2018 Federal Health Insurance Exchange," October 30, 2017.

[59] Brian C. Blase, Paragon Health Institute, Testimony before the Subcommittee on Health of the House Committee on Ways and Means, "Why Health Care Is Unaffordable: The Fallout of Democrats' Inflation on Patients and Small Businesses," 118th Cong., 1st sess., March 23, 2023, pp. 4–5.

[60] Ron Johnson and Mike Lee, letter to U.S. Senate, July 19, 2017.

[61] See generally Michael F. Cannon, "Market Concentration in Health Care: Government Is the Problem, Not the Solution," Cato Institute Briefing Paper no. 139, July 19, 2022.

[62] See *Jacqueline Halbig, et al., v. Sylvia Mathews Burwell, in her official capacity as U.S. Secretary of Health and Human Services*, "Brief of America's Health Insurance Plans as *Amicus Curiae* in Support of Defendants-Appellees and Affirmance," on appeal from the United States District Court for the District of Columbia, No. 1:13-cv-00623, USCA Case #14-5018, filed November 3, 2014, pp. 18, 25. "Kentucky, Maine, Massachusetts, New Hampshire, New Jersey, New York, Vermont, and Washington . . . prohibited risk-based underwriting," which resulted in "an ever-shrinking market" and in some cases "collapse."

[63] See Michael F. Cannon, "Current Exchange Difficulties Are Actually ObamaCare's Fourth Death Spiral," *Forbes*, September 6, 2016.

[64] Government Accountability Office Analysis of Data from the Centers for Medicare and Medicaid Services (CMS).

[65] "CAHI," The Council for Affordable Health Insurance, Center for Advancing Health.

[66] Michael F. Cannon, "End the Tax Exclusion for Employer-Sponsored Health Insurance: Return $1 Trillion to the Workers Who Earned It," Cato Institute Policy Analysis no. 928, May 24, 2022.

67 Had medical prices risen at the rate of general inflation, the "medical services" and "medical commodities" curves would lie flat along the x-axis.

68 "National Health Expenditure Data," U.S. Centers for Medicare & Medicaid Services, last revised September 6, 2023.

69 See Jeffrey A. Singer and Michael F. Cannon, "Drug Reformation: End Government's Power to Require Prescriptions," Cato Institute White Paper, October 20, 2020.

70 See Joseph P. Newhouse and Insurance Experiment Group, *Free for All? Lessons from the RAND Health Insurance Experiment* (Cambridge, MA: Harvard University Press, 1993); Heidi Allen et al., "The Oregon Health Insurance Experiment in the United States," AEA RCT Registry, 2020; and Anup Malani et al., "Effect of Health Insurance in India: A Randomized Controlled Trial," Becker Friedman Institute Working Paper no. 2021-146, December 2021.

71 Bureau of Labor Statistics (BLS), "Producer Price Index by Commodity: Special Indexes: Pharmaceuticals for Human Use, Non-Prescription [WPUSI07006]," Federal Reserve Bank of St. Louis; BLS, "Producer Price Index by Industry: Pharmacies and Drug Retailers: Retailing of Prescription Drugs [PCU4461104461101]," Federal Reserve Bank of St. Louis; and BLS, "Producer Price Index by Commodity: Chemicals and Allied Products: Hormones and Oral Contraceptives [WPU06380105]," Federal Reserve Bank of St. Louis.

72 Advisory Board, "Maryland's Radical All-Payer Model Was Just Extended through 2023," March 24, 2023.

73 West Virginia Health Care Authority, "Rate Review History," WV.gov.

74 James C. Robinson, Timothy T. Brown, and Christopher Whaley, "Reference Pricing Changes the 'Choice Architecture' of Health Care for Consumers," *Health Affairs* 36, no. 3 (March 2017): 524–30.

75 Angela K. Dills, "Telehealth Payment Parity Laws at the State Level," policy brief, Mercatus Center at George Mason University, November 30, 2021. See also "Parity," Center for Connected Health Policy.

76 Nevada Division of Public and Behavioral Health, "States Listed Below Have Some Form of Any Willing Provider Laws," January 27, 2019.

77 Commonwealth Fund, "State Balance-Billing Protections," February 5, 2021.

78 "National Health Expenditure Data," U.S. Centers for Medicare & Medicaid Services, last revised September 6, 2023.

79 Shirley V. Svorny and Michael F. Cannon, "Health Care Workforce Reform: COVID-19 Spotlights Need for Changes to Clinician Licensing," Cato Institute Policy Analysis no. 899, August 4, 2020.

80 Singer and Cannon, "Drug Reformation."

81 Unlike other government price distortions, patents plausibly increase social welfare. Absent government intervention, competitors could acquire and use the knowledge innovators generate without paying for it. If innovators cannot recoup the cost of generating such knowledge, investment in knowledge generation will be suboptimal. Whether health care patents work in practice as theory predicts is an empirical question.

82 David Besanko, David Dranove, and Craig Garthwaite, "Insurance and the High Prices of Pharmaceuticals," NBER Working Paper no. 22353, June 2016, pp. 1, 27.

83 F. A. Hayek, "The Use of Knowledge in Society," *American Economic Review* 35, no. 4 (September 1945): 519–30. "I have deliberately used the word 'marvel' to

shock the reader out of the complacency with which we often take the working of this mechanism for granted."

[84] See Silver and Hyman, *Overcharged* (n. 13); Cannon and Pohida, "Would 'Medicare for All' Mean Quality for All?" (n. 8); Michael F. Cannon, "End the Tax Exclusion for Employer-Sponsored Health Insurance"; and Michael F. Cannon, *Recovery: A Guide to Reforming the U.S. Health Sector* (Washington: Cato Institute, 2023).

Chapter 13: Anti-Price-Gouging Laws

[1] "Hurricane Harvey and Its Impacts on Southeast Texas," National Weather Service, August 2017.

[2] Michelle Fox, "Price Gouging during Hurricane Harvey: Up to $99 for a Case of Water, Texas AG Says," CNBC, August 28, 2017.

[3] "Price Gouging State Statutes," National Conference of State Legislatures, March 10, 2022.

[4] Texas Business and Commerce Code, Title 2 Chapter 17 § 17.4625, May 22, 2019.

[5] "Following the devastation of Hurricane Harvey in Texas, hundreds of incidents of price gouging have been reported to the state attorney general's office. State law prohibits businesses from charging unreasonably inflated prices for necessities after a disaster, and each violation comes with a fine of up to $20,000. What comes closest to your view?" YouGov, September 1, 2017.

[6] S. 4214, Price Gouging Prevention Act, 117th Cong., 2nd sess., May 12, 2022; and Ryan Bourne and Brad Subramaniam, "Elizabeth Warren Forgets That Demand Affects Prices Too," *Cato at Liberty* (blog), Cato Institute, May 16, 2022.

[7] Sabri Ben-Achour, "Combating Lunch Shaming at Schools," *Marketplace Morning Report,* podcast, September 1, 2017; Josh Hendrickson, "Why Price Gouging Laws Aren't So Bad," *Economic Forces* (blog), November 12, 2020.

[8] "Price Gouging," California Governor's Office of Emergency Services, 2023.

[9] "Virginia Post-Disaster Anti-Price Gouging Act," Chapter 46, Code of Virginia.

[10] Isabella Weber and Evan Wasner, "Sellers' Inflation, Profits and Conflict: Why Can Large Firms Hike Prices in an Emergency?" *Review of Keynesian Economics* 11, no. 2 (Summer 2023): 183–213.

[11] Rik Chakraborti and Gavin Roberts, "Anti-Price Gouging Laws, Shortages, and COVID-19: Big Data Insights from Consumer Searches," Elsevier, June 9, 2020.

[12] Rik Chakraborti and Gavin Roberts, "Learning to Hoard: The Effects of Pre-existing and Surprise Price-Gouging Regulation during the COVID-19 Pandemic," *Journal of Consumer Policy* 44, no. 4 (September 2021): 507–29.

[13] Gavin Roberts and Rik Chakraborti, "How Price-Gouging Regulation Undermined COVID-19 Mitigation: Evidence of Unintended Consequences," working paper, Center for Growth and Opportunity, Utah State University, Logan, March 4, 2021.

[14] Luis Cabral and Lei Xu, "Seller Reputation and Price Gouging: Evidence from the COVID-19 Pandemic," *Economic Inquiry* 59, no. 3 (2021): 867–79.

[15] Michael J. Sandel, "'Justice,'" *New York Times*, November 27, 2009.

[16] Michael Hiltzik, "Column: Memo to Economists Defending Price Gouging in a Disaster: It's Still Wrong, Morally and Economically," *Los Angeles Times*, August 28, 2017.

[17] Jeff Ely and Sandeep Baliga, "Price Gouging," *Cheap Talk* (blog), October 29, 2012.

[18] Michael Giberson, "The Problem with Price Gouging Laws," *Regulation*, Spring 2011.

[19] "Price Gouging," Clark Center Forum, June 7, 2022.

[20] "Price Gouging," Clark Center Forum, May 2, 2012.

[21] Casey Klofstad and Joseph Uscinski, "Expert Opinions and Negative Externalities Do Not Decrease Support for Anti-Price Gouging Policies," *Research & Politics* 10, no. 3 (September 20, 2023).

[22] Michael J. Sandel, *Justice: What's the Right Thing to Do?* (New York: Farrar, Straus and Giroux, 2009).

[23] Dwight R. Lee, "The Two Moralities of Outlawing Price Gouging," *Regulation*, Spring 2014.

[24] Alexander P. Reese and Ingo Pies, "What about 'Price Gouging' by Employees?," *Business Ethics Journal Review* 9, no. 3 (May 2021): 14–20.

[25] Hendrickson, "Why Price Gouging Laws Aren't So Bad."

[26] Daniel Kahneman, Jack L. Knetsch, and Richard Thaler, "Fairness as a Constraint on Profit Seeking: Entitlements in the Market," *American Economic Review* 76, no. 4 (September 1986): pp. 728–41; and Harriet Torry, "Bowling for $418? Surge Pricing Creeps into Restaurants, Movies, Gym Class," *Wall Street Journal*, March 12, 2023.

Chapter 14: The West Needs Water Markets

[1] From 2010 to 2020, Nevada grew 15.0 percent and Arizona 11.9 percent, both above the national average of 7.4 percent: "Percent Change in Resident Population for the 50 States, the District of Columbia, and Puerto Rico: 2010 to 2020," Census Bureau, 2020.

[2] Joshua Partlow, "Water Cuts Could Save the Colorado River. Farmers Are in the Crosshairs," *Washington Post*, April 16, 2023.

[3] Gary D. Libecap, "The West Needs Water Markets," Hoover Institution, Stanford, CA, February 7, 2018.

[4] Governor Jerry Brown of California also understood the importance of pricing in California water conservation policy. Adam Nagourney, "California Court Rules Water Pricing Plan Violates Law," *New York Times*, April 21, 2015.

[5] Johnathan H. Adler, "Warming Up to Water Markets," *Regulation* 31, no. 4 (Winter 2008–09): 16.

[6] Gary D. Libecap, "The Problem of Water," *Regulation* 37, no. 3 (Fall 2014): 64–67.

[7] Gary D. Libecap, "The Myth of Owens Valley," *Regulation* 28, no. 2 (Summer 2005): 10–17.

[8] Libecap, "Owens Valley," p. 12.

[9] Libecap, "Owens Valley," p. 11.

[10] Libecap, "Owens Valley," p. 16.

[11] Libecap, "Owens Valley," p. 16.

[12] Libecap, "Owens Valley," p. 17.

[13] Libecap, "The Problem of Water," p. 66.

[14] Joseph L. Sax, "The Public Trust Doctrine in Natural Resource Law: Effective Judicial Intervention," *Michigan Law Review* 68, no. 471 (1970): 471–566; and Michael C. Blumm and Zachary A. Schwartz, "The Public Trust Doctrine Fifty Years after Sax and Some Thoughts on Its Future," *Public Land & Resources Law Review* 44 (2021): 1–48.

[15] Libecap, "The Problem of Water," p. 66.

[16] Libecap, "The Problem of Water," p. 67.

[17] Christopher Flavelle, "A Breakthrough Deal to Keep the Colorado River from Going Dry, for Now," *New York Times*, May 22, 2023.

[18] Andrew B. Ayres, "Easier Said than Done," *Regulation* 45, no. 3 (Fall 2021): 14–17.

[19] Lois Henry, "The Central California Town That Keeps Sinking," *New York Times*, May 27, 2021.

[20] Ayres, "Easier Said than Done," p. 15.

[21] Ayres, "Easier Said than Done," p. 16.

[22] Ayres, "Easier Said than Done," p. 17.

[23] Ayres, "Easier Said than Done," p. 17.

[24] Oliver R. Browne and Xinde James Ji, "The Economic Value of Clarifying Property Rights: Evidence from Water in Idaho's Snake River Basin," *Journal of Environmental Economics and Management* 119 (2023): 102799.

[25] Browne and Ji, "Economic Value of Clarifying Property Rights."

[26] Browne and Ji, "Economic Value of Clarifying Property Rights."

Chapter 15: Minimum Wage Tradeoffs

[1] Nabeel Alsalam et al., "The Effects on Employment and Family Income of Increasing the Federal Minimum Wage," Congressional Budget Office, Washington, July 2019.

[2] Congressional Budget Office, "How Increasing the Federal Minimum Wage Could Affect Employment and Family Income Interactive Tool," August 18, 2022.

[3] Yannet Lathrop, T. William Lester, and Matthew Wilson, "Quantifying the Impact of the Fight for $15: $150 Billion in Raises for 26 Million Workers, with $76 Billion Going to Workers of Color," National Employment Law Project Policy & Data Brief no. 1, July 27, 2021; and Economic Policy Institute, "Why the U.S. Needs a $15 Minimum Wage," January 26, 2021.

[4] Andrew Van Dam, "It's Not Just Paychecks: The Surprising Society-Wide Benefits of Raising the Minimum Wage," *Washington Post*, July 8, 2019.

[5] Jesse Rothstein and Heidi Sherholz, "Full COVID Recovery Requires Raising the Minimum Wage," *The Hill*, February 10, 2021.

[6] David Neumark and Peter Shirley, "Myth or Measurement: What Does the New Minimum Wage Research Say about Minimum Wages and Job Loss in the United States?," National Bureau of Economic Research Working Paper no. 28388, March 2022.

[7] Jeffrey Clemens and Michael Wither, "The Minimum Wage and the Great Recession: Evidence of Effects on the Employment and Income Trajectories of Low-Skilled Workers," *Journal of Public Economics* 170 (February 2019): 53–67; Jeffrey Clemens and Michael R. Strain, "The Heterogeneous Effects of Large and Small Minimum Wage Changes: Evidence over the Short and Medium Run Using a Pre-Analysis Plan," National Bureau of Economic Research Working Paper no. 29264, September 2021; Ekaterina Jardim et al., "Minimum-Wage Increases and Low-Wage Employment: Evidence from Seattle," *American Economic Journal: Economic Policy* 14, no. 2 (May 2022): 263–314; John J. Horton, "Price Floors and Employer Preferences: Evidence from a Minimum Wage Experiment," Elsevier, January 16, 2017; Terry

Gregory and Ulrich Zierahn, "When the Minimum Wage Really Bites Hard: The Negative Spillover Effect on High-Skilled Workers," *Journal of Public Economics* 206 (February 2022): 104582; and Loukas Karabarbounis, Jeremy Lise, and Anusha Nath, "Minimum Wages and Labor Markets in the Twin Cities," National Bureau of Economic Research Working Paper no. 30239, August 2022.

8   The remainder of this chapter's discussion draws in large part on my own recent paper that connects these considerations to a more fully developed analytic framework. See Jeffrey Clemens, "How Do Firms Respond to Minimum Wage Increases? Understanding the Relevance of Non-Employment Margins," *Journal of Economic Perspectives* 35, no. 1 (Winter 2021): 51–72.

9   "Employer Costs for Employee Compensation," Bureau of Labor Statistics news release no. USDL-23-0488, March 17, 2023.

10 Michael S. Dworsky et al., "The Effect of the Minimum Wage on Employer-Sponsored Insurance for Low-Income Workers and Dependents," *American Journal of Health Economics* 8, no. 1 (Winter 2022): 99–126.

11 Mark K. Meiselbach and Jean M. Abraham, "Do Minimum Wage Laws Affect Employer-Sponsored Insurance Provision?," *Journal of Health Economics* 92 (December 2023): 102825.

12 Jeffrey Clemens, Lisa B. Kahn, and Jonathan Meer, "The Minimum Wage, Fringe Benefits, and Worker Welfare," National Bureau of Economic Research Working Paper no. 24635, May 2018.

13 Anne Beeson Royalty, "Do Minimum Wage Increases Lower the Probability that Low-Skilled Workers Will Receive Fringe Benefits?," Joint Center for Poverty Research Working Paper no. 172, May 2001; Kosali Ilayperuma Simon and Robert Kaestner, "Do Minimum Wages Affect Non-Wage Job Attributes? Evidence on Fringe Benefits," *ILR Review* 58, no. 1 (2004): 52–70; Laura Bucila, "Employment-Based Health Insurance and the Minimum Wage," College of the Holy Cross Working Paper Series no. 08-12, September 2008; and Mindy S. Marks, "Minimum Wages, Employer-Provided Health Insurance, and the Non-Discrimination Law," *Industrial Relations* 50, no. 2 (2011): 241–62.

14 Robert Bruce, "These 22 Major Employers Offer Some of the Best Employee Discounts," Penny Hoarder, May 22, 2023.

15 McDonald's, "Implementing the National Employee Discount," September 1, 2020.

16 Haroon Bhorat, Ravi Kanbur, and Benjamin Stanwix, "Minimum Wages in Sub-Saharan Africa: A Primer," *World Bank Research Observer* 32, no. 1 (February 2017): 21–74; Karolina Goraus-Tańska and Piotr Lewandowski, "Minimum Wage Violation in Central and Eastern Europe," *International Labour Review* 159, no. 2 (March 2018): 297–336; Uma Rani et al., "Minimum Wage Coverage and Compliance in Developing Countries," *International Labour Review* 152, no. 3–4 (December 2013): 381–410; Andrea Garnero, "The Dog That Barks Doesn't Bite: Coverage and Compliance of Sectoral Minimum Wages in Italy," *IZA Journal of Labor Policy* 7, no. 1 (2018): 1–24; Andrea Garnero and Claudio Lucifora, "Turning a 'Blind Eye'? Compliance with Minimum Wage Standards and Employment," *Economica* 89, no. 356 (March 2022): 884–907; Jeffrey Clemens and Michael R. Strain, "Understanding 'Wage Theft': Evasion and Avoidance Responses to Minimum Wage Increases," *Labour Economics* 79 (December 2022): 102285; and Jeffrey Clemens and Michael R. Strain, "Does Measurement

Error Explain the Increase in Subminimum Wage Payment Following Minimum Wage Increases?," *Economics Letters* 217 (August 2022): 110638.

[17] Hyejin Ku, "Does Minimum Wage Increase Labor Productivity? Evidence from Piece Rate Workers," *Journal of Labor Economics* 40, no. 2 (April 2022): 325–59; and Decio Coviello, Erika Deserranno, and Nicola Persico, "Minimum Wage and Individual Worker Productivity: Evidence from a Large US Retailer," *Journal of Political Economy* 130, no. 9 (September 2022): 2315–60. Interestingly, the effort margin has been taken seriously in data-driven studies of minimum wages since as early as a 1915 analysis of minimum wage laws in Oregon by Marie Obenauer and Bertha von der Nienburg, who worked at that time for the Bureau of Labor Statistics. See Marie L. Obenauer and Bertha von der Nienburg, *Effect of Minimum-Wage Determinations in Oregon* (Washington: Government Printing Office, July 1915).

[18] Jeffrey Clemens and Michael R. Strain, "Implications of Schedule Irregularity as a Minimum Wage Response Margin," *Applied Economics Letters* 27, no. 20 (2020): 1691–1694.

[19] Nikhil Datta, Giulia Giupponi, and Stephen Machin, "Zero-Hours Contracts and Labour Market Policy," *Economic Policy* 34, no. 99 (July 2019): 369–427.

[20] John J. Horton, "Price Floors and Employer Preferences: Evidence from a Minimum Wage Experiment," Elsevier, January 13, 2017.

[21] Jeffrey Clemens, Lisa Kahn, and Jonathan Meer, "Dropouts Need Not Apply? The Minimum Wage and Skill Upgrading," *Journal of Labor Economics* 39, no. 51 (January 2021): S107–49.

[22] Clemens and Wither, "Minimum Wage and the Great Recession" (n. 7); David Fairris and Leon Fernandez Bujanda, "The Dissipation of Minimum Wage Gains for Workers through Labor-Labor Substitution: Evidence from the Los Angeles Living Wage Ordinance," *Southern Economic Journal* 75, no. 2 (August 2008): 473–96; and Laura Giuliano, "Minimum Wage Effects on Employment, Substitution, and the Teenage Labor Supply: Evidence from Personnel Data," *Journal of Labor Economics* 31, no. 1 (January 2013): 155–94.

[23] Ekaterina Jardim et al., "Minimum-Wage Increases and Low-Wage Employment: Evidence from Seattle," *American Economic Journal: Economic Policy* 14, no. 2 (May 2022): 263–314.

[24] Radhakrishnan Gopalan et al., "State Minimum Wages, Employment, and Wage Spillovers: Evidence from Administrative Payroll Data," *Journal of Labor Economics* 39, no. 3 (July 2021): 673–707.

Chapter 16: Minimum Wages and Poverty

[1] *Lochner v. New York*, 198 U.S. 45 (1905).

[2] *Muller v. Oregon*, 208 U.S. 412 (1908); *West Coast Hotel Co. v. Parrish*, 300 U.S. 379 (1937).

[3] To take another example of what the Supreme Court deemed to be a compelling state interest, in *Muller v. Oregon* (1908), the Court ruled that "the two sexes differ in structure of body, in the functions to be performed by each, in the amount of physical strength . . . then follow extracts from over 90 reports . . .

that long hours of labor are dangerous for women, primarily because of their special physical organization. . . . Perhaps the general scope and character of all these reports may be summed up in what an inspector for Hanover says: 'The reasons for the reduction of the working day to ten hours—(a) the physical organization of women, (b) her maternal functions, (c) the rearing and education of the children, (d) the maintenance of the home—are all so important and so far reaching that the need for such reduction need hardly be discussed.'"

[4] President Franklin D. Roosevelt, "Message to Congress on Establishing Minimum Wages and Maximum Hours," May 24, 1937.

[5] Senator John F. Kennedy, "Fair Labor Standards Speech," delivered in the Senate, August 10, 1960; President Lyndon B. Johnson, "Remarks at the Signing of the Fair Labor Standards Amendments of 1966," September 23, 1966; President William J. Clinton, *Address before Joint Session of the Congress on the State of the Union*, January 24, 1995 (Washington: Government Printing Office), p. 82; and Paul Lewis and Karen McVeigh, "Obama: 'Nobody Who Works Full-Time Should Have to Live in Poverty,'" *The Guardian*, February 12, 2014.

[6] President Joe Biden, interview by Norah O'Donnell at the White House, February 9, 2021, YouTube video, 6:45.

[7] Living Wage Now Act, H.R. 325, 117th Cong., 1st sess., January 15, 2021; Raise the Wage Act of 2021, S. 53, 117th Cong., 1st sess., January 26, 2021.

[8] "Sanders, Scott, 29 Democratic Senators, Introduce Legislation to Raise the Minimum Wage to $17 by 2028, Benefitting Nearly 28 Million Workers across America," Office of Sen. Bernie Sanders news release, July 25, 2023.

[9] Congressional Budget Office, "The Budgetary Effects of the Raise the Wage Act of 2021," February 2021.

[10] Jared Bernstein and Heidi Shierholz, "The Minimum Wage: A Crucial Labor Standard That Is Well Targeted to Low- and Moderate-Income Households," *Journal of Policy Analysis and Management* 33, no. 4 (2014): 1036–43; Arindrajit Dube, "Minimum Wages and the Distribution of Family Incomes," *American Economic Journal: Applied Economics* 11, no. 4 (2019): 268–304.

[11] David Card and Alan B. Krueger, *Myth and Measurement: The New Economics of the Minimum Wage* (Princeton, NJ: Princeton University Press, 1995); and Alan Manning, "The Real Thin Theory: Monopsony in Modern Labour Markets," *Labour Economics* 10, no. 2 (April 2003): 105–31.

[12] Congressional Budget Office, "Budgetary Effects of the Raise the Wage Act."

[13] Jeffrey Clemens and Michael Wither, "The Minimum Wage and the Great Recession: Evidence of Effects on the Employment and Income Trajectories of Low-Skilled Workers," *Journal of Public Economics* 170 (February 2019): 53–67; Jeffrey Clemens and Michael R. Strain, "The Heterogeneous Effects of Large and Small Minimum Wage Changes: Evidence over the Short and Medium Run Using a Pre-Analysis Plan," National Bureau of Economic Research Working Paper no. 29264, September 2021; David Neumark and Peter Shirley, "Myth or Measurement: What Does the New Minimum Wage Research Say about Minimum Wages and Job Loss in the United States?," National Bureau of Economic

Research Working Paper no. 28388, March 2022; and Zachary S. Fone, Joseph J. Sabia, and Resul Cesur, "The Unintended Effects of Minimum Wage Increases on Crime," *Journal of Public Economics* 219 (March 2023): 104780.

14 Card and Krueger, *Myth and Measurement.*

15 "$15 Minimum Wage," Clark Center Forum, September 22, 2015.

16 However, if higher minimum wages make low-skilled jobs less available, they could have the unintended effect of encouraging greater human capital acquisition, which could lead to higher rates of growth. Pierre Cahuc and Philippe Michel, "Minimum Wage Unemployment and Growth," *European Economic Review* 40, no. 7 (August 1996): 1463–82.

17 Joseph J. Sabia, "Minimum Wages and Gross Domestic Product," *Contemporary Economic Policy* 33, no. 4 (January 2015): 587–605; and Joseph J. Sabia, "Do Minimum Wages Stimulate Productivity and Growth?," IZA World of Labor, December 2015.

18 Jeffrey Clemens, "How Do Firms Respond to Minimum Wage Increases? Understanding the Relevance of Non-Employment Margins," *Journal of Economic Perspectives* 35, no. 1 (Winter 2021): 51–72.

19 Thomas MaCurdy, "How Effective Is the Minimum Wage at Supporting the Poor?," *Journal of Political Economy* 123, no. 2 (April 2015): 497–545.

20 The OPM was first established by President Johnson, and poverty thresholds are calculated by the federal government as three times the cost of a minimum food diet in 1963 and adjusted by age and family size. The federal poverty line is set by the Department of Health and Human Services each year, based on a market basket of goods, for each family size and composition (i.e., by age); the U.S. Census Bureau then calculates the number of people living in poverty based on family income and composition. The thresholds are increased each year by the annual national inflation rate via the Consumer Price Index.

21 In addition, the SPM uses a resource-sharing unit that also includes some unrelated individuals who reside in the same household (rather than the OPM, for which the definition of "family" includes only those related by blood, marriage, or adoption) and, importantly, the poverty thresholds employed account for price differences across states. Moreover, unlike the OPM, its thresholds are increased in real terms making it a quasi-relative poverty measure. For instance, a National Academies of Sciences, Engineering, and Medicine panel was created to assess and recommend changes to the SPM. Burkhauser and others offer important recommendations to address the shortcomings of the SPM. Richard V. Burkhauser et al., "Addressing the Shortcomings of the Supplemental Poverty Measure," American Enterprise Institute, Washington, July 2, 2021.

22 Joseph J. Sabia and Robert B. Nielsen, "Minimum Wages, Poverty, and Material Hardship: New Evidence from the SIPP," *Review of Economics of the Household* 13, no. 1 (March 2015): 95–134.

23 David Neumark and William Wascher, *Minimum Wages* (Cambridge, MA: MIT Press, 2008).

24 See, for example: Neumark and Shirley, "Myth or Measurement"; Clemens and Strain, "Heterogeneous Effects of Large and Small Minimum Wage Changes"; Clemens and Wither, "Minimum Wage and the Great Recession"; Doruk Cengiz

et al., "The Effect of Minimum Wages on Low-Wage Jobs," *Quarterly Journal of Economics* 134, no. 3 (August 2019): 1405–54; David Neumark, J. M. Ian Salas, and William Wascher, "Revisiting the Minimum Wage–Employment Debate: Throwing Out the Baby with the Bathwater?," *Industrial & Labor Relations Review* 67, no. 3 (May 2014): 608–48; Sylvia A. Allegretto, Arindrajit Dube, and Michael Reich, "Do Minimum Wages Really Reduce Teen Employment? Accounting for Heterogeneity and Selectivity in State Panel Data," *Industrial Relations* 50, no. 2 (2011): 205–40; and Arindrajit Dube, T. William Lester, and Michael Reich, "Minimum Wage Effects across State Borders: Estimates Using Contiguous Counties," *Review of Economics and Statistics* 92, no. 4 (2010): 945–64.

[25] Card and Krueger, *Myth and Measurement*; Neumark and Wascher, *Minimum Wages*; Richard V. Burkhauser and Joseph J. Sabia, "The Effectiveness of Minimum Wage Increases in Reducing Poverty: Past, Present, and Future," *Contemporary Economic Policy* 25, no. 2 (February 2007): 262–81; and Joseph J. Sabia and Richard V. Burkhauser, "Minimum Wages and Poverty: Will a $9.50 Federal Minimum Wage Really Help the Working Poor?," *Southern Economic Journal* 76, no. 3 (January 2010): 592–23; Sabia and Nielsen, "New Evidence from the SIPP"; MaCurdy, "How Effective Is the Minimum Wage?"; Clemens and Wither, "Minimum Wage and the Great Recession"; Richard V. Burkhauser, Drew McNichols, and Joseph J. Sabia, "Minimum Wages and Poverty: New Evidence from Dynamic Difference-in-Differences Estimates," National Bureau of Economics Working Paper no. 31182, April 2023; David Neumark and William Wascher, "Do Minimum Wages Fight Poverty?," *Economic Inquiry* 40, no. 3 (March 2007): 315–33; and Joseph J. Sabia, "Minimum Wages and the Economic Well-Being of Single Mothers," *Journal of Policy Analysis and Management* 27, no. 4 (Autumn 2008): 848–66.

[26] Burkhauser, McNichols, and Sabia, "Minimum Wages and Poverty"; Card and Krueger, *Myth and Measurement*.

[27] Congressional Budget Office, "Budgetary Effects of the Raise the Wage Act"; Heidi Shierholz, president, Economic Policy Institute, Testimony on "Increasing the Minimum Wage to $15 Per Hour" before the Subcommittee on Oversight, Investigations, and Regulations of the House Committee on Small Business, February 24, 2021; and Ben Zipperer, senior economist, Economic Policy Institute, Testimony on "Gradually Raising the Minimum Wage to $15 Would Be Good for Workers, Good for Businesses, and Good for the Economy" before the House Committee on Education and Labor, February 7, 2019.

[28] Burkhauser, McNichols, and Sabia, "Minimum Wages and Poverty."

[29] We used "synthetic control" methods that select control states that are observably similar in their pretreatment trends in poverty rate.

[30] Sabia and Nielsen, "New Evidence from the SIPP."

[31] Richard V. Burkhauser and T. Aldrich Finegan, "The Minimum Wage and the Poor: The End of a Relationship," *Journal of Policy Analysis and Management* 8, no. 1 (Winter 1989): 53–71.

[32] Richard V. Burkhauser, Kenneth A. Couch, and Andrew J. Glenn, "Public Policies for the Working Poor: The Earned Income Tax Credit versus Minimum Wage Legislation," *Research in Labor Economics* 15 (January 1996): 65–109;

David Neumark and William Wascher, "Does a Higher Minimum Wage Enhance the Effectiveness of the Earned Income Tax Credit?," *Industrial and Labor Relations Review* 64, no. 4 (July 2011): 712–46; and Richard V. Burkhauser and Kevin Corinth, "The Minimum Wage versus the Earned Income Tax Credit for Reducing Poverty," IZA World of Labor, September 2021.

[33] David Card, "Chapter 30—The Causal Effect of Education on Earnings," *Handbook of Labor Economics* 3, part A (1999): 1801–63.

[34] Ryan Bourne, "Government and the Cost of Living: Income-Based vs. Cost-Based Approaches to Alleviating Poverty," Cato Institute Policy Analysis no. 847, September 4, 2018.

Chapter 17: Price Ceilings of Zero

[1] Margaret Jane Radin, "Market-Inalienability," *Harvard Law Review* 100, no. 8 (June 1987): 1849–1937.

[2] Alvin E. Roth, "Repugnance as a Constraint on Markets," *Journal of Economic Perspectives* 21, no. 3 (Summer 2007): 37–58.

[3] Debra Satz, *Why Some Things Should Not Be for Sale: The Moral Limits of Markets* (New York: Oxford University Press, 2010).

[4] "Organ Donation and Transplantation Statistics," National Kidney Foundation, New York, June 18, 2023.

[5] Peter Jaworski, "Liquid Gold: New Zealand's Need for Compensated Plasma Collections," New Zealand Initiative, Wellington, June 2023. See also Peter Jaworski, "Bloody Well Pay Them: The Case for Voluntary Remunerated Plasma Collections," Adam Smith Institute, London, June 13, 2020.

[6] Blood Money: Europe Wrestles with Moral Dilemma over Paying Donors for Plasma, *Politico*, April 21, 2022.

[7] Assisted Human Reproduction Act, S.C. 2004, c. 2 (Can.).

[8] Roger Collier, "Sperm Donor Pool Shrivels When Payments Cease," *Canadian Medical Association Journal* 82, no. 3 (February 2010): 233–34.

[9] Pamela Wallin, "Time to End For-Profit Plasma Donations," Senate of Canada, June 18, 2018.

[10] Richard Morris Titmuss, *The Gift Relationship: From Human Blood to Social Policy* (London: Allen and Unwin, 1970).

[11] For more on the altruism objection to payment, see David Faraci and Peter M. Jaworski, "On Leaving Space for Altruism," *Public Affairs Quarterly* 35, no. 2 (April 2021): 83–93.

[12] Richard H. Chused, *Cases, Materials, and Problems in Property* (New Providence, NJ: LexisNexis, 2010).

[13] This is similar to the worry raised by the philosopher Elizabeth Anderson in the context of commercial surrogacy. She argues that allowing commercial surrogacy would subject this to "market norms"—which include norms of instrumentalism and self-regard, among other considerations—and so may result in surrogate women and the babies that are the products of surrogacy being treated and regarded as commodities. See Elizabeth S. Anderson, "Is Women's Labor a Commodity?," *Philosophy & Public Affairs* 19, no. 1 (Winter 1990): 71–92.

[14] Albert Gore, subcommittee chair, statement on "Procurement and Allocation of Human Organs for Transplantation" before the Subcommittee on Investigations and Oversight of the Senate Committee on Science and Technology, 98th Cong., 1st sess., November 9, 1983.

Part 3: Value

[1] Irina Ivanova, "Rents Are Too Damn High—and a Scourge of 'Junk' Fees Is Making It Worse, Studies Say," CBS News, April 14, 2023; and Derek Headey and Harold Alderman, "The High Price of Healthy Food . . . and the Low Price of Unhealthy Food," *Data Blog*, World Bank, July 23, 2019.

[2] Callie Holtermann, "Are C.E.O.s Paid Too Much?," *New York Times*, May 11, 2021; and Bloomberg Editors, "Low Wages Make Nursing Homes a Hotbed for Covid-19," and Bloomberg, May 15, 2020.

[3] Charity L. Scott, "Shoppers Are Caught Off Guard as Prices on Everyday Items Change More Often," *Wall Street Journal*, February 4, 2022.

[4] Ryan Bourne, "Mark Carney's Value(s) Moans about Free Markets—but His Brave New World Alternative Is a Muddled Farce," *The Telegraph*, March 21, 2021.

[5] Mark Carney, *Value(s): Building a Better World for All* (New York: Hachette Book Group, 2021).

[6] Mark Carney, "From Moral to Market Sentiments: Mark Carney—How We Get What We Value," Reith Lecture, Episode 1 of 4, December 4, 2020.

[7] Carney, "From Moral to Market Sentiments."

[8] F. A. Hayek, *Law, Legislation and Liberty*, vol. 2, Chicago: University of Chicago Press, 1977), p. 64.

[9] F. A. Hayek, *The Constitution of Liberty* (Chicago: University of Chicago Press, 1978), p. 72.

Chapter 18: The Labor Theory of Value

[1] Karl Marx, 1818–1883, *Capital, a Critique of Political Economy* (Chicago: Henry Regnery, 1959).

[2] John Locke, *Second Treatise of Government,* edited by C. B. Macpherson (Cambridge, MA: Hackett Publishing, 1980, originally published in 1690).

[3] Alexandria Ocasio-Cortez (@AOC), "As a person who actually worked for tips & hourly wages in my life, instead of having to learn about it 2nd-hand, I can tell you that most people want to be paid enough to live. A living wage isn't a gift, it's a right. Workers are often paid far less than the value they create," Twitter post, February 16, 2019, 5:37 p.m.

[4] David R. Henderson, "William Stanley Jevons," Econlib, 2023.

[5] Adam Smith, *Wealth of Nations* (Ware, UK: Wordsworth Editions, 2012, originally published in 1776).

[6] Hannah Norman, "Travel Nurses Raced to Help during Covid. Now They're Facing Abrupt Cuts," NBC, May 8, 2022.

[7] Derek Saul, "CEOs Made 324 Times More Than Their Median Workers in 2021, Union Report Finds," Forbes, July 18, 2022.

Chapter 19: Market Prices and Ethical Value

[1] Jack Caporal, "Are You Well-Paid? Compare Your Salary to the Average U.S. Income," *The Ascent,* June 13, 2023.
[2] Mark Carney, *Value(s): Building a Better World for All* (New York: PublicAffairs, 2021).
[3] Charlotte Pickles, "Footballers Seen as Undeserving of the Wealth; Investors as Deserving," UnHerd, July 23, 2017.
[4] Robert Nozick, "Why Do Intellectuals Oppose Capitalism?," *Cato Policy Report* 20, no. 1 (January/February 1998): 1, 9–11.
[5] F. A. Hayek, *Law, Legislation and Liberty, vol. 2* (Chicago: University of Chicago Press, 1976), p. 64.
[6] Thomas Hardy, "Hap," in *Wessex Poems and Other Verses* (London and New York: Harper and Brothers, 1898).

Chapter 20: Market Prices Are Not Corrupting

[1] Oscar Wilde, *Lady Windermere's Fan* (London: Methuen Publishing, 1912).
[2] Uri Gneezy and Aldo Rustichini, "A Fine Is a Price," *Journal of Legal Studies* 29, no. 1 (January 2000): 1–17.
[3] Neda Ulaby, "Dan Ariely Takes on 'Irrational' Economic Impulses," National Public Radio, March 31, 2008.
[4] Adam Smith, *The Wealth of Nations* (Ware, UK: Wordsworth Editions, 2012, originally published in 1776).
[5] Kathy Eden, "'Between Friends All Is Common': The Erasmian Adage and Tradition," *Journal of the History of Ideas* 59, no. 3 (July 1998): 405–19.
[6] Ruth Benedict, *The Chrysanthemum and the Sword* (Boston: Houghton Mifflin, 1946), p. 142.
[7] Herbert Gintis, "Giving Economists Their Due," *Boston Review,* June 25, 2012.
[8] Gintis, "Giving Economists Their Due."
[9] Michael Sandel, *What Money Can't Buy: The Moral Limits of Markets* (New York: Farrar, Straus and Giroux), 2012.
[10] Edward T. O'Donnell, "The Sage of Tammany Hall," *New York Times,* August 28, 2005.
[11] *Encyclopaedia Britannica Online,* s.v. "Jasmine Revolution."

Chapter 21: The Gender Pay Gap

[1] Bureau of Labor Statistics, "Median Earnings for Women in 2022 Were 83.0 Percent of the Median for Men," *Economics Daily,* January 25, 2023.
[2] Jessica Schieder and Elise Gould, "'Women's Work' and the Gender Pay Gap," Economic Policy Institute, Washington, July 20, 2016.
[3] U.S. Department of Labor, "How Overrepresentation in Undervalued Jobs Disadvantaged Women during the Pandemic," fact sheet, March 15, 2022.
[4] White House, "Remarks by President Biden at an Event to Mark Equal Pay Day," March 24, 2021.
[5] Li Zhou, "Kamala Harris's Plan to Close the Gender Wage Gap, Explained," *Vox,* May 21, 2019.

[6] Bureau of Labor Statistics, "Labor Force Statistics from the Current Population Survey. Household Data Annual Averages," Table 18. Employed Persons by Detailed Industry, Sex, Race, and Hispanic or Latino Ethnicity, January 25, 2023.

[7] Jeffrey T. Denning et al., "The Return to Hours Worked within and across Occupations: Implications for the Gender Wage Gap," National Bureau of Economic Research Working Paper no. 25739, April 2019, p. 8.

[8] Andrew Chamberlain, Daniel Zhao, and Amanda Stansell, *Progress on the Gender Pay Gap: 2019* (Mill Valley, CA: Glassdoor, March 27, 2019).

[9] Cody Cook et al., "The Gender Earnings Gap in the Gig Economy: Evidence from Over a Million Rideshare Drivers," working paper, Stanford University, Stanford, CA, May 2020.

[10] "American Time Use Survey Summary," Bureau of Labor Statistics, news release no. USDL-22-1261, June 23, 2022.

[11] "2023 Gender Pay Gap Report," Payscale, Seattle, 2023.

[12] Henrik Kleven, Camille Landais, and Jakob Egholt Søgaard, "Children and Gender Inequality: Evidence from Denmark," National Bureau of Economic Research Working Paper no. 24219, January 2018.

[13] Kleven, Landais, and Søgaard, "Children and Gender Inequality."

[14] Henrik Kleven et al., "Child Penalties across Countries: Evidence and Explanations," National Bureau of Economic Research Working Paper no. 25524, February 2019.

[15] Marianne Bertrand, Claudia Goldin, and Lawrence F. Katz, "Dynamics of the Gender Gap for Young Professionals in the Financial and Corporate Sectors," *American Economic Journal: Applied Economics,* no. 2 (2010): 228–55.

[16] Claudia Goldin, "A Grand Gender Convergence: Its Last Chapter," *American Economic Review* 104, no. 4 (2014): 1091–1119.

[17] Leonardo Bursztyn, Thomas Fujiwara, and Amanda Pallais, "'Acting Wife': Marriage Market Incentives and Labor Market Investments," *American Economic Review* 107, no. 11 (November 2017): 3288–3319.

[18] Gijsbert Stoet and David C. Geary, "The Gender-Equality Paradox in Science, Technology, Engineering, and Mathematics Education," *Psychological Science* 29, no. 4 (April 2018): 581–93.

[19] Claudia Goldin, "A Grand Gender Convergence: Its Last Chapter," *American Economic Review* 104, no. 4 (2014): 1091–1119.

[20] Richard Fry, "Young Women Are Out-Earning Young Men in Several U.S. Cities," Pew Research Center, Washington, March 28, 2022.

[21] Kate Morgan, "Why Young Women Earn More Than Men in Some US Cities," BBC, April 19, 2022.

[22] Carolina Aragao, "Gender Pay Gap in U.S. Hasn't Changed Much in Two Decades," Pew Research Center, Washington, March 1, 2023.

[23] "DeLauro, Murray Introduce the Paycheck Fairness Act," Rosa DeLauro press release, March 9, 2023.

[24] According to the American Bar Association: "The Paycheck Fairness Act will update the class action provisions of the Equal Pay Act. By adopting the current Rule 23 of the Federal Rules of Civil Procedure, class members will automatically

be considered part of the class unless they specifically choose to opt out." "The Paycheck Fairness Act," American Bar Association, Chicago, 2023.

25 Romina Boccia, *The Unintended Consequences of the Paycheck Fairness Act* (Washington: Independent Women's Forum, November 2010).

26 Kleven, Landais, and Søgaard, "Children and Gender Inequality," p. 1.

27 Warren Meyer, "How Labor Regulation Harms Unskilled Workers," *Regulation* 41, no. 2 (Summer 2018):44–50.

Chapter 22: The Pink Tax Is a Myth

1 Kimberly Lankford, "The Pink Tax Costs Women Thousands of Dollars over Their Lifetimes," *U.S. News & World Report,* April 28, 2023.

2 Anna Bessendorf, "From Cradle to Cane: The Cost of Being a Female Consumer: A Study of Gender Pricing in New York City," New York City Department of Consumer Affairs, December 2015.

3 U.S. Congress Joint Economic Committee, "The Pink Tax," December 2016; Government Accountability Office, "Consumer Protection: Gender-Related Price Differences for Goods and Services," August 9, 2018.

4 Michelle Lodge, "Why Does a Woman's Razor Cost $1.08 When a Man's Razor Only Costs 75 Cents?," TheStreet, March 29, 2018; Irina Ivanova, "Like to Smell Nice? Prepare to Pay More—If You're a Woman," CBS News, August 27, 2018; and Belinda Cleary, "Big W Is Slammed as 'Sexist' for Charging $4 More for 'Female' Versions of the Same Soap: 'The Pink Tax Strikes Again,'" *Daily Mail Australia,* December 6, 2022.

5 Sheena Butler-Young, "Are Shoe Brands Charging You More Based on Your Gender?," *Footwear News,* June 20, 2017.

6 California Civil Code § 51.14, September 27, 2022; Pricing Goods and Services on the Basis of Gender Prohibited, Consolidated Laws of New York, Chapter 20, Article 26, § 391-U, October 2, 2020.

7 Sarah Moshary, Anna Tuchman, and Natasha Bhatia Vajravelu, "Gender-Based Pricing in Consumer Packaged Goods: A Pink Tax?," SSRN, March 15, 2023.

8 Kayleigh Barnes and Jakob Brounstein, "The Pink Tax: Why Do Women Pay More?," SSRN, November 4, 2022.

9 Barnes and Brounstein, "Why Do Women Pay More?"

10 Barnes and Brounstein, "Why Do Women Pay More?"

11 Anja Lambrecht and Catherine E. Tucker, "Algorithmic Bias? An Empirical Study into Apparent Gender-Based Discrimination in the Display of STEM Career Ads," SSRN, September 5, 2021.

12 Danielle Kurtzleben, "Women Pay an "Invisible Tax" at the Drugstore, and France Is Investigating It," *Vox,* November 20, 2014.

13 Bessendorf, "From Cradle to Cane."

14 Moshary, Tuchman, and Vajravelu, "Gender-Based Pricing in Consumer Packaged Goods," p. 4.

15 Ryan Bourne, "The 'Gender Tax' Story Doesn't Show What Feminists Think It Shows," Institute of Economic Affairs, London, January 19, 2016.

16 Government Accountability Office, "Consumer Protection."

17 Ellen Byron, "Does Your Razor Need a Gender?," *Wall Street Journal,* February 1, 2020.

18 Emily Peck, "The 'Pink Tax' on Underwear," Axios, February 13, 2023; "Harmonized Tariff Schedule (2023 HTSA Revision 4)," International Trade Commission, last updated April 2023.

Chapter 23: High CEO Pay

1 Timothy Noah, "The Stock Market's Down—but Guess Which Direction CEO Pay Is Going," *New Republic,* April 18, 2023.

2 Aphrodite Papadatou, "'Fat Cat' Friday Recognizes Vast Pay Gap," HRreview, Weybridge, UK, January 4, 2019.

3 Josh Vibens and Jori Kandra, "CEO Pay Has Skyrocketed 1460% since 1978," Economic Policy Institute, Washington, October 4, 2022.

4 Andrew Speke, Harry Window, and Luke Hildyard, "CEO Pay Survey 2022: CEO Pay Surges 39%," High Pay Centre, London, August 22, 2022.

5 In the United Kingdom, this dates back to the 2002 directors' remuneration report; in the United States, to the 2010 Dodd-Frank Act. The European Union's Shareholder Rights Directive, as amended in 2017, gives a comparable say on pay to companies based within the EU.

6 See Fabrizio Ferri and David A. Maber, "Say on Pay Votes and CEO Compensation: Evidence from the UK," *Review of Finance* 178, no. 2 (April 2013): 527–63.

7 Henrik Cronqvist and Rüdiger Fahlenbrach, "CEO Contract Design: How Do Strong Principals Do It?," *Journal of Financial Economics* 108, no. 3 (June 2013): 659–74.

8 "VMware Stock Drops over 7% after News That CEO Pat Gelsinger Will Head to Intel," Business Insider India, January 24, 2021.

9 Dirk Jenter, Egor Matveyev, and Lukas Roth, "Good and Bad CEOs," working paper, London School of Economics, December 2018.

10 Alex Edmans, "Smith & Nephew CEO Quits over Low Pay; Shares Fall 9%," *Grow the Pie* (blog), March 25, 2022.

11 Yu-Kai M. Wang and Kun M. Yang, "The Impact of Executive Job Demands on Dismissal of Newly Appointed CEOs," *Journal of Management and Organization* 21, no. 6 (February 2015): 705–24.

12 Anjli Raval, "LSE Chief Calls for Higher UK Executive Payto Retain Listings" *Financial Times,* May 3, 2023.

13 Raval, "LSE Chief Calls for Higher UK Executive Pay."

14 "SEC Adopts Pay versus Performance Disclosure Rules," Securities and Exchange Commission news release no. 2022-149, August 25, 2022.

15 "New Executive Pay Transparency Measures Come into Force," UK Department for Business, Energy, and Industrial Strategy news release, January 1, 2019.

16 To date, this article has been cited over 10,000 times in the scholarly literature. Michael C. Jensen and Kevin J. Murphy, "Performance Pay and Top-Management Incentives," *Journal of Political Economy* 98, no. 2 (April 1990): 225–64.

17 Jensen and Murphy, "Performance Pay," 227.

[18] Brian J. Hall and Jeffery B. Liebman, "Are CEOs Really Paid Like Bureaucrats?," *Quarterly Journal of Economics* 133, no. 3 (August 1998): 653–91.

[19] Alex Edmans, Xavier Gabaix, and Dirk Jenter, "Executive Compensation: A Survey of Theory and Evidence," in *The Handbook of the Economics of Corporate Governance,* vol. 1, ed. Benjamin E. Hermalin and Michael S. Weisbach (Amsterdam: North Holland, 2017), pp. 383–539.

[20] Ric Marshall and Linda-Eling Lee, "Are CEOs Paid for Performance? Evaluating the Effectiveness of Equity Incentives," MSCI, New York, July 2016.

[21] Lucian Arye Bebchuk and Jesse M. Fried, *Pay without Performance: The Unfulfilled Promise of Executive Compensation* (Cambridge, MA: Harvard University Press, 2004).

[22] Alex Edmans, Tom Gosling, and Dirk Jenter, "CEO Compensation: Evidence from the Field," European Corporate Governance Institute Working Paper no. 771/2021, May 2023.

[23] In 2016, Portland levied a 10 percent surcharge if the CEO earned more than 100 times the median pay of employees, rising to 25 percent for a 250 to 1 ratio. San Francisco is trying something similar. See Christine Ro, "The Push to Penalise Big Corporations with Huge Pay Gaps," BBC, June 14, 2021.

[24] Rupert Neate, "Most Britons Back Curbs on Bosses' Pay, Survey Finds," *The Guardian,* May 3, 2022.

[25] Gary Gorton and Frank Schmid, "Class Struggle inside the Firm: A Study of German Codetermination," National Bureau of Economic Research Working Paper no. 7945, October 2000.

Chapter 24: Dynamic Pricing

[1] Harriet Torry, "Bowling for $418? Surge Pricing Creeps into Restaurants, Movies, Gym, Class," *Wall Street Journal,* March 12, 2023.

[2] Jelisa Castrodale, "This Guy Paid $800 for an Uber Home on New Year's (Surge Prices Reached 9.9x)," *USA Today,* January 5, 2016.

[3] Marco della Cava, "Springsteen Tickets for $4,000? How Dynamic Pricing Works and How You Can Beat the System," *USA Today,* August 17, 2022.

[4] Ron Lieber, "The Case of the $5,000 Springsteen Tickets," *New York Times,* July 26, 2022.

[5] Alan Cross, "In Defence of Ticketmaster's 'Dynamic Pricing' Model for Concert Tickets," Global News, August 14, 2022.

[6] Jordan Crook, "Gett, the Uber without Surge Pricing, Cuts Ride Fares in NYC," *TechCrunch,* March 10, 2015; and Clay Dillow, "Gett Plans to Outmaneuver Uber in NYC without Surge Pricing," *Fortune,* April 24, 2015.

[7] Juan Camilo Castillo, "Who Benefits from Surge Pricing?," working paper, SSRN, August 8, 2022; Peter Cohen et al., "Using Big Data to Estimate Consumer Surplus: The Case of Uber," National Bureau of Economic Research Working Paper no. 22627, September 2016.

[8] Jonathan Hall, Cory Kendrick, and Chris Nosko, "The Effects of Uber's Surge Pricing: A Case Study," *Uber Blog,* September 1, 2015.

9 See, for example, Ningyuan Chen and Guillermo Gallego, "Welfare Analysis of Dynamic Pricing," *Management Science* 65, no. 1 (January 2019): 139–51; Nan Chen and Przemyslaw Jeziorski, "Consequences of Dynamic Pricing in Competitive Airline Markets," working paper, May 2023; and Kevin Williams, "The Welfare Effects of Dynamic Pricing: Evidence from Airline Markets," National Bureau of Economic Research Working Paper no. 28989, July 2021.

10 M. Keith Chen and Michael Sheldon, "Dynamic Pricing in a Labor Market: Surge Pricing and Flexible Work on the Uber Platform," working paper, December 11, 2015.

11 Abel Brodeur and Kerry Nield, "An Empirical Analysis of Taxi, Lyft, and Uber Rides: Evidence from Weather Shocks in NYC," *Journal of Economic Behavior and Organization* 152 (August 2018): 1–16.

12 Chiwei Yan et al., "Dynamic Pricing and Matching in Ride-Hailing Platforms," *Naval Research Logistics* 67, no. 8 (2019): 705–24.

13 Judd Cramer and Alan B. Krueger, "Disruptive Change in the Taxi Business: The Case of Uber," *American Economic Review* 106, no. 5 (May 2016): 177–82.

14 Castillo, "Who Benefits from Surge Pricing?"

15 Natalie Colarossi, "Uber Slammed over Pricing Surge after Brooklyn Subway Shooting," *Newsweek*, April 12, 2022.

16 Vitor Luckerson, "Uber Agrees to Limit Surge Pricing during Emergencies, Disasters," *Time*, July 8, 2014.

17 "Why Uber Will Cost So Much on New Year's Eve," NBC News, December 31, 2013.

18 Z. John Zhang, "Dynamic Pricing: Aim for Transparency," *Wharton @ Work*, Wharton School, University of Pennsylvania, April 2018.

19 "Surging Pricing," Clark Center Forum, January 13, 2014.

INDEX

Note: Information in figures and tables is indicated by *f* and *t*; n designates a numbered note.

ABOUT THE EDITOR

Ryan A. Bourne occupies the R. Evan Scharf Chair for the Public Understanding of Economics at the Cato Institute and is a columnist for *The Times* (UK). He has written on a variety of economic issues, including fiscal policy, inequality, price and wage controls, and infrastructure spending, and is the author of *Economics in One Virus: An Introduction to Economic Reasoning through COVID-19*. He has contributed to numerous books, including *Flaws and Ceilings: Price Controls and the Damage They Cause*; *Taxation, Government Spending, and Economic Growth*; and *A Fiscal Cliff: New Perspectives on the U.S. Federal Debt Crisis*. He is a coauthor, along with Kwasi Kwarteng and Jonathan Dupont, of *A Time for Choosing: Free Enterprise in Twenty-First Century Britain*.

Before joining Cato, Bourne was head of public policy at the Institute of Economic Affairs and head of economic research at the Centre for Policy Studies (both in the United Kingdom). He has extensive broadcast and print media experience and has appeared on BBC News, CNN, Sky News, CNBC, and Fox Business Network. Bourne holds a BA and an MPhil in economics from the University of Cambridge.

ABOUT THE CONTRIBUTORS

Brian C. Albrecht is the chief economist of the International Center for Law & Economics. He has been published in numerous journals and media outlets, and he also writes the *Economic Forces* newsletter. Albrecht earned his MA and PhD in economics from the University of Minnesota. He also has an MSc in the economics of public policy from the Barcelona Graduate School of Economics. He received his BA in physics and political science from St. Olaf College.

Pedro Aldighieri is originally from Brazil and holds a BA and an MA in economics from the Pontifical Catholic University of Rio de Janeiro. He is currently pursuing a PhD in economics at Northwestern University.

Nicholas Anthony is a policy analyst in the Cato Institute's Center for Monetary and Financial Alternatives and a fellow at the Human Rights Foundation. His work has been published in the *Wall Street Journal*, MarketWatch, and Business Insider and by the American Institute for Economic Research and others. Originally from Baltimore, Anthony received a BS in economics and business administration from Towson University and an MA in economics from George Mason University.

David Beckworth is a senior research fellow at the Mercatus Center at George Mason University and a former international economist at the U.S. Department of the Treasury. He also has experience advising congressional staff on monetary policy. He is the author of *Boom and Bust Banking: The Causes and Cures of the Great Recession*, and his work has been cited by numerous publications, including the *Wall Street Journal*, the *Financial Times*, the *New York Times*, *Bloomberg Businessweek*, and *The Economist*.

Eamonn Butler is director of the Adam Smith Institute, a leading think tank in the UK. He holds degrees in economics and psychology, a PhD in philosophy, and an honorary DLitt. A former winner of the Freedom Medal of Freedom's Foundation at Valley Forge and the UK National Free Enterprise Award, Butler is the author of many books, including introductions on the pioneering economists Adam Smith, Milton Friedman, F. A. Hayek, and Ludwig von Mises. He has also published primers on Classical Liberalism, Public Choice, Magna Carta, the Austrian School of Economics, and great liberal thinkers, as well as *The Condensed Wealth of Nations* and *The Best Book on the Market*. His *Foundations of a Free Society* won the 2014 Fisher Prize.

Vanessa Brown Calder is the director of opportunity and family policy studies at the Cato Institute, where she focuses on policies that support family and increase opportunity. Previously, she was executive director and staff director at the U.S. Congress Joint Economic Committee under Sen. Mike Lee of Utah. Calder holds an MA in public policy from Harvard University's John F. Kennedy School of Government and a BS in urban planning from the University of Utah.

Michael F. Cannon is the Cato Institute's director of health policy studies. He has been called "an influential health-care wonk" (*Washington Post*) and "the most famous libertarian health care scholar" (*Washington Examiner*). Cannon is the author of *Recovery: A Guide to Reforming the U.S. Health Sector* (2023), the coeditor of *Replacing Obamacare: The Cato Institute on Health Care Reform* (2012), and coauthor of *Healthy Competition: What's Holding Back Health Care and How to Free It* (2007). He holds an MA in economics and a JM in law and economics from George Mason University and a BA in American government from the University of Virginia.

Jeffrey Clemens is an associate professor of economics at the University of California at San Diego. He is also a research associate at the National Bureau of Economic Research and a CESifo Network fellow. He had two stints at the Stanford Institute for Economic Policy Research, one as a postdoctoral scholar and one as a visiting assistant professor. Clemens's research has been published in numerous academic journals. He holds both a BA and a PhD in economics from Harvard University.

Bryan P. Cutsinger is an assistant professor of economics at the Norris-Vincent College of Business at Angelo State University, where he also serves as the assistant director of the Free Market Institute. He is also a Sound Money Project fellow at the American Institute for Economic Research and a research assistant professor at the Free Market Institute at Texas Tech University. Cutsinger has been published in numerous academic journals. He holds a BA in economics from the University of Colorado at Boulder and an MA and a PhD in economics from George Mason University.

Alex Edmans is a professor of finance at London Business School. Edmans has spoken at the World Economic Forum in Davos, testified in the UK Parliament, and given multiple TED/TEDx talks. He serves as nonexecutive director of the Investor Forum, on the World Economic Forum's Global Future Council on Responsible Investing, and on Royal London Asset Management's Responsible Investment Advisory Committee. His book, *Grow the Pie: How Great Companies Deliver Both Purpose and Profit*, was a *Financial Times* Book of the Year. Edmans has a PhD from the Massachusetts Institute of Technology and was previously a tenured professor at the Wharton School of the University of Pennsylvania and an investment banker at Morgan Stanley.

Peter Jaworski is an associate teaching professor of strategy, ethics, economics, and public policy at Georgetown University's McDonough School of Business. He is cofounder and vice chairman of the board of directors at the Institute for Liberal Studies. He is the coauthor of *Markets without Limits: Moral Virtues and Commercial Interests*. Jaworski has been published in numerous academic journals. He holds a PhD in philosophy from Bowling Green State University, an MA in philosophy from the University of Waterloo, and an MSc in philosophy and public policy from the London School of Economics.

Pierre Lemieux is an economist affiliated with the Department of Management Sciences at the Université du Québec en Outaouais. He is also a senior affiliated scholar at the Mercatus Center at George Mason University. Lemieux is the author of the report "A Primer on Free Trade: Answering Common Objections" and numerous books on economic and political issues. In addition to his many academic articles, he has signed several articles in the international financial press and has also chaired several international academic seminars. He holds an MA in philosophy from the Université de Sherbrooke and an MA in economics from the University of Toronto. Lemieux currently lives in Maine.

Deirdre Nansen McCloskey is a distinguished scholar and Isaiah Berlin Chair in Liberal Thought at the Cato Institute and distinguished professor emerita of economics and of history and professor emerita of English and of communication at the University of Illinois at Chicago. After getting her PhD in economics at Harvard University, she taught at the University of Chicago and the University of Iowa. She has written 24 books and some 400 academic and popular articles.

Jeffrey Miron is vice president for research at the Cato Institute and the director of graduate and undergraduate studies in the Department of Economics at Harvard University. He is an expert on the economics of libertarianism and is the author of *Drug War Crimes: The Consequences of Prohibition* and *Libertarianism, from A to Z*, in addition to numerous op-eds and journal articles. Miron received his PhD in economics from the Massachusetts Institute of Technology.

Liya Palagashvili is a senior research fellow at the Mercatus Center at George Mason University. She previously was an assistant professor of economics at the State University of New York at Purchase and was named one of the Forbes 30 under 30 in Law & Policy in 2016. She has published academic articles, book chapters, and policy papers, and her writing has appeared in media outlets such as the *New York Times* and the *Wall Street Journal*. Palagashvili earned her PhD in economics from George Mason University.

Joseph J. Sabia is chairman of the Economics Department and director of the Center for Health Economics and Policy Studies at San Diego State University. He is an applied microeconomist who specializes in labor, public, and health economics. Sabia's research has appeared in numerous academic journals and has been cited by the *Wall Street Journal*, the *New York Times*, the *Washington Post*, and *USA Today*. Sabia is also a research fellow at the Institute of Labor Economics. He received his PhD in economics from Cornell University.

J. R. Shackleton is a professor of economics at the University of Buckingham and a research and editorial fellow at the Institute of Economic Affairs. He has also served as dean of two business schools and worked as an economist in the UK civil service. Shackleton has published widely in academic and policy journals on labor market issues and is a regular contributor to written and broadcast media. He has authored or edited 12 books and is the editor in chief of *Economic Affairs*. Shackleton was educated at King's College, the

University of Cambridge, and the School of Oriental and African Studies, University of London.

Peter Van Doren is editor of the Cato Institute's quarterly journal *Regulation*. He has taught at the Woodrow Wilson School of Public and International Affairs at Princeton University, the School of Organization and Management at Yale University, and the University of North Carolina at Chapel Hill. His writing has been published in the *Wall Street Journal*, the *Washington Post, Journal of Commerce*, and the *New York Post*. Van Doren has also appeared on CNN, CNBC, Fox News, and Voice of America. He received his bachelor's degree from the Massachusetts Institute of Technology and his MA and PhD from Yale University.

Stan Veuger is a senior fellow in economic policy studies at the American Enterprise Institute and the editor of AEI Economic Perspectives. He is also a fellow at the IE School of Politics, Economics, and Global Affairs and an affiliate of Harvard University's Center for American Political Studies. Veuger's research has been published in leading academic and professional journals, and his writing has been featured in The Bulwark, *Foreign Affairs, Foreign Policy*, the *New York Times, USA Today*, and the *Washington Post*, among other outlets. He received a PhD and an AM in economics from Harvard. He also holds degrees from Erasmus University Rotterdam, Universitat Pompeu Fabra, University of London, and Utrecht University.

ABOUT THE CATO INSTITUTE

Founded in 1977, the Cato Institute is a public policy research foundation dedicated to broadening the parameters of policy debate to allow consideration of more options that are consistent with the principles of limited government, individual liberty, and peace. To that end, the Institute strives to achieve greater involvement of the intelligent, concerned lay public in questions of policy and the proper role of government.

The Institute is named for *Cato's Letters*, libertarian pamphlets that were widely read in the American Colonies in the early 18th century and played a major role in laying the philosophical foundation for the American Revolution.

Despite the achievement of the nation's Founders, today virtually no aspect of life is free from government encroachment. A pervasive intolerance for individual rights is shown by government's arbitrary intrusions into private economic transactions and its disregard for civil liberties. And while freedom around the globe has notably increased in the past several decades, many countries have moved in the opposite direction, and most governments still do not respect or safeguard the wide range of civil and economic liberties.

To address those issues, the Cato Institute undertakes an extensive publications program on the complete spectrum of policy issues. Books, monographs, and shorter studies are commissioned to examine the federal budget, Social Security, regulation, military spending, international trade, and myriad other issues.

In order to maintain its independence, the Cato Institute accepts no government funding. Contributions are received from foundations, corporations, and individuals, and other revenue is generated from the sale of publications. The Institute is a nonprofit, tax-exempt, educational foundation under Section 501(c)3 of the Internal Revenue Code.

CATO INSTITUTE

1000 Massachusetts Ave. NW

Washington, DC 20001

www.cato.org